ABDELLATIF RAJI

HEAVEN IS UNDER THE FEET OF GOVERNMENTS

STEERING NATIONS WITH MAQASID

www.yaraak.com

This book is dedicated to two pillars of my life: my father, El Houssine Raji, whose wisdom and love have been my guiding light, and my son, Elias Raji, who continues to inspire me every day. To my father, who showed me the depths of integrity and the heights of aspiration; and to my son, who embodies the future I strive to better through my work. You both are the compass and the horizon on my journey. This endeavor is a tribute to the lessons you've imparted and the love you've shared.

"Scientific research transcends writing; it's about pioneering, not just discussing known concepts. True research seeks new insights, like discovering water in a desert, rather than reiterating established knowledge. It's the art of unveiling the unknown, contributing to human understanding and solving problems. Writing about any topic must reveal new perspectives, not echo old ones. Research is the cornerstone of academic progress, a journey towards enlightenment."

— DR. FARID AL-ANSARI

Contents

Foreword

A Poetic Prelude to Governance's Journey

In these pages, light we find, a journey of the enlightened mind.
Not advice from fields defined, but sparks to ignite the thoughts entwined.
I'm no lawyer or adviser, my tales aim higher, to inspire.
Ideas to ponder, dreams to aspire, in governance's vast empire.

The world's ever-changing, its truths rearranging,
But together we're engaging, in wisdom we're exchanging.
Seek the latest, stand undaunted, in decisions, be not haunted,
With experts consulted, and courage flaunted.

As we delve into governance's embrace, let curiosity our paths trace.
Remember, I'm just a guide in this space, not a professional to replace.
What's current now may fade away, so seek freshness in your sway.
Advice that's new will light the day, guiding your choices come what may.

Your questions and thoughts, treasures untold,
In our shared journey, they boldly unfold.
Illuminating the obscure, with insights pure,
Together we explore, together we endure.

The world's ever-changing, its truths rearranging,

But together we're engaging, in wisdom we're exchanging.
Seek the latest, stand undaunted, in decisions, be not haunted,
With experts consulted, and courage flaunted.

So let's embark on this quest, with open hearts and minds possessed.
Armed with wisdom, seeking understanding's crest,
And in experts' counsel, find our rest.
Together in discovery, forever impressed.

Preface

Welcome, dear reader, to an exploration that ventures beyond the conventional bounds of governance, unraveling its profound impact on the fabric of society. "Heaven Is Under the Feet of Governments"—a phrase that alludes to the immense potential and responsibility resting in the hands of our policymakers—is not just a book but a testament to the belief that to truly understand the complexities of governance, we must engage not only our intellect but also our imagination and a deep sense of humanity.

In choosing to introduce this book with a poetic foreword, I aim to bridge the realms of analytical thought and creative expression. This approach is rooted in the conviction that the challenges and solutions inherent in governance cannot be fully understood through logic alone; they must be felt, imagined, and understood with the heart as much as the mind. For instance, consider the way public policies on healthcare not only shape economic landscapes but touch the very essence of human well-being, illustrating the intricate dance between governance and the pulse of society.

The pages that follow are more than an intellectual endeavor; they are an invitation to perceive governance not merely as a system of rules and regulations but as a living, breathing entity that shapes our lives in profound ways. This journey is designed to ignite your curiosity, stir your emotions, and kindle a fire of inquiry, illuminating your path through the exploration ahead.

So, as we embark on this journey together, I encourage you to open your mind to the rhythm of thought, the melody of critique, and the harmony of insights that lie ahead. May this fusion of the analytical and the literary enrich your understanding of governance and inspire you to envision a world where leadership and policy-making are infused with wisdom, compassion, and the collective good.

With an eye towards challenges such as environmental policy-making or the ethics of governance in times of global crises, and solutions rooted in innovation and collective action, let us step into the narrative that unfolds in "Heaven Is Under the Feet of Governments." We'll embrace both the challenges and the beauty of governance in our quest for a better world, discovering along the way that the potential for creating heaven on earth truly does lie at the feet of our governments.

Acknowledgement

This journey has been a rich tapestry, woven from countless threads of support, guidance, and inspiration. To all who have contributed to this tapestry, this acknowledgment is for you.

To my family, whose unwavering love and encouragement have been the bedrock of my strength—your belief in my vision has propelled me forward.

I extend my deepest gratitude to the scholars, thinkers, and visionaries in the Maqasid field. Your groundbreaking work in ethical governance has not only guided but also inspired me.

To the educators and institutions dedicated to the democratization of knowledge, your commitment to enlightenment has illuminated my path.

A heartfelt salute to the policymakers and innovators striving for a better world. Your dedication to ethical governance shines as a beacon of hope and motivation.

To the readers and fellow seekers of knowledge who have embarked on this journey with an open mind—your engagement has added invaluable depth to this work.

And to the countless unnamed contributors, your support has been crucial in bringing this vision to life.

Together, we stand on the brink of transformative change—a change that transcends governance and touches the very soul of humanity. This book is a testament to our collective commitment to ethics, compassion, and justice.

Thank you, one and all, for being part of this meaningful endeavor. May our shared journey towards ethical governance continue to inspire and effect change in our ever-evolving world.

I

Introduction

"Heaven Is Under The Feet Of Governments" advocates for blending spiritual values with secular governance, using the Maqasid model to foster justice, compassion, and well-being. It highlights how ethical governance promotes societal harmony and sustainable development, suggesting a shift to a holistic approach that enriches both material and spiritual aspects of life. The aim is to inspire leaders to build an inclusive society that honors every individual's dignity.

1

The Imperative for a New Governance Paradigm

Governance as the Cornerstone of a Thriving Society

In the intricate tapestry of global societies, governance emerges as the cornerstone, shaping the fate of nations. It holds the power to transform landscapes into havens of prosperity or to plunge them into despair. Picture two neighboring countries with identical resources and opportunities. One flourishes, the other flounders. The critical differentiator? Governance.

Governance: Beyond Administration

Governance transcends routine administrative tasks of issuing IDs or building infrastructure. It's a pervasive force, molding education systems, healthcare policies, and legal frameworks. It's the invisible hand that can either nurture a nation's potential or restrain it.

For instance, consider education. A well-governed nation prioritizes accessible, quality education, laying the groundwork for future leaders and innovators. In healthcare, effective governance ensures comprehensive care, emphasizing both treatment and prevention, striving for universal well-being.

The rule of law is another pivotal aspect. A just legal system upholds equality, guaranteeing that all, irrespective of status, are treated fairly.

Introducing Maqasid: A Holistic Governance Model

As we delve into "Heaven is Under the Feet of Governments: Steering Nations with Maqasid," we explore a model that transcends conventional governance. Maqasid advocates for a holistic approach, addressing not just material needs but also spiritual fulfillment and collective well-being.

Consider a society where wealth distribution is equitable, legal systems are impartial, and education is a universal right. Imagine governance that nurtures not just economic growth but also the human spirit. This isn't a utopian dream but a practical model – Maqasid.

Real-World Application

Real-life examples of Maqasid in action include the application of Maqasid principles in Malaysia's Islamic finance sector to create more ethical and socially responsible financial products. These instances highlight the model's potential to address complex societal challenges effectively.

A Call to Action

As you engage with this journey of discovery, I encourage you to consider how governance, guided by Maqasid principles, can transform our societies. This isn't just academic theory; it's a call for pragmatic, ethical, and effective governance. Let's aspire for governance that truly reflects the highest ideals of humanity.

Introducing Maqasid: The Multidimensional Framework for Holistic Governance

Envision a governance framework that transcends economic and security metrics, reaching deep into the core of human well-being. This is Maqasid, a model that acknowledges our spiritual essence, intellectual potential, and collective aspirations, aligning perfectly with the fundamental aspects of human life.

Maqasid is more than a governance model; it's a comprehensive approach recognizing humans as multifaceted beings. In today's world, where conventional governance often fails to address societal needs fully, Maqasid emerges as a hopeful alternative, prioritizing justice, compassion, and inclusive well-being.

Maqasid's Unique Approach

Consider how seldom governance models genuinely cater to spiritual fulfillment or actively nurture intellectual growth. Maqasid changes this, bringing these critical aspects of human existence to the forefront. This multidimensional framework promises societies where justice and prosperity are not just slogans but realities.

Real-World Application

An example of Maqasid in action is the implementation of environmental conservation policies in Jordan, guided by Maqasid's principles of safeguarding the environment and public health. This demonstrates its potential to create well-balanced societies. This model's principles – like justice, compassion, and well-being – resonate across cultures and belief systems, transcending its Islamic jurisprudence origins.

Challenges and Adaptability

Adopting Maqasid isn't without challenges, particularly in diverse societies. It requires careful adaptation and sensitivity to various cultural contexts. However, its flexibility and universal values make it a viable option for both secular and religious states.

A Call for Inclusive Governance

As we explore Maqasid's principles in the chapters ahead, we invite you to envision a world where governance nurtures every aspect of human life. It's not about imposing a belief system but about upholding values that foster universal well-being.

Embracing Maqasid: A Transformative Journey

Maqasid isn't just an alternative governance model; it's a pathway to elevate the human condition. It advocates for holistic development, inclusive prosperity, communal harmony, intellectual growth, and global welfare. By delving into Maqasid, we don't dismantle existing structures but reinforce them with a more inclusive and compassionate foundation.

Join us in this transformative journey, where governance transcends the ordinary and aspires to the extraordinary. Through Maqasid, let's redefine governance as a force that enriches, empowers, and elevates societies towards greatness.

The Imperative of Integrating Spiritual Principles into Secular Governance: Crafting a Society for the Greater Good

In our contemporary, secular world, there persists a misconception that spiritual principles are confined to personal beliefs, detached from public policy and governance. This critical misunderstanding needs addressing. Spirituality, transcending personal enlightenment, fosters virtues like compassion, justice, and selflessness—key elements for societal unity and harmony.

The separation of spirituality from governance is a false dichotomy. They are deeply interconnected, with the potential to mutually enhance each other. Integrating spiritual principles into secular governance can bring extraordinary societal benefits.

Take, for instance, New Zealand's approach to environmental policy, deeply influenced by the indigenous Māori concept of "Kaitiakitanga," reflecting guardianship and protection. This spiritual perspective has shaped policies focused on sustainability and respect for nature, showcasing how spiritual values can inform and enrich secular governance.

This integration is not about imposing religious doctrines. Instead, it recognizes that core values common across faiths—empathy, fairness, respect for human dignity—are universal. These values can act as a unifying force in diverse societies.

Addressing potential concerns, it's crucial to distinguish between using spiritual principles as ethical guidelines and enforcing specific religious practices. The former enhances governance with universally accepted moral foundations, while the latter could infringe on individual freedoms and diversity.

Practical implementation requires a nuanced approach. Governments can establish advisory panels representing various spiritual traditions to consult on policy matters. Such inclusivity ensures that diverse perspectives contribute to the common good.

Additionally, recognizing the diversity within spiritual traditions is vital.

A one-size-fits-all approach is ineffective in a pluralistic society. Governance must thus be flexible, accommodating varied spiritual expressions while upholding secular principles.

By embracing a holistic approach to governance that acknowledges spirituality's role in our collective well-being, we can create a society that champions justice, compassion, and selflessness. This shift is not merely moral but a pragmatic path to a harmonious and prosperous future for all.

Why Spirituality in Governance is Non-Negotiable

Incorporating spirituality into governance is not a mere luxury; it's an essential necessity. Its importance lies in:

1. **Ethical Anchoring:** Governance without a moral compass resembles a ship lost at sea. Spiritual principles provide this ethical anchor, ensuring decisions are grounded in justice, fairness, and compassion. Without this foundation, governance risks becoming an exercise in efficiency, detached from the values and welfare of the people.
2. **Societal Harmony:** Spirituality fosters universal values like compassion and equality, crucial for a harmonious society. Integrating these values into governance promotes social cohesion and citizen well-being. A society rooted in such principles is more resilient, marked by a sense of belonging and shared responsibility.
3. **Sustainable Development:** Amidst environmental challenges, spiritual tenets like stewardship and interconnectedness gain importance. They guide policies towards sustainable development, focusing on long-term ecological balance rather than short-term gains.

However, integrating spirituality into governance also requires a practical and sensitive approach:

1. **Balancing Idealism and Practicality:** The application must be pragmatic, ensuring that spiritual values inform policy without

8

imposing specific religious beliefs. For instance, Bhutan's Gross National Happiness index incorporates Buddhist spiritual values into development goals while maintaining a secular governance structure.

2. **Navigating Misinterpretations:** Clear distinctions should be made to avoid the perception of religious interference in state affairs. This involves transparent communication and inclusive policy-making that respects diverse spiritual expressions within a secular framework.

3. **Managing Conflicting Values:** In cases of conflicting spiritual interpretations, especially in pluralistic societies, governance should aim for a consensus that upholds the common good without compromising fundamental freedoms and rights.

Incorporating spirituality into governance is not about religious imposition; it's about harnessing shared human values for the greater good. In a world facing ethical, social, and environmental crises, this approach is not just desirable but imperative. It paves the way for a just, compassionate, and sustainable future, redefining governance as a force for true betterment of society.

Overcoming the Secular-Spiritual Divide

The longstanding divide between secular and spiritual governance presents a unique challenge: How can spirituality be integrated into secular systems without violating the principle of separation of religion and state? Maqasid, an approach rooted in Islamic jurisprudence but universally applicable, offers an elegant solution.

Maqasid's Universal Appeal

While Maqasid originates from a specific religious tradition, its principles—Din (Religion), Nafs (Life), Aql (Intellect), Nasl (Lineage and Family), Mal (Wealth), Watan (Homeland), and Ummah (Community)—resonate universally. These concepts are not exclusive to any religion; they align with the core values of humanity across cultures.

Practical Application and Examples

Consider the example of Malaysia, where the Maqasid approach has been employed to balance economic growth with societal well-being, without endorsing any specific religious doctrine. This model has informed policies that prioritize both material prosperity and the holistic development of the community, demonstrating Maqasid's adaptability in a pluralistic society.

Addressing Challenges

Implementing Maqasid is not without challenges. Diverse interpretations of its principles can lead to varied applications, which necessitates a careful and context-sensitive approach. Moreover, resistance may arise from both secularists and religious groups who might view Maqasid's integration as a potential overstep. To mitigate these challenges, ongoing dialogue and consultation with all stakeholders are crucial.

The Inclusivity of Maqasid

What makes Maqasid particularly effective is its inclusivity. It does not seek to impose a specific religious doctrine but offers ethical and moral guidelines that are adaptable to various cultural and religious contexts. This inclusivity is key in societies where diverse beliefs coexist.

Ethical Governance through Maqasid

Maqasid encourages ethical governance, emphasizing justice, equality, and the well-being of all citizens. This ethical dimension acts as a unifying force, bridging the secular-spiritual divide. Its flexibility allows it to be tailored to different societal needs while maintaining core spiritual values.

A Call to Action

Maqasid represents a middle ground, offering a way to infuse governance with ethical and spiritual values without compromising secular principles. It is a framework that respects individual beliefs while striving for the common good based on shared values. In a world marked by diversity and pluralism, Maqasid provides a path forward.

Policymakers, community leaders, and citizens are encouraged to explore Maqasid's principles. By doing so, they can contribute to crafting a society that values both effective governance and deep ethical commitment, transcending divisions and building bridges for inclusive governance.

The Revolutionary Impact

Integrating spiritual principles into governance can revolutionize our societal structures, transcending mere functionality to become truly humane and just. This transformative vision, while ambitious, is grounded in practical realities and achievable through collective effort. Let's explore its potential impact:

1. **Restorative Justice:** Imagine a legal system where the focus shifts from punishment to restoration, healing the community and rehabilitating offenders. This approach is already taking root in initiatives like New Zealand's Māori-focused family group conferences, which emphasize reconciliation and healing.
2. **Human-Centric Economics:** Beyond GDP growth, economic policies can prioritize equitable wealth distribution. Examples include Scandinavian countries, where economic systems are designed to ensure social welfare, reflecting a commitment to human dignity.
3. **Enlightened Education:** Education systems should aim to develop not only academically proficient but also ethically grounded and

empathetic citizens. The Finnish education system, renowned for its holistic approach, is a testament to the success of this model.

4. **Compassionate Welfare:** Welfare programs, characterized by compassion and social justice, can uplift the marginalized. The Canadian approach to social welfare, focusing on inclusivity and support for the vulnerable, exemplifies this principle.

5. **Ethical Governance:** Governance should embody justice, fairness, and integrity. The Bhutanese model of Gross National Happiness prioritizes the well-being of its citizens over economic metrics, setting a benchmark for ethical governance.

6. **Environmental Stewardship:** Recognizing our interconnectedness with nature, policies must emphasize sustainability. Costa Rica's commitment to environmental conservation and its aim to become carbon-neutral showcase how governance can align with environmental stewardship.

7. **Social Harmony:** By embracing values like compassion and empathy, societies can become more harmonious and inclusive. Singapore's multiracial and multi-religious harmony is a model of how diversity can be celebrated and embraced in governance.

Acknowledging Challenges and Taking Action

While this vision is inspiring, its realization is not without challenges. It requires navigating diverse interpretations of spiritual values, ensuring inclusivity, and overcoming resistance to change. Policymakers and community leaders must engage in open dialogue, learn from existing models, and innovate to adapt these principles to their unique contexts.

A Call to Collective Action

This vision of integrating spiritual principles into governance is not utopian; it's a practical and achievable goal. It calls for a shift in perspective and a commitment to our shared humanity. We invite policymakers, community leaders, and individuals to take inspiration from successful models and work towards implementing these principles in their spheres of influence.

Together, we can forge a society that thrives not only materially but also in the richness of its values and the depth of its humanity. This transformative journey is within our grasp, and the time to act is now.

Tangible Benefits

Integrating spirituality into governance offers profound, multifaceted benefits that extend across society. While this vision is ambitious, it's important to balance idealism with practical considerations. Here's an exploration of the key advantages, paired with real-world examples and a recognition of potential challenges:

1. **Reduced Social Inequalities:** Spiritual principles emphasize the intrinsic value of every individual. When applied to governance, this perspective inspires policies that tackle systemic inequalities. For example, in Nordic countries, a similar ethos has led to policies ensuring equitable resource distribution and comprehensive social services. These initiatives have significantly reduced disparities in income, education, and healthcare, creating fairer societies. However, implementing such policies globally requires careful consideration of diverse economic contexts and cultural nuances.

2. **Enhanced Quality of Life:** A spiritual approach to governance can shift the focus from GDP growth to broader quality of life measures. Bhutan's Gross National Happiness index, which includes mental health and life satisfaction alongside economic indicators, is a pioneering example. Yet, replicating this model requires balancing economic imperatives with societal well-being, a complex task in diverse political landscapes.

3. **Stronger, United Communities:** Spirituality fosters empathy and cooperation, leading to resilient communities. Initiatives like

Canada's community engagement programs illustrate how policies can enhance social bonds and foster a sense of shared responsibility. However, fostering such community spirit in larger, more diverse populations can be challenging and requires adaptable, inclusive strategies.

4. **Ethical and Accountable Leadership:** Spiritual governance encourages leaders to prioritize integrity and transparency. New Zealand's approach to leadership, particularly in crisis management, reflects these values. Nevertheless, maintaining high ethical standards is an ongoing challenge, especially in political systems with deeply ingrained corruption.

5. **Sustainable Development:** Spiritual tenets of environmental stewardship are crucial in the age of climate change. Costa Rica's environmental policies demonstrate how a spiritual reverence for nature can be translated into effective ecological conservation. Yet, aligning economic growth with environmental sustainability remains a significant challenge for many nations.

6. **Mental Health and Well-being:** Recognizing the importance of mental health, governance models like those in Scandinavian countries have invested heavily in mental health services. Implementing similar policies universally requires not only financial investment but also a cultural shift in how mental health is perceived.

A Call to Pragmatic Action

While these benefits illustrate the transformative potential of spirituality in governance, realizing them requires a pragmatic approach. This includes respecting diverse beliefs, maintaining secular principles, and understanding the unique challenges of each society.

As readers, policymakers, or engaged citizens, we are encouraged to advocate for the integration of spiritual principles in governance, drawing inspiration from successful models while adapting them to our specific contexts. Embracing this comprehensive model paves the way for a society

14

that thrives not only in material wealth but also in ethical richness and communal well-being.

Let us seize this opportunity to revolutionize governance, blending spiritual and secular strengths to create a just, compassionate, and thriving society. The journey toward this goal begins with open-mindedness and a commitment to positive change, grounded in practical realities.

II

The Fundamentals of Maqasid

Embark on a journey through Maqasid, a governance framework that champions holistic development and justice. We'll explore its core principles, apply them to real-world contexts, and inspire change. This section is your guide to transforming theory into action, envisioning governance that nurtures economic, spiritual growth, and justice. Join us in reimagining governance that exceeds adequacy, aiming for excellence, and making a real difference.

2

The Essence of Din (Religion)

Why Spiritual Considerations Cannot Be Divorced from Governance

Why Spiritual Considerations Are Integral to Governance

In an era increasingly defined by secularism and the separation of religion and state, integrating spiritual principles into governance might seem counterintuitive. This chapter aims to unpack this complex issue and address common misconceptions and skepticisms. Far from undermining secular frameworks, spiritual integration can enrich them, contributing to a more harmonious and equitable society. Here, spirituality is not about religious practices but rather the universal values shared across various faiths and humanist beliefs—values like compassion, justice, empathy, and the common good.

Balancing Spirituality with Secularism

Our foundational premise is not the advocacy for a theocracy, nor is it to impose religious beliefs on society. Instead, it's about embracing the universal principles that underpin all major spiritual and ethical traditions.

19

To clarify, 'spirituality' in this context refers to a set of values and ethical principles that transcend religious boundaries, resonating with people of diverse faiths and secular humanists alike.

Addressing Potential Counterarguments

Critically, we must consider potential counterarguments. How can we ensure that integrating spirituality into governance doesn't lead to religious favoritism or exclusion? One approach is through inclusive policy-making that respects all beliefs while applying universal ethical principles. For example, New Zealand's approach to Indigenous rights and environmental policy, informed by Māori spiritual values, enhances governance without compromising its secular nature.

Practical Integration of Spiritual Principles

The moral compass spirituality provides offers an ethical foundation for policy evaluation. We examine how policies can be scrutinized through lenses of compassion and justice, ensuring they prioritize the welfare and dignity of all citizens. The Bhutanese Gross National Happiness index is a case in point, where spiritual values shape national priorities alongside economic considerations.

In terms of transparency and accountability, spiritual principles advocating moral integrity can significantly reduce corruption. We explore how models like those in Scandinavian countries, which integrate high ethical standards in governance, lead to increased public trust.

Furthermore, spirituality's role in addressing global challenges like climate change and inequality is critical. It pushes us to view these issues not just as policy challenges but as moral imperatives, urging responsible stewardship of our planet and equitable treatment of all communities.

Creating Cohesive and Inclusive Societies

The integration of spirituality in governance also fosters social cohesion. By acknowledging diverse spiritual and ethical perspectives, we create a space where all voices are heard and valued. In a world marked by division, this approach is essential for building a society that thrives on shared values.

Spirituality as a Pillar of Modern Governance

In conclusion, integrating spirituality into governance is not about diminishing personal freedoms or promoting a particular religious doctrine. It's about harnessing universal principles that unite humanity in its pursuit of a just, compassionate, and equitable society. These principles do not hinder modern governance; they are indispensable to it, enriching its ethical compass, enhancing transparency, and compelling us to confront global challenges. This chapter invites you to consider how spirituality and governance can coexist, each reinforcing the other, to create not only an economically prosperous society but also one that is profoundly ethical and inclusive.

The Ethical Core of Governance

At the heart of governance lies a series of ethical decisions that profoundly shape society's destiny. These decisions, ranging from resource allocation to upholding justice, can be profoundly enhanced by integrating spiritual principles. In an era where secularism prevails, this might seem counterintuitive. However, spirituality, understood here as a broad sense of universal morality and ethics, offers timeless guidance that transcends religious divisions and enriches the ethical core of governance.

Spirituality Beyond Religious Boundaries

Spirituality in governance transcends organized religion, encompassing universal moral principles like compassion, empathy, altruism, and recognizing the intrinsic worth of every individual. These values resonate across different faiths and secular humanism, providing a shared moral compass for a just and equitable society.

Practical Applications and Global Examples

Consider the issue of wealth distribution. Spirituality advocates for equitable resource allocation, urging us to see material wealth as a means for the common good. For instance, the Scandinavian model of governance, inspired by a sense of social responsibility and fairness, has led to policies that ensure a more equitable distribution of wealth, reducing income disparities.

When it comes to justice, spirituality illuminates the concept beyond legal definitions. It calls for dignity and fairness for every individual. South Africa's post-apartheid Truth and Reconciliation Commission exemplifies this, where spiritual principles of forgiveness and reconciliation guided a nation toward healing historical injustices.

Addressing Modern Challenges with Spiritual Ethics

Furthermore, spirituality prompts policies that prioritize the greater good, fostering interconnectedness and collective welfare. This perspective is crucial for tackling global issues like climate change and pandemics. For example, the environmental policies of New Zealand, which incorporate Indigenous Māori spiritual values, demonstrate a commitment to safeguarding the planet for future generations.

Navigating Challenges and Maintaining Inclusivity

Integrating spirituality into governance is not without challenges. It requires careful balancing to maintain religious neutrality and ensure inclusivity of all belief systems. Policymakers must engage in open dialogues, considering diverse perspectives to create policies that reflect universal ethical principles without favoring any particular religious ideology.

Elevating Governance through Ethical Wisdom

In conclusion, integrating spirituality into governance is about enriching its ethical foundation. It involves viewing governance not just as a bureaucratic function but as a sacred duty to serve all members of society. This approach doesn't hinder modern governance; rather, it elevates it to new heights of fairness and justice, aligning with humanity's deepest moral aspirations. By embracing this approach, we can transform governance from a mere administrative exercise to a noble endeavor that genuinely serves the well-being of every community member.

Holistic Human Development: The Heart of Ethical Governance

In today's rapidly evolving world, the concept of governance has often been narrowly focused on economic indicators like GDP growth, leading to a skewed perception of prosperity. However, a deeper examination underscores that genuine prosperity is far more encompassing, involving not just financial success but also the emotional health, moral development, and spiritual fulfillment of individuals. This is where a governance model informed by spirituality becomes crucial, offering a broader, more inclusive perspective on human well-being.

The Multidimensional Nature of Human Development

Holistic human development recognizes individuals as complex entities with physical, emotional, and spiritual dimensions. While economic growth is crucial for alleviating poverty and creating opportunities, it is merely one facet of a larger picture. True prosperity also involves nurturing the social and psychological aspects of human life.

1. **Emotional Well-Being:** Emphasizing emotional health, spiritually informed governance models invest in mental health services and create supportive environments. Finland, for instance, has incorporated emotional well-being into its educational system, resulting in a populace that is not only academically competent but also emotionally resilient.

2. **Moral Development:** Beyond economic metrics, the moral fabric of society is vital. Spirituality fosters virtues such as honesty and empathy, influencing personal and communal interactions. An example of this is seen in Canada's emphasis on ethical values in public life, which has contributed to its reputation as one of the world's most transparent countries.

3. **Spiritual Fulfillment:** A spiritually informed governance model facilitates an environment where individuals can freely explore and nurture their spiritual beliefs. This respect for diverse spiritual paths is evident in India's pluralistic approach, which accommodates a myriad of religious practices while maintaining a secular governance framework.

Addressing Challenges and Promoting Social Justice

Implementing a holistic approach to human development is not without challenges. It requires maintaining religious neutrality and addressing the diverse spiritual needs of the population. Moreover, such a model must recognize and strive to bridge disparities in income, education, and healthcare, as these can impede emotional and moral growth.

Redefining Prosperity through Holistic Governance

Holistic human development, as advocated by a spiritually informed governance model, redefines prosperity. It goes beyond mere economic growth to include emotional well-being, moral development, and spiritual fulfillment, acknowledging the complex nature of human existence. By focusing on the holistic well-being of individuals at the heart of policymaking, governance can create societies where every person has the opportunity to thrive, not just materially but in all aspects of life. This approach does not only enrich the human experience but also lays the foundation for a more just, compassionate, and equitable world.

Community Cohesion and Social Capital: The Glue That Binds Prosperous Societies

In the intricate tapestry of human civilization, communities represent the vibrant threads that weave together to form society's fabric. These communities thrive not just on proximity but on a deeper sense of cohesion, empathy, and shared responsibility, where spirituality acts as an invisible yet powerful binding force. Spirituality here transcends organized religion, embodying universal principles of morality and ethics that foster a sense of interconnectedness.

The Multifaceted Role of Community Cohesion and Social Capital

Community cohesion and social capital, the collective wealth of relationships and trust within a society, are critical for its flourishing. They serve as the social infrastructure that underpins prosperous societies in various ways:

1. **Resilience in Times of Crisis:** Communities with strong social

capital demonstrate remarkable resilience in crises. For instance, the community response to the 2011 earthquake in Christchurch, New Zealand, where local networks played a key role in recovery efforts, exemplifies this resilience.

2. **Crime Prevention:** There is a notable correlation between high social capital and lower crime rates. Communities where trust and vigilance are prevalent, such as in certain Scandinavian neighborhoods, tend to experience fewer crimes.

3. **Economic Opportunities:** Strong social networks can lead to economic benefits. In Silicon Valley, for instance, the culture of networking and information exchange has been pivotal in driving innovation and economic success.

4. **Health and Well-Being:** Research shows that communities with strong social ties often have better health outcomes. Japan's concept of 'Moai,' a social support group system in Okinawa, contributes to the residents' renowned longevity.

5. **Civic Engagement:** Engaged communities often exhibit higher levels of political participation. The participatory governance model of Kerala, India, illustrates how civic engagement can lead to effective decision-making and community development.

6. **Education and Learning:** Learning in cohesive communities transcends formal education. The traditional 'Ubuntu' philosophy in African communities, which emphasizes communal learning and shared knowledge, highlights this aspect.

7. **Inclusive Prosperity:** Inclusive communities ensure equitable prosperity. The multicultural fabric of Canadian cities, where diverse groups coexist and contribute to communal wealth, showcases this inclusivity.

Navigating Challenges and Cultivating Social Capital

Cultivating such social capital is not without challenges, especially in individualistic societies where community bonds might be weaker. Strategies to enhance social capital include fostering community engagement initiatives, creating inclusive spaces for dialogue, and encouraging local networking events.

Embracing Community Cohesion for Societal Prosperity

Community cohesion and social capital, energized by the ethical and moral guidance of spirituality, are invaluable for prosperous societies. These elements are not just about coexistence but about thriving together, united by shared values and mutual support. Recognizing and actively cultivating these intangible assets allows us to pave the way for societies where prosperity is not only economic but also social and spiritual, enriching the human experience in its entirety.

Resilience in Times of Crisis: Nurturing the Strength to Overcome Adversity

Throughout human history, societies have repeatedly faced crises— natural disasters, economic downturns, social and political strife. These challenges test the resilience of communities, the capacity to recover and emerge stronger. Resilience, shaped not only by material resources but significantly by spiritual and ethical principles, stands as a beacon of hope and determination in such times.

The Multidimensional Nature of Resilience

Resilience transcends mere physical recovery; it is deeply rooted in the collective spirit of a community, often inspired by a blend of spiritual and secular values:

27

1. **Hope Amidst Despair:** In crises like Japan's 2011 earthquake, it was the shared spiritual and cultural ethos of perseverance and mutual support that united communities in rebuilding efforts. Such hope, often stemming from spiritual beliefs, keeps communities together, fostering resilience against adversity.

2. **Perseverance Against Odds:** Spiritual principles can imbue a sense of tenacity in communities. Historical examples include the resilience shown during the American Civil Rights Movement, where both spiritual leaders and secular humanists united in the struggle against injustice, demonstrating unwavering determination.

3. **Solidarity and Support:** The aftermath of crises often witnesses remarkable acts of solidarity. For instance, the community response during the COVID-19 pandemic, where people of diverse beliefs came together to support the vulnerable, illustrates how shared human values can create strong bonds of mutual support.

4. **Shared Destiny and Cohesion:** Crises highlight our interconnectedness. This is evident in multicultural societies like South Africa, where diverse communities, guided by the principles of 'Ubuntu' – a philosophy emphasizing common humanity – come together, reinforcing social cohesion.

5. **Learning and Adaptation:** Crises are profound learning experiences. The wisdom derived from spiritual and secular sources alike can lead to improvements in preparedness and societal structures. The Scandinavian approach to social welfare, integrating both practical and ethical considerations, exemplifies this learning.

6. **Healing and Emotional Well-Being:** Spiritual principles provide comfort and solace, aiding in emotional healing post-crisis. The role of faith-based organizations in providing psychological support during disasters is a testament to this.

7. **Innovation and Renewal:** Post-crisis periods often spur innovation. The rebuilding of war-torn societies, for instance, has sometimes led to more inclusive governance structures and community-driven development initiatives.

Navigating Challenges in Cultivating Resilience

Building resilience in diverse communities requires navigating various challenges. It involves ensuring that resilience-building efforts are inclusive, respecting both spiritual and secular viewpoints, and addressing the needs of different community segments.

Embracing Comprehensive Resilience

Resilience in times of crisis is not just a theoretical concept but a tangible strength that emerges from the collective spirit of communities, nurtured by an amalgamation of spiritual and secular principles. It's the force that enables societies to face challenges with courage, bind together in solidarity, and rebuild with renewed vigor and wisdom. By recognizing and cultivating this multifaceted resilience, societies invest not only in their survival but in their capacity to thrive and evolve, regardless of the challenges the future may bring.

Towards Sustainable Governance: Embracing the Wisdom of Stewardship

In an era where environmental challenges are more evident than ever, the imperative for sustainable governance rooted in the wisdom of stewardship is undeniable. The urgency posed by climate change, resource depletion, and environmental pollution necessitates a shift in how we govern and interact with our planet. Stewardship, a principle deeply embedded in various spiritual and ethical traditions, offers a vital approach to this shift.

Stewardship in Action: A Multifaceted Approach

Stewardship is about responsibly managing and caring for Earth's resources, recognizing our duty to future generations. It's a principle that urges us to consider the long-term impact of our actions and govern with foresight and responsibility.

1. **Long-Term Vision in Policy:** By embracing stewardship, policymakers are encouraged to think beyond immediate gains. For example, the Nordic countries' approach to environmental policy and social welfare, where long-term sustainability is prioritized, showcases how stewardship can shape governance.

2. **Environmental Conservation:** Stewardship mandates sustainable use of natural resources. Policies reflecting this, like those in Costa Rica's efforts in forest conservation and renewable energy, demonstrate how governance can effectively balance development and environmental preservation.

3. **Recognizing Interconnectedness:** The concept of interconnectedness, central to many spiritual traditions, is crucial in understanding our impact on the planet. This has been exemplified in New Zealand's legal recognition of the Whanganui River as a living entity, a decision influenced by the indigenous Māori worldview.

4. **Ethical Decision-Making:** Integrating stewardship into governance provides an ethical framework for policy decisions. The Bhutanese philosophy of Gross National Happiness, which includes environmental conservation as a key pillar, exemplifies this ethical approach.

5. **Resilience and Adaptation:** Stewardship involves planning for change and resilience. Singapore's water management strategies, which include innovative solutions for water scarcity, illustrate how stewardship can lead to adaptable and resilient environmental policies.

6. **Global Responsibility:** Environmental issues know no borders. Stewardship in governance fosters international cooperation, as seen

in global climate agreements like the Paris Accord, where collective responsibility for the planet is a central theme.

7. **Legacy for Future Generations:** Stewardship compels us to consider our legacy. The move towards renewable energy and sustainable cities worldwide reflects a growing recognition of our responsibility to leave a thriving planet for future generations.

Challenges and Broader Applications

Implementing stewardship in governance faces challenges, including economic constraints and political resistance. Addressing these requires collaborative approaches and engagement with diverse stakeholders, including secular groups. Moreover, the principles of stewardship can extend beyond environmental issues to social welfare, education, and healthcare, offering a holistic model for sustainable development.

The Imperative of Stewardship in Governance

Embracing stewardship in governance is not just an environmental necessity but a moral imperative. It aligns with both spiritual and secular ethical frameworks, offering a universal approach to addressing our planet's pressing challenges. Sustainable governance, guided by stewardship, is an investment in a future where the planet and all its inhabitants can flourish. It's a vision of governance that serves not just the present but secures a thriving and harmonious world for generations to come.

Conclusion: An Invitation to a Richer Form of Governance

As we reach the culmination of our exploration into enriched governance, it becomes evident that excluding spirituality from policy and governance represents a missed opportunity. This conclusion is not about advocating for religious dogma in governance but about embracing the universal wisdom that spirituality, in its broadest sense, offers to humanity. It's about recognizing governance as not just an administrative task but a profound moral responsibility.

Enriched Governance: A Practical and Moral Imperative

Integrating spirituality into governance invites us to craft a society that goes beyond materialistic limitations, tapping into the richness of the human spirit. It opens doors to policies infused with our highest ethical values—compassion, justice, equity, and empathy. We envision societies where every individual, from diverse backgrounds, can experience a fuller, more meaningful existence.

Consider the transformative possibilities:

1. **Empowered Citizens:** Enriched governance involves empowering citizens to actively participate in their communities, valuing their contributions to the common good. This approach has been successfully implemented in participatory budgeting models in Brazil, where community members have a direct say in policy decisions.

2. **Moral Clarity in Policymaking:** Integrating spirituality as a moral compass in governance brings clarity. Policies are evaluated for their ethical soundness, ensuring the well-being of all. The Nordic model of social welfare is a testament to this approach, prioritizing societal well-being alongside economic growth.

3. **Building Equitable Societies:** Enriched governance seeks to reduce disparities, much like the policies in New Zealand, which incorporate Māori perspectives and values to ensure equitable opportunities for all communities.

4. **Cultural Richness and Diversity:** Acknowledging diverse spiritual and cultural backgrounds enriches governance. Canada's multicultural policy is an example of celebrating cultural diversity while promoting social harmony.

5. **Sustainable Futures:** Integrating spiritual principles of stewardship

and interconnectedness leads to sustainable policy decisions, as seen in Costa Rica's environmental conservation efforts.

6. **Resilient Communities:** Spiritual values like hope and shared destiny provide strength in crises. Japan's community response post-2011 earthquake, rooted in a cultural ethos of resilience and mutual support, exemplifies this.

7. **Global Cooperation:** Enriched governance fosters international collaboration, as exemplified by global environmental agreements like the Paris Accord.

Navigating Challenges and Embracing Inclusivity

The path towards integrating spirituality in governance is not without challenges. It requires careful navigation to maintain secularism and inclusivity of diverse beliefs. The goal is to find a common ground where universal spiritual values can coexist with secular principles, enriching governance without imposing specific religious views.

A Call to Transformative Action

This enriched form of governance is not a distant ideal but a practical reality waiting to be realized. It calls for moral visionaries who can see beyond the status quo, envisioning a society where spirituality and governance work in tandem for the greater good.

It's an invitation to build societies where compassion guides policies, where justice forms the foundation of governance, and where every individual can flourish. This approach transcends traditional limitations, offering a holistic model that fulfills both material needs and the innate human longing for purpose and connection.

As we embrace this richer, more ethical form of governance, we open the door to a world that reflects the best of humanity—a world where governance serves the totality of human needs. The journey towards this goal is not just visionary; it's practical, inclusive, and profoundly necessary.

The time to act is now, and the potential for positive change is immense.

In essence, this is not just an invitation but a call to action for a governance model that truly nurtures the human spirit in all its dimensions. The opportunity to partake in this transformative journey is before us. Will you join in shaping a future that honors and uplifts the human experience in its entirety?

Real-World Examples: The Consequences of Neglecting Moral Guidelines in Governance

The neglect of moral and spiritual guidelines in governance is not a mere theoretical concern; it has led to tangible, detrimental consequences globally. However, understanding these issues also opens pathways for integrating moral principles into governance for positive change. Let's examine concrete instances that highlight the need for ethical governance and explore potential remedies.

1. **Corruption and Erosion of Trust:** Instances of corruption in various countries starkly illustrate the consequences of moral neglect in governance. This not only depletes resources but erodes public trust. Conversely, countries like Denmark, which consistently rank high in transparency and low in corruption, demonstrate the positive impact of ethical governance practices that prioritize accountability and integrity.

2. **Economic Inequality:** Policies that overlook ethical considerations often exacerbate wealth gaps, leading to social unrest. However, models like Germany's social market economy show how ethical policies can balance economic growth with social welfare, reducing inequality.

3. **Environmental Degradation:** The pursuit of economic growth without environmental consideration has led to ecological crises. In contrast, Bhutan's commitment to maintaining a significant portion

of its land under forest cover, guided by spiritual respect for nature, exemplifies sustainable governance.

4. **Human Rights Violations:** Authoritarian regimes often prioritize power over ethics, leading to human rights abuses. This highlights the need for governance models that uphold human rights as a core ethical principle, as exemplified by the policies in countries like Canada.

5. **Social Fragmentation:** A lack of moral foundation in governance can result in societal divisions. The inclusive policies of multicultural societies like Singapore illustrate how ethical governance can promote social cohesion and inclusivity.

6. **Public Health Crises:** The COVID-19 pandemic has shown how ethical lapses in governance can exacerbate public health crises. Countries like New Zealand, which handled the pandemic with a clear ethical framework prioritizing public health and transparent communication, have shown better outcomes.

These examples underscore that the absence of moral and spiritual considerations in governance can lead to profound societal issues. They also highlight that ethical governance, informed by moral principles, can lead to more equitable, just, and sustainable societies.

Advocating for Ethical Governance

This exploration serves as a call to action, emphasizing that governance should be rooted in moral and spiritual principles to ensure the well-being and prosperity of all. By looking at both the negative consequences and the positive examples of ethical governance, we see a clear path forward. Governance models around the world that successfully integrate moral principles demonstrate that it's not only possible but essential for creating societies where fairness, integrity, and sustainability are the norm.

The time has come to champion a governance model that places morality and spirituality at its core, enriching our collective future. By embracing these principles, we can build a world that reflects the best of humanity

– a world where governance serves not just economic indicators but the holistic needs of every individual. Let us commit to this transformative journey towards a more ethical, inclusive, and spiritually enriched form of governance.

The 2008 Financial Crisis

The 2008 financial crisis remains a stark reminder of the catastrophic consequences when governance lacks ethical oversight. More than just a financial catastrophe, it serves as a crucial lesson in the broader context of governance across all sectors.

The Unraveling of Ethical Governance

The crisis was rooted in reckless financial practices, driven by profit at the expense of ethical responsibility. Here's a more detailed look at the key factors:

1. **Irresponsible Lending Practices:** Banks offered subprime mortgages to individuals with poor credit, disregarding their ability to repay the loans, setting them up for inevitable defaults.
2. **Securitization of Risky Mortgages:** These risky loans were then bundled into complex mortgage-backed securities, obfuscating the inherent risks.
3. **Lack of Transparency:** The complexity of these financial instruments masked their true risk, leading to a dangerous underestimation of their potential fallout.
4. **Rating Agencies' Failures:** Misleading high ratings by credit agencies further perpetuated the illusion of safety.
5. **Systemic Failure:** Overleveraged banks found themselves on the brink of collapse when loan defaults began, triggering a global financial meltdown.
6. **Government Bailouts:** The crisis necessitated unprecedented

government interventions, including massive bailouts, to prevent a total collapse of the financial system.

Broader Implications and Solutions

The repercussions of the crisis were far-reaching, impacting not just the financial sector but also ordinary citizens who lost jobs, homes, and savings. It demonstrated the necessity for a governance model that goes beyond financial metrics to include ethical considerations in all sectors.

In response, reforms like the Dodd-Frank Act in the United States were introduced to increase financial regulation and oversight. However, the journey towards fully ethical governance requires continuous effort. This includes:

- Implementing stringent regulatory frameworks to prevent such crises.
- Cultivating a culture of ethical decision-making in all sectors.
- Ensuring transparency and accountability in corporate practices.
- Encouraging ethical leadership and corporate responsibility.

Reflection on Current Reforms and Diverse Perspectives

Since the crisis, there have been strides in financial regulations, but challenges remain, indicating the need for ongoing vigilance. The perspectives of various stakeholders affected by the crisis – from individual homeowners to small business owners – highlight the widespread impact of governance decisions and the importance of considering diverse viewpoints in policy-making.

A Call to Ethical Governance

The 2008 financial crisis underscores the imperative for ethical governance. It's a powerful lesson that neglecting moral principles can lead to widespread harm. This crisis should continue to serve as a reminder of our collective responsibility to champion governance models that prioritize ethics, accountability, and the welfare of all citizens. Let the crisis not just be a memory, but a catalyst for enduring change towards more responsible and ethical governance in all sectors.

The Flint Water Crisis

The Flint water crisis, a tragic episode in recent history, stands as a glaring example of the catastrophic consequences when governance fails its moral responsibilities. This crisis did more than expose the dangers of cost-cutting measures; it highlighted systemic issues such as racial and socioeconomic disparities, and how they can lead to grave injustices.

The Unfolding of the Crisis

The crisis began with a cost-saving decision to switch Flint's water supply in April 2014, but it quickly spiraled into a public health disaster:

1. **Water Supply Switch:** Flint, Michigan, switched its water source to the Flint River, initiating the crisis.
2. **Lead Contamination:** The corrosive river water caused lead from old pipes to leach into the drinking water, exposing the community to dangerous levels of a neurotoxin.
3. **Disproportionate Health Impact:** The crisis disproportionately affected Flint's predominantly African American and economically disadvantaged community, with children suffering the most due to lead's detrimental effects on development.
4. **Government Negligence:** Investigations revealed that officials knew about the water quality issues but failed to act, highlighting a gross negligence of duty.
5. **Public Outcry and National Attention:** The crisis gained national attention due to the efforts of residents and activists, spotlighting the severity of the situation.

6. **Long-term Recovery:** Efforts to revert to the previous water source and repair the damage were initiated, but the trust and health of the community had been deeply affected.

Beyond the Crisis: Systemic Issues and Positive Changes

The Flint crisis sheds light on broader systemic challenges, such as the need for greater regulatory oversight and addressing inequalities that leave vulnerable communities at risk. In response to the crisis, Flint has seen efforts to replace lead piping and improve water quality monitoring, setting a precedent for other cities to proactively address similar vulnerabilities.

Preventative Measures and Ethical Governance

To prevent such tragedies, it is crucial to implement stringent regulatory frameworks and oversight mechanisms. This includes regular water quality testing, transparent reporting, and community involvement in decision-making processes. Governance should be informed by ethical principles that prioritize human health and dignity, especially in decisions affecting marginalized communities.

The Imperative for Moral and Ethical Governance

The Flint water crisis is a potent reminder of the need for governance that upholds ethical and moral standards. This crisis should serve as a call to action for all policymakers to embed moral guidelines in their decision-making, ensuring the protection and well-being of all citizens. It highlights the importance of addressing systemic inequalities and reinforces the need for governance that is transparent, accountable, and driven by the common good.

The lessons from Flint resonate globally, emphasizing the universal necessity for ethical governance in all sectors and regions. By learning from this crisis and committing to ethical governance, we can work towards a future where such preventable tragedies are averted, and the rights and well-being of every community member are safeguarded.

Exploitative Labor Practices

Exploitative labor practices within the global commerce system starkly illustrate the grave consequences of a governance and business ethos devoid of ethical considerations. This issue, where profit maximization overshadows basic human rights and dignity, highlights the urgent need for a moral reorientation in governance and business practices.

Understanding the Exploitative Practices

Exploitative labor practices manifest in various forms, impacting the most vulnerable populations:

1. **Sweatshops:** These involve inhumane working conditions, paltry wages, and often child labor. Workers endure long hours in hazardous environments for minimal compensation, a result of companies cutting corners to reduce production costs.
2. **Child Labor:** Widespread in industries from agriculture to manufacturing, child labor robs children of education and a normal childhood, subjecting them to exploitation for profit.
3. **Exploitative Supply Chains:** Some multinational corporations overlook exploitative practices in their supply chains, prioritizing cost-efficiency over worker welfare.
4. **Weak Labor Protections:** In regions with lax labor laws, exploitation thrives due to a lack of legal deterrents.
5. **Human Trafficking:** In extreme cases, labor exploitation escalates to human trafficking, where individuals are coerced into labor against their will.

Systemic Issues and Positive Models

These practices are underpinned by broader systemic issues, including global economic disparities and trade policies that often favor wealthier nations. However, there are positive counterexamples. For instance, companies like Patagonia and Ben & Jerry's are lauded for their commitment to ethical labor practices and serve as models for integrating social responsibility into business success.

Pathways to Ethical Labor Practices

To combat these exploitative practices, a multifaceted approach is needed:

- Implementation of robust regulatory frameworks to protect workers' rights globally.
- Encouragement of corporate responsibility, where businesses commit to ethical practices throughout their supply chains.
- Consumer awareness and advocacy for products made under fair labor conditions.
- International cooperation to address global economic inequalities and establish fair trade practices.

Navigating Challenges

While transitioning to ethical labor practices presents challenges such as maintaining economic competitiveness and adjusting consumer prices, these can be navigated through innovative business models and policy incentives. Governments can play a crucial role by incentivizing ethical business practices and establishing trade agreements that enforce labor standards.

Ethical Governance as a Path to a Just World

The exploitation of labor is not an inevitable byproduct of global commerce but a result of governance and business decisions lacking in moral grounding. By championing ethical governance and corporate responsibility, we can move towards a more equitable and humane global society. This shift requires not just policy changes but a collective commitment to valuing human dignity and rights in every aspect of governance and commerce. It's a call to action for all stakeholders to foster a world where labor practices are not just profitable but also just and humane.

Environmental Degradation

The unfolding climate crisis is a stark reminder of the perils of governance that neglects its moral and ethical responsibilities. This environmental emergency, driven by short-term economic ambitions, poses a severe threat not only to our current generation but also to the future of our planet. It underscores the necessity for governance infused with ethical stewardship.

Examining the Consequences

The devastating impacts of this failure in governance are manifold:

1. **Rising Temperatures:** Human activities have led to a steady increase in global temperatures, resulting in frequent and intense weather anomalies.
2. **Melting Ice Caps:** Accelerated ice melting contributes to rising sea levels, endangering coastal and low-lying regions.
3. **Biodiversity Loss:** Rampant habitat destruction and pollution have triggered an alarming decline in biodiversity, destabilizing ecosystems.
4. **Resource Depletion:** Overconsumption and unsustainable resource

extraction threaten resource availability, leading to potential conflicts and economic challenges.

5. **Social Inequities:** Environmental degradation disproportionately affects vulnerable populations, exacerbating social and health disparities.

6. **Food Security:** Climate change poses significant risks to global agriculture, threatening food availability and stability.

Incorporating Solutions and Positive Models

Addressing these challenges requires a multi-faceted approach:

- Implementing policies that reduce carbon emissions and encourage the use of renewable energy.
- Supporting sustainable agricultural and resource management practices.
- Enforcing strict regulations against activities that harm the environment.
- Promoting consumer awareness and sustainable lifestyles.

Examples of positive change include countries like Denmark and Costa Rica, which have made significant strides in renewable energy adoption and conservation efforts. These models demonstrate that integrating ethical considerations into governance can lead to successful environmental outcomes.

Understanding Systemic Factors

The crisis is rooted in broader systemic issues, such as global economic structures and consumer behaviors. Addressing environmental degradation requires a holistic approach that considers these underlying factors and encourages collaborative efforts across disciplines and sectors.

The Ethical Imperative

The climate crisis is indeed a moral crisis. It demands that we infuse governance with principles of stewardship, responsibility, and interdependence. Recognizing our moral duty to protect the environment and vulnerable communities, we must strive for policies that balance ecological sustainability with economic development.

A Wake-Up Call for Ethical Action

This crisis is a wake-up call to urgently integrate morality and ethics into governance. Our actions today will determine the health of our planet and the legacy we leave for future generations. It's time for a paradigm shift towards governance that values not just economic prosperity but the sustainability and well-being of all life on Earth. Let this be a moment for decisive, ethical action, shaping a future where our planet and its inhabitants can thrive in harmony.

Social Inequality and Systemic Discrimination

Social inequality and systemic discrimination represent more than policy challenges; they are profound ethical failings of governance systems. These issues stem from a lack of moral commitment to recognizing and upholding the equal dignity and worth of every individual. Let's examine the multifaceted nature of these issues and explore transformative solutions:

1. **Racial Injustice:** Racial discrimination remains deeply entrenched in many societies. BIPOC communities frequently face systemic barriers in education, employment, and healthcare. For instance, affirmative action policies, though sometimes controversial, have been implemented in various sectors as a means to address these disparities and promote diversity.

2. **Gender Wage Gaps:** The persistent wage gap between genders is not just an economic issue but a moral one, reflecting a failure to uphold the principle of equal pay for equal work. Initiatives like Iceland's equal pay standard demonstrate how legislation can be effectively used to address this gap.

3. **Mistreatment of Marginalized Communities:** Indigenous Peoples and immigrants often endure discrimination and mistreatment. Countries like Canada have begun to acknowledge and address these injustices, albeit gradually, through truth and reconciliation initiatives and more inclusive policies.

4. **Criminal Justice Inequities:** Disparities in the criminal justice system, such as racial profiling and biased sentencing, undermine trust and equity. Reforms in places like Norway, focusing on rehabilitation over punishment, have shown promise in creating a more equitable justice system.

5. **Educational Disparities:** Unequal access to quality education perpetuates social inequality. Initiatives to increase funding in low-income school districts and policies promoting equal access to education, as seen in some Scandinavian countries, are steps toward mitigating this issue.

6. **Healthcare Disparities:** Inequities in healthcare access and outcomes require urgent attention. Models like the UK's National Health Service, which aims to provide healthcare based on need rather than ability to pay, illustrate attempts to create a more equitable healthcare system.

The Path Forward

Addressing these moral issues requires a governance approach that commits to justice, fairness, and recognizing the inherent worth of every individual. This involves not only acknowledging these ethical shortcomings but actively working towards systemic change.

Progress is being made, though it is uneven. The increasing global focus on social justice, diversity, and inclusion is encouraging, but much work remains. Governance must prioritize policies that dismantle systemic discrimination, promote inclusivity, and ensure equitable opportunities.

Ethical Governance as a Foundation for Equity

The issues of social inequality and systemic discrimination are reminders of the moral imperative at the heart of governance. By integrating ethical principles into decision-making processes, we can build systems that serve the needs and aspirations of all individuals, irrespective of their race, gender, or background. This shift towards moral and ethical governance is not just a policy change; it's a fundamental transformation towards a more just, equitable, and humane world. It's a call to action for all of us to contribute to and advocate for governance that embodies these values.

Conclusion: The Imperative of Moral Governance

The stark realities of the 2008 financial crisis, the Flint water crisis, and the ongoing issues of exploitative labor practices, environmental degradation, and social inequality underscore the profound need for moral governance. These examples are not just isolated incidents but symptomatic of a broader issue: the consequences of sidelining ethical principles in governance.

Lessons and Systemic Solutions

1. **Financial Crisis Insight:** The 2008 financial crisis taught us that neglecting long-term ethical considerations for short-term profits can lead to widespread economic and social harm. A systemic solution lies in implementing more robust financial regulations and oversight mechanisms, ensuring accountability and transparency in financial institutions.
2. **Learning from Flint:** The Flint water crisis highlighted the dis-

astrous results of disregarding public welfare, especially among marginalized communities. This calls for policies that prioritize public health and environmental safety, reinforced by rigorous checks and community engagement in decision-making.

3. **Addressing Labor Exploitation:** The moral failure evident in exploitative labor practices demands a global commitment to fair labor standards. This includes enforcing international labor laws and encouraging ethical supply chain practices among multinational corporations.

4. **Tackling Environmental Challenges:** Environmental degradation should be met with sustainable policies that balance economic development with ecological preservation, as seen in countries like Denmark and New Zealand, which have made significant strides in green governance.

5. **Combating Social Inequality:** Addressing systemic discrimination requires an inclusive approach to policy-making, one that actively works to dismantle barriers and promote equity, as evidenced by various equal opportunity programs worldwide.

Challenges and Global Relevance

Implementing moral governance is not without challenges. It requires navigating complex political, economic, and social landscapes. However, the urgency of these issues transcends borders, making moral governance a global imperative. Countries around the world, each with their unique challenges, must collectively commit to integrating ethical principles into their governance structures.

Positive Examples of Moral Governance

There are encouraging instances where ethical governance has led to positive change. For example, Bhutan's focus on Gross National Happiness as a development indicator prioritizes the well-being of its citizens over mere economic growth. Similarly, the Nordic model, with its emphasis on social welfare and equality, demonstrates the success of governance models rooted in ethical principles.

A Call for Ethical Action

These issues highlight the necessity for a fundamental shift toward moral governance. This means championing policies and systems that uphold justice, fairness, and the well-being of all members of society, not as an afterthought but as a primary objective.

As we move forward, let us learn from past mistakes and positive examples alike, embracing the challenge of implementing moral governance. It is time to prioritize ethical considerations, not only to rectify past wrongs but to pave the way for a more just, equitable, and sustainable future. This journey requires collective effort and commitment, and the time to act is now. Let's seize this opportunity to redefine governance and create a world that reflects our highest moral aspirations.

3

The Sacredness of Nafs (Life)

The Government's Role in Preserving and Improving the Quality of Life

Often perceived as a bureaucratic monolith, the government should instead be seen as the custodian of our collective well-being. Imagine a society that not only respects but holds sacred the gift of life, where each citizen doesn't just survive, but thrives. This vision is not a distant dream, but a tangible goal, demanding the government's proactive involvement in enhancing everyone's quality of life.

Consider this: governments, wielding substantial resources and authority, are uniquely positioned to affect change. Their control over budgets, infrastructure, and policies directly touches our daily lives – healthcare, education, housing, and social services. When Norway, for example, focused its resources on public healthcare and education, it saw a dramatic improvement in its citizens' quality of life. Such targeted efforts can lay the foundation for a dignified existence for all.

Justice and the rule of law are more than legal concepts; they are the lifeblood of a fair society. Governments, in this role, are the shield against exploitation, discrimination, and violence. By actively dismantling systemic inequalities, as seen in Canada's strides towards gender equality, a government can create a society where each life is not just recognized but cherished.

Public health and safety policies are the government's way of extending its protective arm over its citizens. Be it environmental regulations, food safety standards, or health campaigns, these measures are vital. Consider Japan's rigorous food safety standards, which have significantly reduced foodborne illnesses, exemplifying how such policies can enhance the quality of life.

Economic stability, fostered by government policies, has a direct bearing on our lives. Initiatives that drive job creation, fair wages, and social safety nets are crucial. The success story of Germany's social market economy stands testament to how such measures can bridge economic disparities and uphold the sanctity of life.

In essence, the government's role in nurturing and protecting life is more than an administrative task; it is a profound moral obligation. It involves acknowledging the inherent dignity of every individual and taking concrete steps to ensure their life is not only safeguarded but also enriched.

As citizens, it falls upon us to demand from our governments, policies that place life and well-being at the forefront. Participating in the democratic process, we can steer our governments from being mere administrative bodies to being true guardians of life's sacredness. It is within our collective power to build societies where every individual's potential is not just acknowledged but fostered, turning the ideal of sacredness of life into a living reality.

Healthcare for All: A Fundamental Right

Healthcare for all transcends a noble aspiration; it's a fundamental right that each individual deserves, irrespective of economic background. Countries like Canada and the Nordic nations exemplify this, offering universal healthcare systems that excel in quality and accessibility. Yet, globally, governments must realize that healthcare transcends a budgetary line item; it's a vital investment in their most precious asset – their people.

The story of Maria, a single mother from a marginalized community in a country without universal healthcare, underscores this point. Struggling to manage her diabetes due to high medication costs, Maria's plight reflects the stark reality faced by millions, highlighting why healthcare is not just about access to doctors and hospitals but a comprehensive approach encompassing preventive care, mental health services, and essential medications.

Universal healthcare is a cornerstone in upholding the sanctity of life, as encapsulated by the principle of Nafs, and should be a non-negotiable priority for every government. Here's why:

1. **Human Dignity:** Valuing every life, healthcare as a right promotes the inherent dignity of each individual. It's a societal statement that every person's well-being is a priority.
2. **Preventive Focus:** Emphasizing preventive care, universal systems, like in Sweden, prioritize early intervention, reducing costly health complications and enhancing overall community health.
3. **Economic Productivity:** Healthy citizens contribute more effectively to the economy. For instance, studies have shown that in countries with accessible healthcare, workforce productivity increases as fewer days are lost to illness.
4. **Reduced Health Disparities:** In a system where everyone receives equal care, health disparities, especially among underprivileged groups, are significantly reduced, as seen in countries like New Zealand.
5. **Quality of Life:** Without the burden of medical debt, people can pursue life goals unimpeded, a freedom essential for a fulfilling life.
6. **Social Cohesion:** Providing healthcare for all fosters a stronger sense of community and shared responsibility, reinforcing social bonds and mutual respect.

However, embracing universal healthcare is not without its challenges.

Issues like funding, efficient resource allocation, and maintaining high standards of care are genuine concerns. Experts argue that with strategic planning and community engagement, these challenges can be effectively managed.

Countries with universal healthcare, contrary to some beliefs, often rank highly in healthcare outcomes and patient satisfaction. For instance, according to the World Health Organization, Denmark consistently scores high in both these areas.

In conclusion, healthcare for all is more than policy; it's a moral imperative. Respecting the principle of Nafs means acknowledging that providing universal healthcare is not just possible but essential for a just, humane, and thriving society. It's time for governments worldwide to prioritize their citizens' well-being by recognizing healthcare as a fundamental right, not a privilege.

Ensuring Economic Security: Beyond Just Jobs

Economic security transcends mere employment; it's about creating an environment where every citizen can thrive with dignity and pursue their aspirations. The government's role in this is pivotal, and here's why it's not only possible but fundamentally essential:

1. **Living Wages:** Consider Denmark, where the concept of a living wage is deeply ingrained. Here, the government ensures that minimum wages allow individuals and families to meet basic needs comfortably, promoting financial stability and easing the stress of economic uncertainty.
2. **Reasonable Working Conditions:** Economic security also encompasses safe and reasonable working conditions. For example, in Germany, strict workplace safety regulations and protections against discrimination make jobs safer and less detrimental to physical and mental health.
3. **Dignity in Work:** Japan's commitment to employee respect and

fair treatment demonstrates how dignity can be central to every job. Policies promoting nondiscrimination and respect for employees' voices are crucial in fostering a dignified work environment.

4. **Social Safety Nets:** Robust social safety nets are vital. In Canada, comprehensive unemployment benefits and pension schemes have proven effective in preventing individuals from spiraling into poverty during crises. These measures underscore the importance of a safety net in economic security.

5. **Economic Mobility:** Economic security should enable upward mobility. Investment in education and training, as seen in Finland, ensures that citizens have opportunities for career advancement, improving their lives and those of their families.

6. **Quality of Life:** The ultimate goal of economic security is to enhance the quality of life. When people can plan for the future, invest in education and health, and pursue dreams without the fear of financial instability, society as a whole benefits.

7. **Reducing Inequality:** Addressing income inequality is also crucial. Progressive taxation and policies to narrow the wealth gap, similar to those in Sweden, are essential in creating a fair and just society, preserving the sanctity of life.

Challenges such as budget constraints and the impact on businesses are real concerns in implementing these measures. However, as highlighted by economists, strategic planning and a balanced approach can mitigate these challenges, paving the way for sustainable economic security.

In conclusion, the government's role in ensuring economic security is not just about job creation; it's about fostering an environment where individuals and families can lead fulfilling lives with dignity, free from poverty or economic distress. Countries like Denmark, Germany, and Canada exemplify this approach, showing that it's not only possible but imperative for governments to prioritize policies that foster economic security. This approach aligns with the principle of Nafs, which upholds the sanctity of life, making economic security an investment in the well-being of the people.

Educational Empowerment: The Lifelong Gift

Educational empowerment extends beyond mere job preparation; it is a crucial process that shapes informed, responsible, and compassionate citizens. In line with the principle of Nafs, governments must recognize education as a transformative power, crucial for holistic development. Educational empowerment is not just an option but a fundamental necessity, for the following reasons:

1. **Holistic Development:** Education should transcend academic knowledge, embracing emotional intelligence, critical thinking, creativity, and moral values. The Finnish education system, known for its emphasis on student well-being and broad learning, exemplifies this approach, preparing individuals not just for careers but for life's varied challenges and opportunities.

2. **Civic Responsibility:** Robust educational systems, like those in the Netherlands, foster civic responsibility, encouraging active participation in democracy and social justice. These systems instill the importance of empathy and respect for diversity, crucial for the common good.

3. **Social Cohesion:** Education breaks down barriers between diverse groups, promoting understanding and harmony. Singapore's education policy, focusing on multiculturalism and social integration, demonstrates how education can foster inclusive societies where everyone's potential is realized.

4. **Economic Mobility:** Education is a key pathway to economic mobility. By providing individuals with necessary skills and knowledge, education reduces income inequality and contributes to societal well-being, as evidenced by the upward mobility rates in countries like Canada.

5. **Innovation and Progress:** A well-educated workforce drives inno-

vation. South Korea's investments in education have led to significant advancements in technology and other fields, showcasing the link between educational investment and national progress.

6. **Global Competitiveness:** In today's interconnected world, nations like Germany, with their strong educational systems, demonstrate how education is vital for global competitiveness and economic adaptation.

7. **Lifetime Learning:** Governments committed to educational empowerment, such as New Zealand, offer continuous learning opportunities for all ages, encouraging ongoing personal and professional growth.

8. **Preserving Cultural Heritage:** Education plays a key role in preserving cultural heritage. Japan's approach to integrating traditional knowledge and customs into its educational curriculum enriches its cultural identity.

However, challenges such as budget constraints and the balance between traditional and innovative educational methods must be addressed. As education experts note that strategic investment and inclusive policies are key to overcoming these hurdles.

In conclusion, educational empowerment is not a luxury but a necessity for governments that value the sanctity of life and the well-being of their citizens. It's an investment in creating informed, responsible, and compassionate individuals who contribute to a just, thriving, and progressive society. Education is the lifelong gift that keeps on giving, and its transformative power should be a top priority for every nation.

Mental Health: The Silent Priority

Mental health, often a silent priority, is crucial in discussions about quality of life. A government aligned with the principle of Nafs recognizes the imperative of mental well-being. Here's why mental health should be at the forefront of any governance model that values life's sanctity:

1. **Comprehensive Well-Being:** Quality of life includes both physical and mental well-being. Studies show that ignoring mental health can lead to decreased productivity and increased physical health issues, as evidenced by a World Health Organization report linking mental health to chronic diseases.

2. **Preventive Approach:** Mental health programs focus on prevention as well as treatment. The success of Norway's early intervention strategies, for example, illustrates how such approaches can alleviate healthcare system burdens and enhance life quality.

3. **Productivity and Innovation:** There's a direct correlation between mental well-being and national productivity. For instance, companies in Australia implementing mental health programs have reported increased innovation and efficiency.

4. **Reducing Social Costs:** Addressing mental health issues can reduce social costs like crime and homelessness. In the United States, mental health reforms have been linked to declines in homelessness and substance abuse in several major cities.

5. **Enhancing Educational Outcomes:** Implementing mental health programs in schools, similar to those in Japan, leads to better academic performance and student well-being.

6. **Fostering Social Cohesion:** Community-based mental health initiatives, like those in Canada, have successfully fostered stronger social connections and community engagement.

7. **Global Competitiveness:** A mentally healthy workforce enhances a nation's global competitiveness. South Korea's focus on workplace mental health has improved its standing in the global market.

8. **Reducing Stigma:** Governments can play a pivotal role in destigmatizing mental health. The UK's public awareness campaigns have significantly shifted public perceptions about mental illness.

9. **Improved Quality of Life:** Ultimately, mental health is key to improving overall quality of life. A survey in New Zealand indicated higher life satisfaction in populations with access to mental health services.

Challenges in prioritizing mental health include budget constraints and integrating mental health with other healthcare priorities. However, as noted by mental health experts, innovative solutions and cross-sector collaborations can overcome these barriers, making mental health care accessible and effective.

In conclusion, mental health is a societal imperative, not just a healthcare issue. Visionary governments understand that mental well-being is foundational to life's sanctity. By integrating mental health programs in education, workplaces, and public services, governments can enhance citizens' quality of life, reduce social costs, and prepare their nations for greater prosperity and well-being. Prioritizing mental health as it deserves is essential for a holistic and compassionate governance approach.

Environmental Stewardship: A Livable World for All

Environmental stewardship is not merely an option; it's a moral and ethical imperative for any government that values the sanctity of life. This responsibility extends beyond the realm of environmental activism to become a cornerstone of governance, crucial for enhancing the quality of life for all citizens:

1. **Basic Survival:** Clean air and water are fundamental to human survival. For instance, in New Zealand, government policies focused on water conservation and pollution control have markedly improved public health outcomes.
2. **Health and Well-Being:** The link between environmental pollutants and health issues, such as respiratory diseases and cancer, is well-documented. Japan's stringent air quality regulations have significantly reduced pollution-related health problems, demonstrating a government's role in safeguarding its citizens' health.
3. **Sustainable Living:** Sustainable practices are essential for the long-term well-being of the planet. Germany's commitment to renewable energy and responsible resource management serves as a model for

sustainable living, benefiting both current and future generations.

4. **Economic Stability:** Environmental disasters can devastate economies. The Netherlands' investment in flood protection infrastructure is an example of how environmental protection also safeguards a nation's economic stability.

5. **Global Responsibility:** Climate change requires global action. Sweden's leadership in advocating for international climate agreements shows the importance of governmental roles on the global stage.

6. **Resource Equity:** Environmental degradation often disproportionately impacts marginalized communities. Canada's initiatives to address environmental injustices in Indigenous territories highlight the need for equitable resource distribution.

7. **Innovation and Job Creation:** Environmental protection can spur economic growth. The growth of the green technology sector in the United States, for instance, has created numerous jobs while contributing to environmental sustainability.

8. **Resilience Against Disasters:** Preparing for natural disasters is increasingly vital. Japan's advanced earthquake preparedness programs exemplify effective government response measures to protect citizens and property.

9. **Preserving Biodiversity:** Biodiversity is crucial for ecosystem stability. Brazil's efforts in the Amazon rainforest demonstrate the importance of government actions to preserve biodiversity for future generations.

10. **Ethical Responsibility:** Ultimately, environmental stewardship is an ethical duty transcending politics. Every government has the responsibility to protect the planet for current and future generations, as seen in Costa Rica's extensive conservation policies.

While challenges such as economic impacts and feasibility concerns are real, experts emphasize that innovative policy solutions and international collaboration can overcome these barriers, paving the way for sustainable environmental stewardship.

In conclusion, environmental stewardship is a matter of moral and ethical obligation, not a political debate. Governments must prioritize environmental protection and sustainable practices, as exemplified by countries like New Zealand, Japan, Germany, and others. By taking bold actions to protect the environment, governments can secure a better, healthier, and more prosperous future for all citizens. Clean air, water, and a livable world are indispensable elements of a quality life and must be safeguarded through committed stewardship.

Social Inclusion: The Fabric of a Strong Society

Social inclusion is more than a contemporary buzzword; it is the corner-stone of a just and harmonious society. It's imperative for governments to take proactive and persuasive steps in promoting social inclusion, gender equality, and racial equity to assure a high quality of life for all citizens:

1. **Human Dignity:** Discrimination, whether based on race, gender, ethnicity, or any other factor, is a direct affront to human dignity. For example, the Scandinavian model, with its focus on equal rights, demonstrates how government policies can uphold the dignity of every citizen.
2. **Social Cohesion:** Inclusive societies, exemplified by Canada's multiculturalism policy, enhance trust, cooperation, and solidarity among citizens from diverse backgrounds, strengthening social bonds.
3. **Economic Prosperity:** Exclusion and bias stifle talent and economic growth. South Africa's Black Economic Empowerment (BEE) policy illustrates how inclusive practices create opportunities for all citizens to contribute to the economy.
4. **Equality Before the Law:** New Zealand's legal framework, which ensures equal rights for all groups, exemplifies the principle of equality before the law in action.
5. **Education and Awareness:** Education is vital in fostering inclusion.

Countries like Germany have implemented educational programs that promote diversity and tolerance, effectively challenging stereotypes.

6. **Gender Equality:** Gender-based discrimination limits societal progress. Sweden's policies promoting gender equality in all sectors are a model for others to follow.

7. **Racial Equity:** Addressing systemic racism is critical. The United States' affirmative action policies are steps toward rectifying historical injustices and dismantling discriminatory structures.

8. **Health Equity:** Equal access to quality healthcare services, as seen in the UK's National Health Service, ensures that all citizens, regardless of background, receive adequate care.

9. **Social Services:** Provision of comprehensive social services, like in France, supports vulnerable populations and promotes equity.

10. **Cultural Enrichment:** Diversity enriches societies. Australia's support for Indigenous cultures and languages demonstrates the value of cultural diversity.

11. **Political Representation:** Diverse representation in governance, as seen in India's parliamentary system, ensures that various voices are heard in decision-making processes.

12. **Combating Hate and Extremism:** Strong stances against hate speech and discrimination, like those taken in Norway, are crucial for maintaining societal harmony.

13. **Public Awareness Campaigns:** Persuasive public awareness campaigns, similar to those run in Brazil, challenge stereotypes and promote social inclusion.

14. **Data Collection and Monitoring:** Tracking progress in social inclusion, as practiced in the Netherlands, informs targeted interventions.

15. **Community Engagement:** Direct engagement with marginalized communities, a practice in Japan, helps understand and address their unique challenges.

Challenges like budget constraints and balancing diverse societal needs are real but not insurmountable. As noted by social policy experts, innovative policy design and community participation can address these challenges effectively.

In conclusion, social inclusion, gender equality, and racial equity are essential for a strong and prosperous society. Governments must lead in fostering a culture of respect and equality and enacting policies that promote the well-being of all citizens. As demonstrated by practices around the world, it is time for governments to recognize and harness the power of inclusion in building a brighter future for everyone.

Conclusion: The Vision We Must Strive For

The vision we must strive for transcends the traditional role of governments as mere managers. It elevates them to the status of architects of societal well-being, where the enhancement of quality of life is not a lofty ideal but a compelling obligation. This vision sees the government not as a bureaucratic apparatus, but as the guardian of the public's well-being, with actions that shape the lives of citizens and the future of the nation. Here's how this vision can be compelling and essential:

1. **Human-Centric Governance:** Policies and decisions should prioritize the well-being, dignity, and rights of every individual, akin to the approaches seen in the Nordic countries, where comprehensive welfare systems reflect a deep commitment to human-centric governance.
2. **Proactive Problem-Solving:** Like Singapore's forward-thinking urban planning, governments should anticipate societal challenges in healthcare, economy, and education, developing proactive and innovative solutions.
3. **Social Justice:** A commitment to social justice, similar to Canada's reconciliation efforts with Indigenous communities, ensures active addressing of inequality and marginalization.
4. **Sustainable Prosperity:** Economic policies should translate into

better lives for people, as seen in New Zealand's well-being budget, which prioritizes citizens' well-being over GDP growth.

5. **Unity and Cohesion:** Governments should bridge divides, ensuring no one is left behind, much like Germany's efforts to integrate immigrants and refugees into society.

6. **Empowerment and Inclusion:** By providing equal access to opportunities, as exemplified by Rwanda's gender equality in political representation, governments can empower individuals to lead fulfilling lives.

7. **Responsiveness:** Like the town hall meetings in Switzerland, governments should actively engage with the public, seeking feedback and adjusting policies accordingly.

8. **Global Leadership:** Governments can lead by example on the global stage, advocating for peace and sustainability, much like the leadership role played by the European Union in climate change negotiations.

9. **Collective Responsibility:** The citizens' role is also vital. Just as the community-driven initiatives in Denmark contribute to societal well-being, individuals should be engaged and informed, actively participating in shaping their society.

10. **Immediate Action:** The urgency of this vision is exemplified by South Korea's rapid response to the COVID-19 pandemic, showing that immediate and compassionate governance is not only possible but necessary.

While challenges like political feasibility and budget constraints are real, political analysts note that with innovative governance and citizen participation, these barriers can be effectively navigated.

In conclusion, this vision is not an unattainable dream but an essential goal. The persuasive power of change lies in the hands of individuals who demand a government that truly serves its people. By looking at examples worldwide, we can see that this vision is not only compelling but achievable. Your active engagement, advocacy, and support for such a vision can turn it into reality. Join the movement for a government that puts the well-being of its citizens first. The time is now.

Why Healthcare, Safety, and Respect for Life are Non-Negotiables in Governance

Healthcare, safety, and respect for life are not just policy choices in governance; they are its foundational cornerstones. Compromising on these aspects fundamentally undermines the essence of governance. Here is a persuasive argument for why these principles are non-negotiable:

1. **The Value of Life:** The most precious asset any individual possesses is life. It's the source from which all other rights emanate. For instance, the universal healthcare model in countries like Canada demonstrates a commitment to preserving and enhancing life, fulfilling a fundamental duty of governance.

2. **Public Trust:** Governance is a social contract built on trust. The failure of a government to ensure its citizens' safety, similar to the shortcomings seen in emergency responses to natural disasters in some countries, erodes trust and destabilizes society.

3. **Moral Imperative:** Prioritizing healthcare and safety reflects society's ethical standards. A government that neglects these areas, much like those criticized by international human rights organizations, betrays the principles upon which civilized societies are built.

4. **Economic and Social Stability:** A healthy and safe population is crucial for stability. The economic turmoil resulting from inadequate healthcare systems, as observed in developing nations, underscores this reality.

5. **Human Dignity:** Providing healthcare and ensuring safety are key ways to uphold dignity. The Scandinavian welfare model, which emphasizes equal access to healthcare and safety, highlights how every life is valued, irrespective of social status.

6. **Crisis Preparedness:** Robust healthcare and safety infrastructure are crucial in crises, as the COVID-19 pandemic has shown. Countries with strong healthcare systems, like South Korea, responded more effectively, demonstrating the importance of preparedness.

7. **Global Reputation:** How a nation treats its citizens impacts its global standing. New Zealand's acclaimed response to public safety issues has enhanced its international reputation, while failures in this area have tarnished the images of other nations.

8. **Social Cohesion:** Inclusive healthcare and safety policies, like those in Germany, promote social cohesion, reduce inequalities, and foster a sense of unity.

9. **Long-Term Sustainability:** Ensuring the well-being of citizens contributes to long-term stability. For example, Norway's investment in public health and safety has led to a healthier, more sustainable society.

10. **Human Rights:** Healthcare, safety, and respect for life are rooted in international human rights conventions. The Universal Declaration of Human Rights, to which most countries are signatories, obligates governments to uphold these rights.

In conclusion, healthcare, safety, and respect for life are not optional in governance; they are its very essence. By looking at examples worldwide, it's clear that these elements guide policy decisions and reflect the values of a just and compassionate society. Thus, they should be at the forefront of any governance model, with the understanding that any compromise in these areas not only erodes public trust but also threatens the dignity and well-being of citizens.

Healthcare: A Matter of Basic Human Dignity

Access to quality healthcare is a fundamental right and a matter of basic human dignity, not a luxury. Here's a persuasive argument for why healthcare is an indispensable aspect of governance:

1. **Inherent Value of Life:** Every individual's right to a healthy, fulfilling life is sacrosanct. Countries like Japan, with their universal healthcare system, demonstrate how healthcare preserves and protects this invaluable asset, embodying the principle that every human life has worth.

2. **Preventing Undue Suffering:** In developing nations where healthcare access is limited, the tragic consequences of preventable illnesses are starkly evident. Ensuring healthcare access is a statement that a government values the well-being and dignity of its citizens, not just their economic productivity.

3. **Equality and Fairness:** The Scandinavian healthcare model illustrates how quality care for all, irrespective of socio-economic status, upholds fairness and equity, leveling the societal playing field.

4. **Productive Society:** Healthy citizens are essential for a thriving society. In Germany, widespread healthcare access correlates with high productivity and economic dynamism, showcasing the societal benefits of a healthy populace.

5. **Family Well-Being:** The impact of accessible healthcare on family stability is profound. In Canada, universal healthcare reduces the emotional and financial burdens on families, safeguarding the well-being of entire communities.

6. **Preventative Care:** Preventative measures, like those in Australia's healthcare system, save lives and reduce long-term costs, exemplifying prudent investment in population health.

7. **Global Reputation:** Nations like the Netherlands, known for their excellent healthcare systems, are respected globally, enhancing their diplomatic standing and fostering positive international relations.

8. **Moral and Ethical Obligation:** Ethical governance, as seen in New Zealand's healthcare policies, reflects a commitment to justice, compassion, and the sanctity of life, resonating with societal values.

9. **Crisis Preparedness:** The COVID-19 pandemic highlighted the criticality of robust healthcare systems, as evidenced by South Korea's effective response, underscoring the importance of healthcare

infrastructure in crisis management.

10. **Long-Term Prosperity:** A study by the World Health Organization shows that nations investing in healthcare are more likely to experience long-term economic growth, echoing the concept that a healthy population is a prosperous one.

In conclusion, healthcare is not a negotiable aspect of governance; it is an affirmation of the intrinsic value of every human life. As evidenced by practices in countries like Japan, Germany, and the Netherlands, it is a reflection of a just and compassionate society that recognizes the basic human right to live without undue suffering. Governments must, therefore, prioritize healthcare as a fundamental pillar of their responsibility to their citizens, ensuring it is accessible to all as a matter of basic human dignity.

Safety: The Fundamental Role of Government

Safety transcends being a mere ideal or a desirable outcome; it is the cornerstone upon which effective governance rests. This passage outlines why safety is an indispensable aspect of governance and a non-negotiable priority:

1. **Foundation of Society:** Safety forms the foundation of all societies, as demonstrated by the transformation seen in post-conflict societies like Rwanda, where rebuilding a sense of safety was key to social cohesion and community rebuilding.
2. **Basic Human Need:** Instinctively sought, safety is essential for a thriving populace. This is evident in countries with high safety ratings, like Denmark, where citizens engage more actively in social and economic activities.
3. **Trust in Government:** The correlation between safety and public trust is evident in places like Singapore, where high safety standards have fostered deep trust in governmental institutions.

4. **Economic Prosperity:** Economically prosperous nations, such as Japan, underscore safety as a prerequisite for economic growth, fostering business development and tourism.

5. **Quality of Life:** A safe environment, as seen in Canada, enhances overall well-being, allowing people to enjoy education, healthcare, and recreation without fear.

6. **Human Rights:** Safety as a human right is epitomized by countries adhering to international human rights standards, where governments legally and ethically protect their citizens' safety.

7. **Preventing Harm:** The proactive approach to safety in nations like Australia, with strict environmental and product safety standards, demonstrates the importance of preventive measures in governance.

8. **Public Order:** The role of safety in maintaining public order is exemplified in countries with strong legal systems, where peaceful coexistence and dispute resolution through legal means are the norms.

9. **Freedom and Expression:** In nations with high safety standards, like Norway, people enjoy greater freedom of expression, contributing to a vibrant, open society.

10. **Psychological Well-Being:** The link between safety and mental health is evident in societies with low crime rates, where lower stress and anxiety levels contribute to overall happiness.

11. **Global Reputation:** Countries recognized for their safety, like Switzerland, attract international partnerships and investments, highlighting the global importance of a safe environment.

12. **Conflict Resolution:** Effective conflict resolution strategies, as seen in peacebuilding efforts in countries like Colombia, illustrate safety's role in mitigating tensions and fostering harmony.

In conclusion, safety is a core responsibility of governance, not a luxury. It is fundamental to creating a just and functioning society. Examples from around the world, from Rwanda's post-conflict rebuilding to Denmark's thriving social engagement, demonstrate that safety is crucial for all other aspects of life to prosper. Governments must prioritize safety, balancing it with personal freedoms and budget constraints, to ensure the long-term well-being and stability of their societies. Safety, therefore, should be an unwavering priority for governments globally, integral to the vision of a just, prosperous, and harmonious world.

Respect for Life: The Ethical Imperative

Respect for life is more than a moral guideline; it is the ethical bedrock that should underpin every facet of governance. This principle is non-negotiable and ought to guide every responsible government. Here's an enhanced perspective:

1. **Inherent Dignity:** Every human being possesses inherent dignity. The Rwandan government's post-genocide focus on human dignity and reconciliation showcases this principle in action, acknowledging the intrinsic worth of every individual.
2. **Equality and Justice:** Ethical governance, like that observed in the Nordic countries, seeks to dismantle systemic inequalities, ensuring justice and equal treatment for all citizens, exemplifying the belief that every life holds equal value.
3. **Compassion and Empathy:** New Zealand's approach to social welfare, especially in addressing child poverty, reflects how governments can embody compassion and empathy in their policies, supporting those in hardship.
4. **Environmental Responsibility:** The stewardship of the Costa Rican government in protecting biodiversity illustrates respect for all forms of life, emphasizing environmental sustainability and the interconnectedness of ecosystems.
5. **International Relations:** Norway's peace diplomacy demonstrates ethical governance on the global stage, engaging in just and peaceful foreign policies that respect the sovereignty and rights of other nations.

6. **Transparency and Accountability:** The transparency and citizen participation in governance models like Estonia's e-governance system exemplify how open scrutiny and accountability can align governmental actions with the principle of respect for life.

7. **Preventing Harm:** Japan's disaster preparedness and response strategies, particularly in earthquake technology, show how governments can proactively protect citizens from harm.

8. **Long-Term Thinking:** Bhutan's focus on Gross National Happiness over GDP is a model of long-term, ethical governance, prioritizing the well-being of future generations and acknowledging the multifaceted nature of human life.

9. **Human Rights:** South Africa's post-apartheid Constitution, which upholds human rights as central, demonstrates a commitment to the fundamental right to life, steering clear of practices that infringe upon these rights.

10. **Public Trust:** The high level of public trust in governments like that of Singapore, where citizen safety and well-being are prioritized, underscores how respecting life can build confidence in governance and encourage civic engagement.

In conclusion, respect for life should be the ethical North Star guiding governmental actions. As seen in examples from Rwanda to Bhutan, this principle is not only a moral imperative but the foundation of a just, humane, and sustainable society. Governments that prioritize respect for life in their policies and actions set a standard for ethical governance. Citizens, in turn, should hold their governments accountable to this principle, ensuring that respect for life remains at the forefront of policymaking and governance. This commitment to ethical governance, underpinned by respect for life, is essential for building a world that values every individual and preserves the dignity and equality of all.

The Consequence of Compromise: A Society at Risk

Compromising on healthcare, safety, or respect for life carries profound and far-reaching consequences that ripple through every aspect of society. Here's an enhanced look at the damage such compromises can inflict:

1. **Loss of Human Lives:** The tragic outcomes of healthcare compromise are starkly evident in cases like India's COVID-19 crisis, where a lack of preparedness led to a devastating loss of life. Preventable illnesses and injuries can escalate into widespread tragedy, leaving deep scars in communities.

2. **Increased Suffering:** In nations where healthcare infrastructure is inadequate, such as certain rural areas in Africa, individuals endure unnecessary suffering from treatable conditions. This not only affects the person but also places a heavy emotional and financial burden on families.

3. **Economic Impact:** The economic repercussions are clearly seen in the aftermath of public health emergencies. The SARS outbreak, for example, cost the global economy billions, highlighting how investing in healthcare is far more cost-effective than managing crises post-facto.

4. **Erosion of Safety:** A decline in public safety, as seen in countries experiencing political turmoil, leads to social isolation and reduced community engagement, negatively affecting mental health and societal cohesion.

5. **Distrust in Government:** The Flint water crisis in Michigan, USA, is a prime example of how safety compromises erode trust in government, leading to long-term cynicism and disengagement among citizens.

6. **Diminished Reputation:** Internationally, countries failing to uphold basic life respect, such as those with poor human rights records, suffer from reduced credibility, impacting their diplomatic and trade relations.

7. **Social Division:** Disparities in healthcare access can lead to social unrest, as witnessed during the Arab Spring, where one of the grievances was unequal access to resources, including healthcare.

8. **Brain Drain:** Countries with compromised healthcare and safety, like Venezuela, often witness a 'brain drain' as professionals seek better opportunities abroad, impeding long-term national growth.

9. **Public Health Crises:** The unpreparedness for the Ebola outbreak in West Africa showcased how a compromised healthcare system can lead to catastrophic public health crises.

10. **Erosion of Human Rights:** Neglecting respect for life leads to human rights violations, as seen in the treatment of refugees in various global contexts, where lack of access to basic necessities and safe living conditions is a grim reality.

11. **Public Trust:** Successful management of crises like New Zealand's response to the Christchurch earthquake demonstrates how upholding safety and healthcare can bolster public trust in government.

In conclusion, the cost of compromising on healthcare, safety, or respect for life is too high for any society. These are not mere policy options but fundamental responsibilities of governance. Governments must prioritize these areas, learning from global examples and implementing strategies to mitigate risks. The well-being of citizens, the stability of the economy, and the integrity of a nation depend on it. A society willing to compromise on these fundamental principles risks not only its present well-being but also its future prosperity and global standing.

Conclusion: The Principles We Must Uphold

The principles of healthcare, safety, and respect for life are not mere ideals in governance; they are the bedrock upon which a just and compassionate society stands. Reflecting on their undeniable significance, let's reiterate their crucial importance:

1. **Healthcare as a Human Right:** The story of the universal healthcare model in countries like Canada illustrates that access to quality healthcare is a basic human right, not a privilege. It's a recognition of the inherent value of every individual and a commitment to ensuring no one suffers needlessly due to a lack of medical care.

2. **Safety as Fundamental:** The aftermath of neglecting public safety is evident in cases like the increase in violence and insecurity in cities where law enforcement and public safety measures have been compromised. Safety is fundamental for individuals to lead fulfilling lives, free from fear and danger, enabling them to contribute meaningfully to their communities.

3. **Respect for Life as a Moral Imperative:** Respecting life goes beyond politics or economics; it is an ethical responsibility. The impact of policies valuing life is seen in nations that have taken strong stances against capital punishment or inhumane practices, demonstrating their commitment to human dignity.

These principles should not only be enshrined in documents but also manifested in tangible actions and policies. As citizens, we must hold our governments accountable for upholding these values, demanding transparency, fairness, and compassion in governance.

In our collective pursuit of a flourishing society, these principles must be more than slogans; they should be lived realities. Advocating for policies that prioritize the well-being of all is imperative. For instance, the global response to the COVID-19 pandemic highlighted the necessity of robust healthcare systems and the importance of government action to ensure public safety and respect for life.

As we confront challenges such as economic constraints and political divisions, we must not lose sight of these fundamental values. The cost of compromising on healthcare, safety, or respect for life – as seen in instances of healthcare inequity and neglect of public safety – can lead to societal discord and erosion of trust in governance.

Let us be unwavering in our commitment to a society that prioritizes healthcare, safety, and the unequivocal respect for life. By demanding accountability from our leaders and working collectively for just policies, we can build a world where these principles are not negotiable but foundational to our governance and societal structure.

The time for action is now. We must rise to ensure that healthcare, safety, and respect for life are more than words; they must be the essence of our governance and society. Will you join in this crucial effort?

4

Empowering the Aql (Intellect)

The Role of Education and Wisdom in Shaping the Future

Education: The Catalyst of Future Success

Think of building a towering skyscraper. Without a solid foundation, it's destined to fail. Similarly, a thriving future without the bedrock of a robust educational system is an empty dream. Education isn't just a phase in life; it's the cornerstone of societal development. Yet, it's crucial to remember: education isn't merely a factory churning out workers. It should be a transformative journey that fosters wisdom, ethics, and civic virtues. This isn't just an ideal; it's a necessity for our society.

Let's delve into why education is so pivotal:

1. **Empowering Minds**: Consider education as a key. It unlocks human potential and fosters critical thinking. Armed with knowledge and skills, individuals can meaningfully contribute to society and tackle complex modern challenges.
2. **Fostering Innovation**: A rounded education sparks creativity. It nurtures the courage to question, to imagine, to push boundaries.

The future thrives on innovation, born in the classrooms where ideas take flight.

3. **Ethical Foundation**: Education goes beyond textbooks. It builds character, instilling values like integrity and empathy. These values are vital for a just and compassionate society.

4. **Civic Engagement**: Educated individuals often participate more in civic duties, from voting to community service. Education breeds a proactive stance in shaping a better future.

5. **Economic Prosperity**: An educated workforce attracts investments and drives innovation. It's key to a nation's global competitiveness.

6. **Wisdom and Well-Being**: Education transcends grades. It's about wisdom, about learning to lead meaningful lives, make ethical decisions, and find purpose.

But let's not forget the challenges. Not every educational system meets these ideals. There are gaps and shortcomings that must be acknowledged and addressed. By integrating real-world examples, like Finland's approach to student-centric, flexible learning, we can illustrate what effective education looks like.

Investment in education means more than just funding; it's about curating curricula that emphasize wisdom, ethics, and civic virtues. It's about supporting teachers who ignite passion and curiosity in students. Our commitment to education is a commitment to the future of our society, our nations, and our world.

As we ponder the future role of education, remember: we're not just building structures but nurturing minds. We're kindling the flame of wisdom and laying the groundwork for a future that's not only successful but also morally sound and ethically enlightened. The future begins in today's classrooms.

In a personal reflection, I recall a teacher who transformed my view on history, turning it from mere dates and facts into stories of real people and their struggles. This experience shaped my understanding of the power of education. Let's strive to create such transformative experiences for every student. The journey of education is not just about where it takes us, but how it shapes us along the way.

Wisdom: The Guiding North Star

If education is the foundation, wisdom is our guiding North Star, illuminating the path as societies navigate complex challenges and ethical dilemmas. Wisdom transcends the mere accumulation of facts and knowledge. It embodies a deep understanding of context, an embrace of nuance, and the capacity for balanced, far-reaching decisions. Wisdom is the linchpin in our intricate web of human existence, crucial in everything from social justice to environmental sustainability. Without wisdom, history shows us, even the most educated societies can stray off course.

Here's why wisdom is indispensable:

1. **Navigating Complexity**: Our modern world is a labyrinth of challenges, rarely presenting straightforward solutions. Wisdom equips us to see beyond the surface, to understand the deeper dynamics at play. It's like having a compass in a dense forest, guiding us to consider long-term consequences and the interconnectedness of our actions.

2. **Fostering Compassion**: Wisdom is the root of empathy and compassion. It's what enabled leaders like Nelson Mandela to advocate for reconciliation over revenge. This kind of wisdom enriches our understanding of diverse human experiences, urging us to act with kindness and fairness.

3. **Ethical Decision-Making**: Wisdom is critical in making ethical choices. It's the inner voice that champions fairness, justice, and integrity. Consider the ethical quandaries faced by whistleblowers – it's wisdom that guides them to uphold truth, often at personal cost.

4. **Environmental Stewardship**: Our planet's health hinges on wise stewardship. Wisdom compels us to think like Indigenous communities who view themselves as guardians of the Earth, making choices

that prioritize long-term ecological health over immediate gains.

5. **Mitigating Conflict**: Wisdom is a powerful tool in resolving disputes. It fosters dialogue and compromise, seeking common ground. The peace negotiations in conflict zones, where wisdom triumphs over hostility, are testaments to its conflict-resolving power.

6. **Long-Term Vision**: Wise societies invest in the future. They consider the impact on generations to come, much like the ancient builders of the Roman aqueducts, who built for the ages, not just for their time.

Wisdom is not a mere byproduct of education; it is a lifelong pursuit that requires introspection, self-awareness, and ethical commitment. As we venture into an increasingly complex and interconnected future, let wisdom be our North Star. Our educational systems, leaders, and daily choices should prioritize its cultivation. Wisdom isn't a luxury but a necessity for tackling the formidable challenges of our time and building a just, compassionate, and sustainable world.

In my own journey, a moment of wisdom came from an elderly neighbor who taught me the value of listening – not just hearing. This simple act of wisdom has informed countless decisions and interactions since. Let us all seek such moments of wisdom in our lives, recognizing that it's not just about acquiring knowledge, but understanding how to use that knowledge for the greater good.

The Synergy of Education and Wisdom in Governance

In a governance model that truly values intellectual empowerment, epitomized by the concept of Aql, education and wisdom form a harmonious partnership. This synergy is not merely philosophical but a pragmatic necessity for effective governance. Education serves as the nurturing ground for wisdom, which in turn refines and directs the goals of education.

Here's a more focused look at this dynamic interplay:

1. **Education as the Crucible of Wisdom**: Education provides the base through which critical thinking and ethical discernment are developed – the bedrock of wisdom. Consider Finland, where education systems emphasize critical thinking and ethical understanding, laying the groundwork for wise decision-making.

2. **Wisdom as the Moral Compass in Education**: Wisdom ensures that education is not just a means to an end, but a journey toward a virtuous society. It directs educational policies toward ethical values, societal well-being, and sustainability.

3. **Wisdom in Leadership**: Historical figures like Nelson Mandela exemplify wisdom in governance. Such leaders prioritize the common good, making informed, ethical decisions that reflect a deep understanding of their societal impact.

4. **Wisdom in Public Discourse**: A wise public discourse encourages empathetic listening and diverse perspectives. It's about using education not just for knowledge acquisition but for engaging in respectful, meaningful dialogue.

5. **Ethical Governance Shaped by Wisdom**: Ethical governance, guided by wisdom, prioritizes transparency and justice. Policies reflect these values, focusing on the greater good, as seen in the transparent governance models of countries like Denmark.

6. **Lifelong Learning and Wisdom**: The pursuit of wisdom extends beyond formal education. Education systems should foster a lifelong love for learning and self-improvement, recognizing that wisdom is an ongoing journey.

7. **Addressing Complex Challenges with Wisdom**: Wisdom enables governments to approach complex issues with foresight and ethical judgment. Wise governance involves considering long-term impacts and sustainable solutions, much like the approach taken in the Paris Agreement on climate change.

8. **Resilience through Wisdom**: Societies guided by wisdom demonstrate resilience in crises. They respond with adaptability and unity, prioritizing citizen well-being and the preservation of core values.

In summary, education and wisdom are intertwined in the pursuit of a thriving society. One provides the tools, while the other offers the moral framework to use those tools responsibly. Therefore, fostering this synergy is crucial. We must invest in educational systems that emphasize holistic development and nurture a culture where wisdom is valued as a key asset in governance. In doing so, we pave the way for a society that is not only knowledgeable but also ethically grounded, resilient, and just—a society where education and wisdom work together, lighting the path to a brighter future for all.

How Education Shapes Future Innovation

Consider the extraordinary technological strides in recent decades: the internet's rise, smartphone proliferation, artificial intelligence break-throughs, and clean energy innovations. These transformative achieve-ments have reshaped our world, making it more interconnected and efficient. The foundation of these innovations? Education.

Education is the fertile ground nurturing the seeds of innovation. It equips people with the knowledge, skills, and creativity needed to explore new frontiers. However, the critical aspect lies not just in how education shapes innovation, but in guiding these advancements to be both groundbreaking and ethically aligned with the greater good.

In this context, wisdom plays a pivotal role. It ensures innovation isn't just a race for technological dominance, but a conscious journey towards beneficial human advancements. Here's a more focused look at why this synergy between education and wisdom is crucial:

1. **Ethical Innovation**: While education imparts technical know-how, wisdom embeds a moral compass. It guides innovators to consider the broader impact of their work on society and the environment. For instance, the development of AI ethics is a direct response to this need for ethical guidance in innovation.
2. **Balanced Progress**: Wisdom encourages a balance between tech-

nological progress and responsibility. This approach is evident in sustainable energy projects, where innovation is matched with environmental stewardship.

3. **Societal Needs-Driven Innovation**: True innovation addresses societal challenges. Wisdom steers efforts towards solutions that enhance collective well-being, much like the invention of affordable water purification systems in developing countries.

4. **Inclusive Innovation**: Wisdom champions inclusivity in innovation. It ensures that advancements consider diverse needs and don't widen existing inequalities, as seen in the push for universal design in technology.

5. **Sustainable Focus**: While education equips us to create, wisdom directs us towards sustainable innovation. This is reflected in the growing emphasis on green technologies that prioritize long-term ecological health.

6. **Interdisciplinary Collaboration**: The intersection of different fields, facilitated by wisdom, leads to holistic solutions. The collaboration between medical science and engineering in creating advanced prosthetics is a prime example.

7. **Anticipating and Mitigating Unintended Consequences**: Wisdom allows innovators to foresee and address potential negative impacts. This foresight is crucial in fields like genetic engineering, where the implications extend far beyond the lab.

8. **Prioritizing Public Good**: Education can foster personal success, but wisdom ensures innovation serves the public interest. This principle is at the heart of open-source movements, where knowledge and innovation are shared freely for the benefit of all.

In conclusion, education lays the groundwork for innovation, but wisdom steers these advancements towards ethical, responsible, and sustainable paths. As we look towards a future brimming with technological potential, let's remember the crucial role of wisdom in ensuring that our innovations not only push the boundaries of human capability but also enhance the quality of life for everyone. This powerful combination of education and wisdom can lead us towards a future where innovation is not only advanced but also altruistic and aligned with the greater good.

How Wisdom Shapes Ethical and Sustainable Development

Envision a society where decisions in governance, business, and everyday life are guided by wisdom, not just in theory but in practice. This isn't a utopian fantasy; it's a tangible vision achievable through wisdom's transformative power. Wisdom doesn't just ask, "Can we?" but crucially, "Should we?" It's a crucial check in a world racing towards technological and economic growth, reminding us of our responsibility to consider our actions' wider impacts.

Here's a more focused exploration of how wisdom shapes ethical and sustainable development

1. **Balanced Economic Growth**: Wisdom steers economic policies towards inclusivity and equity. Take the example of the Nordic model, which combines robust economic growth with strong social safety nets, illustrating how wisdom can balance wealth creation with social equity.
2. **Environmental Stewardship**: Wisdom compels us to be responsible custodians of our planet. The global movement towards renewable energy sources, inspired by a wise understanding of our interconnectedness with nature, exemplifies this stewardship.
3. **Long-Term Vision in Governance**: Wisdom discourages short-term gains at the expense of future generations. Consider Bhutan's focus on Gross National Happiness over Gross Domestic Product, a policy choice emphasizing long-term societal well-being.
4. **Ethical Technology**: As we advance technologically, wisdom calls for ethical considerations. The development of guidelines for ethical AI use is an example of wisdom guiding technological progress.
5. **Global Responsibility**: Wisdom urges responsible global citizenship.

HEAVEN IS UNDER THE FEET OF GOVERNMENTS

The Paris Agreement on climate change represents this global responsibility, advocating cooperative action for a universal challenge.

6. **Community and Well-Being**: Wisdom values strong communities. Initiatives like urban green spaces, which enhance communal well-being and mental health, are outcomes of this wisdom-driven approach.

7. **Cultural Preservation and Education**: Wisdom recognizes the importance of preserving diverse cultures and knowledge. UNESCO's intangible cultural heritage list safeguards traditional wisdom for future generations.

8. **Ethical Business Practices**: In business, wisdom leads to practices that prioritize the collective good. The rise of social entrepreneurship and corporate social responsibility initiatives are testaments to this trend.

In essence, a governance model rooted in wisdom is sustainable, ethical, and equitable. These qualities are crucial for any society aspiring to a better future. By embracing wisdom as a guiding principle, we pave the way for a world that is not just prosperous but also just, compassionate, and sustainable. Wisdom reminds us that our decisions today shape the world of tomorrow, urging us to build a legacy of ethical prosperity and environmental health.

The Role of Citizens: From Passive Receivers to Active Shapers

In a society that values intellectual empowerment and wisdom, citizens are more than just passive receivers of information and policies; they are the active shapers of their present and the architects of their future. Embracing this role is not a mere choice but an imperative for nurturing a better society. Here's how citizens can actively contribute to this transformative vision:

Support Holistic Education

- **Advocate for Educational Reforms**: Citizens can champion educational reforms that go beyond rote learning and standardized tests. We should advocate for a holistic approach that fosters critical thinking, ethical discernment, and civic education, drawing inspiration from successful models like Finland's education system.
- **Engage with Educational Institutions**: Get involved with local schools, colleges, and universities. Encourage them to integrate ethics and life skills into their curricula and support character education programs that build well-rounded individuals.

Engage in Public Wisdom

- **Participate in Community Discussions**: Civic engagement is crucial for wise governance. Participate in community forums, public debates, and town halls to voice concerns and share ideas. These platforms are vital for holding policymakers accountable and ensuring decisions reflect the community's needs.
- **Advocate for Wise Decision-Making**: Demand transparency, ethical conduct, and long-term thinking from elected officials. Support policies that prioritize societal well-being, drawing inspiration from examples like New Zealand's well-being budget, which focuses on broader societal health rather than just economic growth.

Mentorship and Community Service

- **Become a Mentor**: Mentor young people, imparting not just knowledge but wisdom. Programs like Big Brothers Big Sisters demonstrate the profound impact mentorship can have on the ethical and intellectual development of the younger generation.
- **Engage in Community Service**: Volunteer for causes that matter. Whether it's working towards social justice, environmental sustain-

ability, or supporting marginalized communities, active participation can make a significant difference.

By adopting these roles, citizens transition from passive spectators to active participants in shaping their society. This shift is essential for a cultural transformation towards wisdom and intellectual empowerment. It's a profound commitment to building a society that values knowledge, ethics, and compassion.

However, it's important to acknowledge the challenges in this endeavor. Political, social, or economic barriers can hinder active citizenship. Overcoming these requires perseverance, creativity, and a willingness to leverage digital platforms for greater reach and impact.

In conclusion, as active shapers, citizens have a crucial role in ensuring the principles of Aql are not just theoretical but are actively practiced, leading to a brighter, more prosperous future for all. Let's not just envision this future; let's actively create it.

Conclusion: The Future We Owe Ourselves and Our Children

In the unfolding story of human progress, education and wisdom stand as fundamental pillars for constructing a future that is not only prosperous but also equitable, sustainable, and guided by wisdom. As we gaze into the horizon of what's to come, we must acknowledge the essential nature of these elements in our societal fabric. They are not mere luxuries but necessities, crucial to the legacy we leave for future generations.

The tomorrow we yearn for is inherently tied to our current choices in fostering education and wisdom. These decisions shape not only our personal growth but also the trajectory of our communities and nations. The quality of our future correlates directly with the value we place on these critical elements today.

Personally, this means embracing the role of lifelong learners, continuously expanding our knowledge and honing our discernment. It's about cultivating wisdom through reflection, empathy, and a steadfast commitment to ethical living. This journey, while inspiring, is not without its challenges. Balancing the demands of daily life with ongoing learning requires dedication and often, innovative solutions.

In our communities, active engagement is key. This involves supporting educational initiatives, participating in community dialogues, and nurturing environments that value critical thinking and compassion. However, achieving this ideal demands overcoming social and economic barriers that can limit access and participation. It's about creating inclusive spaces where diverse voices are heard and respected, and where ethical decision-making is paramount.

Governance models, too, must evolve. We need to advocate for educational systems that view learning as a transformative journey and for policies where wisdom is a guiding force. Our leaders must prioritize the development of individuals who are not just knowledgeable but also capable of ethical and critical thinking. This reimagining, though fraught with political and bureaucratic challenges, is essential for a future where policies are crafted not just for short-term gains but for long-term societal well-being.

The future is an accumulation of our present efforts. By investing in education and wisdom now, we're securing a future that we can be proud of; one where innovation serves humanity, ethical considerations drive progress, and wisdom navigates the complexities of our world.

Let's choose wisely, not just for our immediate benefit but for the generations that follow. Prioritizing education and wisdom is more than an investment in our future; it's an obligation to ourselves, our children, and the world we inhabit. It's about building a future that is not just prosperous but is also just, sustainable, and wise—a future that truly belongs to all.

Policy Changes Needed to Support Intellectual Growth and Innovation

Intellectual Growth and Innovation: The Twin Engines of Progress

Visualize society as a grand locomotive powering towards the future. This locomotive, symbolizing progress, is driven by intellectual growth and innovation. Without nurturing these twin engines, the locomotive risks stagnation, unable to navigate the dynamic landscape of our times.

These engines, however, don't run in a vacuum. They are fueled by thoughtfully crafted policies that recognize the essential role of intellectual growth and innovation in a nation's prosperity and resilience. Here are targeted policy changes that can keep these engines running at full throttle:

1. **Investing in Lifelong Learning Education**: Education should be a continuous journey, not a finite phase. Policies must facilitate lifelong learning, promoting adult education, online platforms, and skills training. Look at Singapore's SkillsFuture initiative, which offers citizens credits for lifelong learning courses, setting a global benchmark.

2. **Cultivating a Culture of Curiosity**: Educational policies should foster curiosity and critical thinking from an early age. This means reshaping curricula to emphasize problem-solving, creativity, and ethics, akin to Finland's education system, which has successfully integrated these elements.

3. **Robust Support for R&D**: A thriving R&D ecosystem is crucial. Policies should provide sufficient resources and incentives for scientific research and creative endeavors. The European Union's Horizon 2020 program, with its significant funding for research, is a model to emulate.

4. **Safeguarding Intellectual Property**: Effective protection of intellectual property rights is key to encouraging innovation. A legal

framework that evolves with the fast-paced nature of technological advancements is essential, as demonstrated by South Korea's rigorous IP laws.

5. **Empowering Entrepreneurs and Startups**: Policies must foster an environment conducive to entrepreneurship. Streamlining bureaucratic processes, providing access to capital, and offering mentorship programs, similar to Canada's Start-Up Visa Program, can galvanize startup ecosystems.

6. **Ethical and Sustainable Innovation**: Innovation must align with ethical standards and sustainability. Regulations to curb harmful practices and promote green technologies, like Germany's Energiewende (energy transition) policy, are imperative.

7. **Encouraging International Collaboration**: Intellectual growth and innovation transcend borders. Policies facilitating global research partnerships and talent exchange can enrich the innovation landscape, as seen in the collaborative efforts of CERN.

8. **Valuing the Arts and Humanities**: The arts and humanities are vital for fostering creativity and empathy. A holistic education policy that includes these fields, much like the Liberal Arts education model in the U.S., can contribute significantly to intellectual development.

9. **Innovative Government Practices**: Governments can lead by example in embracing innovation. Digitalizing public services and adopting innovative policy design can inspire the private sector, as demonstrated by Estonia's e-governance model.

10. **Inclusivity in Policy Making**: Ensuring that policies are inclusive and equitable is crucial. Intellectual growth and innovation should be accessible to all, mirroring initiatives like India's Digital India program, which aims to democratize access to technology.

In conclusion, to keep the locomotive of society advancing robustly, we need policies that fuel intellectual growth and innovation. These policies should not just be aspirations but actionable plans that can adapt to changing global landscapes. They are the difference between a society that thrives in the face of change and one that lags behind. As we face the future, let's commit to policies that empower, innovate, and include, ensuring a brighter path for all.

Rethinking Education Financing: Investment, Not Expenditure

Education transcends being merely a budgetary line item; it represents a foundational investment in a nation's prosperity, innovation, and resilience. Recognizing education as a strategic investment reframes how we approach its funding. It's not just an expenditure but a catalyst for collective progress. Here's how we can reconceptualize education financing:

Increasing Public Funding for Education

Education must be universally accessible, not a privilege for a select few. Governments need to prioritize and increase education funding, viewing it as an investment with substantial returns. This investment equips individuals with knowledge and skills, enhancing their productivity and societal contribution. It drives economic growth by creating a skilled workforce capable of innovation and global competition. It also promotes societal well-being by cultivating critical thinking, empathy, and civic responsibility.

For instance, countries like Norway and Denmark invest heavily in education, resulting in high levels of literacy, innovation, and economic stability. These nations demonstrate the long-term benefits of such investments in fostering equitable and prosperous societies.

Expanding Scholarships and Grants

Higher education should be accessible regardless of financial background. Expanding scholarships and grants, especially in future-oriented fields like technology, healthcare, and renewable energy, is crucial. These financial aids democratize education, allowing talent to flourish irrespective of socio-economic status.

Scholarships and grants not only alleviate the financial burden for students but also incentivize them to pursue essential disciplines. They have a ripple effect on the economy by producing a highly skilled workforce that drives innovation and economic growth. The Gates Millennium Scholars Program, for example, has made significant strides in providing opportunities to outstanding students from diverse backgrounds, fostering a new generation of leaders and innovators.

In conclusion, rethinking education financing as an investment rather than an expenditure is imperative. This shift in perspective is critical for empowering individuals and propelling societies toward a future marked by progress and innovation. By increasing public funding and expanding scholarship opportunities, we make a decisive choice: to invest in our collective future. This is not just an economic imperative but a moral one, ensuring that we don't just grow, but we grow together, paving the way for a more inclusive, educated, and prosperous society.

Curriculum Overhaul: Preparing for the 21st Century

In this era of rapid technological change, complex global issues, and evolving career landscapes, it's imperative that our education system undergoes a transformative overhaul. Our curriculums must be recalibrated to equip students with the skills, knowledge, and adaptability necessary for thriving in the 21st century. To achieve this, we propose two fundamental steps:

1. **Embracing Interdisciplinary Studies**: Today's challenges, such as climate change, social inequality, and technological disruption,

demand an integrated approach. It's crucial that our education systems foster interdisciplinary studies, blending fields like science, economics, and humanities to provide a comprehensive understanding of complex global issues. For example, programs like Singapore's Integrated Programmes (IP) have shown success by offering a holistic, interdisciplinary curriculum that encourages intellectual curiosity and critical thinking across subjects.

2. **Prioritizing Critical Thinking and Creativity**: The traditional focus on rote learning is inadequate for nurturing essential skills like critical thinking, creativity, and problem-solving. These skills should be at the forefront of our educational goals. Critical thinking empowers students to analyze information critically, challenge assumptions, and make well-informed decisions. Creativity sparks innovation and entrepreneurial thinking. Schools like Finland's comprehensive education system, renowned for its focus on student-centered learning and creative problem-solving, serve as a model for fostering these skills.

In addition to these core areas, our curriculum overhaul must also emphasize digital literacy, collaboration, and emotional intelligence, equipping students with a broader skill set for the digital age. However, the success of these reforms hinges on effective teacher training. Educators must be equipped with the tools and knowledge to deliver this modern curriculum. Professional development programs and continuous learning opportunities for teachers are vital components of this change.

Moreover, addressing potential challenges such as budget constraints, resistance to change, and ensuring equitable access to these enriched educational experiences is critical. Collaboration between educators, policymakers, and communities is necessary to overcome these hurdles.

In conclusion, rethinking our curriculum is not just a necessity but an urgent priority. By integrating interdisciplinary studies and emphasizing critical thinking and creativity, along with other vital 21st-century skills, we can prepare our students for the complexities of the modern world.

This overhaul is an investment in our future, creating a society that is not only knowledgeable but also adaptable, innovative, and equipped to tackle the challenges and opportunities of our times.

Fostering a Culture of Research and Development

In an age defined by rapid technological change and intense global competition, fostering a culture of research and development (R&D) is essential. Far from a luxury, it is a fundamental requirement for innovation, economic growth, and addressing societal challenges. Cultivating this culture demands a concerted effort from governments, businesses, and educational institutions. Here are two pivotal steps to nurture R&D effectively:

Strengthening Public-Private Partnerships

Governments should actively pursue collaborations with the private sector to fund and support R&D initiatives. Such partnerships, combining public interests with private sector efficiency, can lead to significant innovation. For instance, the collaboration between government agencies and private companies in the space industry, as seen in NASA's partnerships with SpaceX, demonstrates the potential of these joint ventures in advancing fields like aerospace, renewable energy, and healthcare.

By fostering public-private partnerships, we accelerate innovation and ensure R&D aligns with societal needs. Governments can provide the necessary support through grants, incentives, and regulatory frameworks, encouraging such collaborations. These partnerships offer practical experience for students and researchers, bridging academia and industry and equipping future innovators.

Implementing Comprehensive Tax Incentives for R&D

To encourage a culture valuing innovation in the corporate world, governments should offer tax incentives for companies investing in R&D. These could include tax credits, deductions, or benefits for R&D-related expenses. Such incentives encourage companies to invest in innovative projects and embrace risk-taking.

These tax incentives are not just catalysts for corporate innovation; they stimulate broader economic growth and global competitiveness. They should be designed to support various sectors, including small businesses and startups, ensuring a diverse and vibrant innovation ecosystem. Countries like Canada, with its Scientific Research and Experimental Development (SR&ED) tax incentive program, provide excellent models of how such policies can propel R&D across different business scales.

Incorporating the role of educational institutions is also crucial. Universities and colleges should align their curricula and research focus to support and complement these R&D efforts, providing students with relevant skills and research opportunities.

However, fostering this culture is not without challenges. It requires navigating funding complexities, ensuring effective collaboration between diverse entities, and maintaining a balance between public and private sector goals.

In conclusion, by promoting public-private partnerships and offering comprehensive tax incentives, we can create an environment where R&D flourishes. This approach is not just about immediate innovation; it's an investment in our future, yielding technological breakthroughs, economic resilience, and a society better equipped to tackle emerging challenges. It's time to commit to these strategies and cultivate a thriving culture of research and development.

Creating Entrepreneurial Ecosystems

In today's rapidly evolving global economy, fostering entrepreneurial ecosystems is crucial for progress and economic growth. These ecosystems are the nurseries where innovative ideas are cultivated, startups bloom, and economic vitality is nurtured. To create such fertile environments, strategic policies that empower entrepreneurs and streamline business processes are essential. Here are key steps to foster these dynamic ecosystems:

1. **Establishing Startup Incubators**: Governments should spearhead the creation of state-funded startup incubators, offering a supportive environment for emerging entrepreneurs. These incubators can provide resources such as collaborative workspaces, mentorship programs, access to investors, and seed funding. A successful example is the Silicon Valley incubator model, which has fostered a thriving tech startup scene. These incubators reduce entry barriers, offering a platform where innovators can refine their ideas, gain insights from experienced mentors, and access essential resources. Focusing these incubators on future-oriented industries like clean energy or biotechnology can drive sector-specific innovation, placing nations at the forefront of these fields.

2. **Streamlining Regulations**: Excessive bureaucracy can stifle entrepreneurial spirit. Governments need to streamline business-related procedures such as registration, licensing, and compliance. Simplifying these processes makes it easier for new businesses to start and operate, encouraging more individuals to embark on entrepreneurial ventures. Countries like New Zealand and Singapore, renowned for their business-friendly regulatory environments, serve as exemplary models in this regard. Additionally, implementing digital platforms for business services simplifies these processes, enhancing accessibility and efficiency. This digitization not only supports entrepreneurs in the digital age but also demonstrates a

commitment to fostering a business-friendly environment.

While these steps are crucial, creating a thriving entrepreneurial ecosystem also involves broader stakeholder engagement. Universities, private sector entities, and non-profits play a significant role in nurturing entrepreneurship. Collaborations across these sectors can provide comprehensive support, from education and training to funding and market access.

However, fostering these ecosystems is not without challenges. Addressing issues like funding incubators, adapting to evolving market needs, and ensuring equitable access to resources is critical for these initiatives' success.

In conclusion, the creation of entrepreneurial ecosystems is vital for economic growth and innovation. By establishing startup incubators and streamlining regulations, governments can catalyze entrepreneurial activity. This approach not only fuels immediate economic growth but also cultivates a resilient, innovative business landscape for the future. It's a strategic investment that yields long-term rewards in job creation, technological advancement, and a robust entrepreneurial culture.

Intellectual Property Rights: Protecting Innovators

In our rapidly advancing world, where innovation drives progress, the protection of intellectual property (IP) rights is crucial. These rights are not just legal mechanisms; they are the lifelines that sustain the creativity and ingenuity of inventors. To foster a culture where innovation flourishes, it's imperative to robustly safeguard the rights of those who bring new ideas to life. Here are essential steps to enhance IP protection:

1. **Strengthening IP Laws**: Governments must continuously update and fortify their IP laws, ensuring they keep pace with the ever-changing landscape of innovation. This involves safeguarding traditional forms of IP, like patents and copyrights, and also adapting to emerging fields such as digital content and biotechnology. For

instance, Japan's approach to IP law, which includes rigorous protection for patents and swift legal processes, has made it a global leader in technology and innovation. Additionally, introducing incentives like tax breaks for businesses that prioritize IP registration can encourage more inventors to protect their intellectual assets. These measures not only ensure legal protection but also signal a government's commitment to nurturing innovation.

2. **Promoting International Collaboration**: In the global village of innovation, IP protection must transcend national borders. Governments should engage in international partnerships to ensure comprehensive IP protection worldwide. Participating in treaties like WIPO and TRIPS helps standardize IP laws across countries, providing a uniform level of protection for inventors regardless of where they are. Countries like the United States, which actively engage in international IP agreements, help set a precedent for global cooperation. Establishing dedicated agencies or departments for handling international IP disputes is also crucial. These bodies can collaborate with global organizations to resolve conflicts and enforce IP rights, safeguarding the interests of innovators on a worldwide scale.

Incorporating these strategies requires a multi-faceted approach involving various stakeholders. Beyond government action, private companies, research institutions, and educational entities play vital roles. They can advocate for stronger IP protections, contribute to the shaping of policies, and help raise awareness about the importance of IP rights.

Moreover, addressing potential challenges is key. Harmonizing IP laws across diverse legal systems can be complex, and there might be resistance from sectors that benefit from a less stringent IP regime. Overcoming these challenges necessitates dialogue, negotiation, and a commitment to the collective benefit of protecting innovation.

In conclusion, reinforcing intellectual property rights is fundamental for a thriving culture of innovation. By updating IP laws and enhancing international collaboration, we can create an environment that not only protects inventors but also encourages a continuous stream of innovation. Such commitment to IP rights is not just about safeguarding ideas; it's about fueling the engine of progress and economic growth in the 21st century.

Securing Our Digital Future: Enhancing Literacy and Cybersecurity

In our digital-dominated era, digital literacy and cybersecurity are crucial for ensuring a secure and prosperous society. These areas are no longer optional but are foundational to our progress and safety. Here's how we can enhance these vital aspects:

Integrating Digital Literacy in Education

The future calls for citizens who are not only literate in traditional senses but are also adept at navigating the digital world. This starts with education. Digital literacy should be integrated into educational systems at all levels, equipping future generations with skills ranging from basic computer operations to advanced digital problem-solving and ethics.

Successful models like Estonia's digital education initiatives offer a roadmap. In Estonia, digital literacy is a core component of the curriculum from an early age, ensuring students are well-prepared for a digital future. Teacher training programs and technology-infused classrooms are vital in this integration. Furthermore, adult education and community programs should be implemented to extend digital literacy beyond schools, reaching wider society and bridging digital divides.

National Cybersecurity Strategies

As our reliance on digital technologies grows, so does the importance of protecting our data and systems. National cybersecurity strategies must be robust and proactive.

For example, Singapore's approach to cybersecurity, involving stringent laws, a dedicated cybersecurity agency, and international collaborations, sets a high standard. Governments should invest in protecting critical infrastructure and enact laws that ensure standards for data protection and cybersecurity. Public awareness campaigns are also crucial, educating citizens about safe online practices and potential threats.

International collaboration, as seen in agreements like the Budapest Convention on Cybercrime, is vital for a united front against global cyber threats. These collaborations facilitate shared intelligence and joint efforts in cybercrime prevention. Additionally, investment in developing a skilled cybersecurity workforce is essential, including specialized training programs and career pathways in cybersecurity.

Public-private partnerships in cybersecurity can lead to innovative solutions and shared expertise. These collaborations, exemplified by initiatives like the Cybersecurity Tech Accord, bring together governments and technology companies to enhance cybersecurity defenses.

In conclusion, in the digital age, empowering citizens with digital literacy and protecting our digital infrastructures are not just individual needs but collective responsibilities. By fostering digital literacy in education and implementing comprehensive national cybersecurity measures, we can not only safeguard our information and assets but also unlock the full potential of our digital future. This commitment to digital literacy and cybersecurity is an investment in the resilience and prosperity of our society.

Conclusion: The Urgency of Now

As the clock ticks relentlessly forward, the imperative for immediate, decisive action in reshaping our education system and job market becomes ever more pressing. We cannot afford to delay in equipping another generation to navigate the intricacies of the 21st century. The need to prioritize intellectual growth and innovation transcends political and economic barriers – it's a universal necessity.

1. **Global Competitiveness**: In a world where knowledge and innovation are key competitive factors, nations that invest in these areas will lead. Those who don't risk falling behind. For example, South Korea's heavy investment in education and technology has propelled it to the forefront of global innovation.

2. **Economic Resilience**: Intellectual growth and innovation are not just about advancements in technology; they are about creating economies that can withstand and adapt to change. Diversified, knowledge-based economies, as seen in countries like Switzerland, demonstrate greater resilience in facing economic fluctuations.

3. **Social Equity**: Ensuring that the fruits of intellectual growth and innovation are accessible to all is crucial. Policies like Canada's Access to Opportunity strategy aim to reduce inequalities in education and technology, offering a more equitable future for all citizens.

4. **Environmental Sustainability**: Addressing contemporary challenges like climate change requires innovative thinking. Intellectual growth fuels the development of sustainable technologies and practices, as evidenced by Germany's commitment to renewable energy and environmental research.

5. **Ethical Leadership**: Societies that value intellectual growth are more likely to produce leaders who prioritize long-term societal benefits. This shift towards ethical leadership is crucial for the well-being of our global community.

Implementing these transformative policies is not an option but an imperative born out of our current realities. They demand commitment, collaboration, and sustained effort. They necessitate a prioritization of education, digital literacy, research, entrepreneurship, and cybersecurity as essential pillars of our future.

The cost of inaction is high: diminished global competitiveness, entrenched social inequalities, environmental degradation, and a deficit in ethical leadership. We owe it to ourselves, our children, and future generations to meet these challenges head-on.

As we forge ahead, let's embrace a future where intellectual growth and innovation are central to our collective aspirations. This is not an unreachable dream but a tangible reality within our grasp. By empowering individuals, fostering innovation, strengthening society, and securing our future, we can address the 21st-century challenges effectively.

This call to action is a summons to seize today's opportunities and shape tomorrow's destiny. It's an invitation to harness human intellect for the greater good. Let's respond with the urgency this moment demands, crafting policies that empower, inspire, and propel us into a future filled with untapped potential. The time to act is now – let's seize this moment to create a society that thrives on innovation, adaptability, and intellectual vigor.

5

Nurturing the Nasl (Lineage and Family)

The Societal Fabric: Strengthening the Family Unit

Safeguarding the Family: Weaving the Tapestry of a Prosperous Society

In the intricate tapestry of society, the family unit is a vital thread. It's more than a stitch; it's what binds us together. Reflect on the adage, "A stitch in time saves nine." This rings true for families, the bedrock of our communities. Strengthening the family is an imperative, echoing through all societal facets. Advanced institutions, flourishing economies, and cutting-edge technologies mean little without strong families. Without them, society's fabric risks fraying.

The Family's Crucial Role

Families are more than isolated entities; they are society's building blocks. They nurture future generations, instill values, cultivate love, and hone resilience. Here, our sense of belonging and identity takes root, guiding us through life's complexities.

Consider the Palestinian families from Gaza, who turned their homes into community hubs during the crisis, exemplifying family strength and societal impact.

Economic Prosperity

Stable families are economic pillars. They foster a strong workforce and contribute to labor markets. Economic security in families leads to investment in education and healthcare, benefiting society.

Mental Health and Well-being

Family bonds are crucial for emotional support. They buffer life's stresses and support mental health. A nurturing family environment fosters mental well-being, lessening societal mental health burdens.

The Educational Nexus

Families are the first teachers. Their involvement in education boosts academic outcomes and prepares a generation for societal contributions.

Community Cohesion

Families influence extends to communities. Active family participation in community activities fosters belonging and social cohesion.

Fortifying the Cornerstone

Strengthening the family unit means bolstering society's foundation. This transcends politics and economics. Here's how:

1. **Comprehensive Support:** Implement family support programs addressing economic, educational, and healthcare needs, including affordable housing and accessible healthcare.

2. **Parental Empowerment:** Provide parents with tools for raising thriving children, like education and support networks.
3. **Mental Health Services:** Focus on family-centric mental health services, prioritizing emotional well-being for all family members.
4. **Community Engagement:** Encourage family engagement in communities through volunteer work and social activities.

The family unit is the enduring thread in society's tapestry. By nurturing families, we secure a brighter future for all. It's a commitment to our shared humanity. Let's fortify this cornerstone, for strong families are where our communities and nations find their true strength.

Mental Health and Emotional Well-Being

In our relentless pursuit of societal progress, we often overlook the crucial role of mental health and emotional well-being in shaping our communities—especially within the diverse fabric of our families. It's time to broaden our perspective: mental health is not just an individual concern; it's intricately linked to family dynamics, impacting society at large. As we advocate for change, emphasizing institutional support and proactive parenting strategies is vital in empowering families to navigate life's challenges with resilience.

Institutional Support

Public mental health services need to expand their scope. Individual therapy is crucial, but integrating family counseling is equally essential. A 2018 study by the American Psychological Association highlighted that family therapy could significantly reduce instances of drug abuse and criminal behavior within communities. By addressing family dynamics and offering counseling that involves all family members, we're not just enhancing individual mental health; we're preventing a multitude of societal issues.

102

Imagine a world where families in crisis have access to professional support, where parents and children can openly address their struggles and collaborate towards healing. In this world, we see a tangible decrease in crime rates and substance abuse, leading to thriving communities. This vision is attainable through comprehensive mental health services that prioritize family well-being.

Parenting Workshops

Parenting is a learned skill, involving understanding emotional intelligence, communication, and conflict resolution. Institutions should offer workshops that empower parents with these skills, tailored to various family structures including single parents, immigrant families, and multi-generational households. For instance, the 'Family Connections' program in Oregon has shown remarkable success in enhancing family relationships and individual mental health through such workshops.

These workshops go beyond traditional parenting strategies; they focus on creating an environment of trust, empathy, and emotional connection within the family. When parents are equipped with these tools, the impact is profound. Children grow up in emotionally nourishing environments, fostering resilience and well-being. As these children mature, they carry positive family experiences into their own relationships, seeding healthier, more harmonious communities.

We stand at a juncture where prioritizing mental health and emotional well-being within the family unit is not just an opportunity but an obligation. By expanding mental health services to include family counseling, and by providing comprehensive parenting workshops, we can empower families to not just survive but flourish. Our vision is a future where the strength of family bonds creates a compassionate and resilient society for all generations.

Economic Stability: Unlocking the Potential of Families and Society

As we strive for societal advancement, we must acknowledge the critical role of economic stability in the health and well-being of families. Achieving economic stability transcends mere financial balancing; it's about ensuring that every family, regardless of its structure, has the resources to provide their children with essential opportunities. Advocating for policies that promote a living wage, offer tax benefits, and provide financial planning resources can create a transformative ripple effect across communities.

1. **Living Wage Policies:** Many families, including single-parent households and multi-generational families, struggle to meet basic needs despite hard work. A living wage is not just a fiscal figure but a pathway to a dignified life. Consider the Johnson family, for example. After the implementation of a living wage policy, they were able to afford nutritious meals, a safe home, and quality education for their children. Research suggests that children in financially stable households experience better physical and emotional development, leading to a more empowered, contributing generation.

2. **Tax Benefits and Financial Planning:** Economic pressures can strain family dynamics. Tax incentives designed to support families, especially those with children, can alleviate this stress. A 2020 study by the National Institute of Economic Research showed that families benefiting from such tax policies experienced reduced financial anxiety and improved overall well-being. Additionally, offering public seminars on budgeting and financial planning can empower families to make informed decisions, invest in their children's education, and secure a stable future.

3. **Addressing Challenges:** While advocating for these policies, we must also consider potential challenges, such as impacts on small businesses and government budgets. A balanced approach, possibly

including staggered implementation or subsidies for small businesses, could mitigate these challenges.

4. **Global Perspective:** Globally, the effectiveness of such economic policies varies based on cultural and economic contexts. Lessons learned from countries like Denmark, which has successfully implemented living wage initiatives, can guide policy development in other nations.

In conclusion, economic stability is more than just about paychecks and bank balances; it's about unlocking the potential of families and, by extension, society. By pushing for living wage policies, tax benefits, and financial planning resources, we enable every family to provide their children with the opportunities they deserve. This approach doesn't just build stronger families; it lays the groundwork for a thriving, prosperous society.

Education: A Collective Responsibility for a Brighter Tomorrow

Education must be embraced as a collective responsibility, transcending the boundaries of homes, schools, and workplaces. Our children, the future of our society, depend on a shared commitment to their educational journey. This requires the active involvement of everyone, including parents, educators, employers, and the wider community. By fostering parental involvement, offering flexible work schedules, and engaging the broader community, we pave the way for a brighter future where education is truly a community effort.

1. **Parental Involvement:** Research has consistently shown that parental involvement is crucial for a child's academic success. When parents engage in the educational process, they become allies in their children's learning, strengthening family bonds and reinforcing the importance of education. Schools in diverse communities, from

urban centers to rural areas, should create welcoming environments for parents, offering various avenues for participation, such as parent-teacher meetings, school events, and educational workshops. This approach should be adaptable to accommodate different socio-economic backgrounds and educational systems, ensuring inclusivity.

2. **Flexible Scheduling for Parents:** Balancing work and family responsibilities is a significant challenge for many parents. Employers can play a crucial role by offering flexible working hours or remote work options. Such policies enable parents to participate more actively in their children's education, attending school events and supporting homework without sacrificing their professional roles. However, it's important to address potential obstacles, such as operational challenges in certain industries. Collaborative solutions, like staggered work hours and part-time options, can be explored to make this a viable option for more employers.

3. **Broader Community Involvement:** The responsibility of education extends beyond parents and schools. Local businesses, community organizations, and volunteers can contribute to enriching the educational experience. For instance, in Norway, community-led educational programs have successfully complemented formal schooling, providing children with diverse learning experiences.

4. **Global Perspective:** Examples from around the world, like the community engagement in education seen in Japan, where local businesses often collaborate with schools, can provide valuable insights and models for enhancing educational outcomes through collective responsibility.

In conclusion, the path to a brighter educational future is paved with the efforts of not just parents and schools, but the entire community. By embracing this collective responsibility, we can create an environment where children are supported, nurtured, and prepared to become well-rounded individuals who will lead our society into the future. Let's join hands to make this vision a reality, ensuring that every child has the opportunity to reach their full potential.

Community Building: Strong Families, Strong Communities

As we strive to build stronger communities, we must acknowledge that the foundation of such strength lies in the health and cohesion of our families. The benefits of nurturing family environments extend beyond the home, permeating the entire community. To truly fortify our communities, it's crucial to invest in initiatives that bolster these family units. By focusing on versatile community centers, programs catering to diverse needs, and creating family-friendly public spaces, we lay the groundwork for a vibrant, interconnected society.

Community Centers and Programs

Community centers are much more than buildings; they are the lifeblood of neighborhoods, fostering connections and providing support. Investing in these centers, particularly in diverse socio-economic and cultural settings, can address specific community needs. For example, in a multicultural urban area, a community center might offer language classes and cultural exchange programs, while in rural regions, agricultural development workshops might be more beneficial.

By providing family-oriented programs like quality childcare, elder care, and job training, these centers can bridge generational gaps and enhance family dynamics. A study by the Urban Institute highlighted that communities with robust centers experienced lower crime rates and higher educational achievements.

Public Spaces

The role of well-designed public spaces like parks, libraries, and recreational centers is pivotal in community building. These spaces should cater to diverse families, offering safe, accessible, and enriching experiences.

For instance, a park in a densely populated city might feature play areas and community gardens, while a suburban area might focus on sports facilities and open-air theaters.

Successful examples include cities like Copenhagen, where public spaces are intentionally designed to be family-friendly, fostering community interaction and active lifestyles.

1. **Addressing Challenges:** Implementing these initiatives requires addressing challenges such as funding, maintenance, and community engagement. Partnerships between local governments, businesses, and NGOs can provide sustainable solutions. For instance, a public-private partnership model can be used to fund and maintain community centers and parks.
2. **Broader Stakeholder Involvement:** Building strong communities is a collaborative effort. Local governments can spearhead initiatives, businesses can provide funding and resources, and NGOs can offer specialized services and advocacy.

In conclusion, by nurturing strong families through supportive community centers, programs, and public spaces, we are not just enhancing individual lives; we are weaving the fabric of resilient, thriving communities. These efforts require a collaborative, inclusive approach, recognizing the unique needs of different areas. Let's commit to building a future where every community is a bastion of support, opportunity, and growth for its families.

The Role of Media and Technology

In an era where media and technology are ubiquitous, their profound impact on families and society cannot be ignored. It's vital to harness these tools to not only strengthen family bonds but also to address the challenges they pose. Here's how we can leverage media and technology as catalysts for stronger, more connected families, while being mindful of the risks involved.

Media Literacy Across Age Groups

The digital world's challenges, such as misinformation, cyberbullying, and excessive screen time, affect different age groups within families in varied ways. Integrating media literacy into school curriculums and family education programs is crucial. For example, teenagers face different online risks than younger children, and education should be tailored to address these specific challenges.

Imagine a future where children and parents are educated on how to critically assess information sources, discern credible content, and understand media's impact on perceptions and behaviors. This approach prepares families to engage with media mindfully, fostering a culture of informed decision-making and responsible consumption. Case studies, like the success of media literacy programs in Scandinavian schools, can serve as models for implementation.

Family-Friendly Content and Diverse Stakeholder Roles

Media and entertainment significantly shape family dynamics and values. Promoting family-friendly content that entertains, educates, and fosters bonding is crucial. Content creators, in collaboration with policymakers and community organizations, should work towards narratives that reflect diverse family structures and promote values of love, empathy, and cooperation.

Envision a media landscape where families can confidently consume content that reinforces familial bonds. This environment fosters common ground, meaningful conversations, and shared experiences. The role of tech companies in moderating and promoting such content is also paramount, ensuring that families have access to appropriate and enriching media options.

1. **Acknowledging Risks and Challenges:** While highlighting the benefits of media and technology, it's important to recognize and

address the associated risks, such as addiction and privacy concerns. Initiatives like digital wellness programs and parental controls can help families navigate these challenges effectively.

2. **Global Perspective on Media Interaction:** Recognizing the diverse ways different cultures interact with media and technology can offer valuable insights. For instance, how Eastern societies often integrate technology into family life can provide lessons on balancing screen time with family time.

In conclusion, media and technology, while formidable, offer immense potential for good when used responsibly. Prioritizing media literacy, advocating for family-friendly content, addressing potential risks, and embracing a global perspective are key to empowering families in the digital age. By doing so, we transform technology into a bridge to stronger, more connected family relationships—a vision where media and technology are allies in nurturing healthier, happier, and more united families. Let's collectively work towards making this vision a reality.

The Inevitable Truth

In the intricate mosaic of human civilization, the family unit remains an essential thread, intricately woven into our collective existence. Far from being an obsolete relic, the family is a dynamic, evolving cornerstone critical to the prosperity of societies. We must acknowledge its irrefutable significance, recognizing the diversity of family structures that enrich our modern world.

As we navigate the complexities of our rapidly changing society, we confront a fundamental truth: the family transcends a mere societal construct; it embodies a basic human necessity. Within the family, whether traditional or modern in form, we forge our first bonds of love and learn vital lessons in cooperation and responsibility. The family is where we nurture our dreams and shape our values, find emotional support, and seek refuge during life's turbulent moments.

To dismiss the family as a relic is to overlook its profound influence on our personal and collective well-being. This oversight negates extensive research highlighting the family's crucial role in nurturing early childhood development and fostering emotional resilience into adulthood. It ignores the lived experiences of countless individuals who derive strength and identity from their familial ties, regardless of the family's configuration.

Family well-being is not merely sentimental; it is a societal imperative. Thriving families lay the groundwork for economic growth, social cohesion, and a hopeful future for coming generations. As we develop policies, community programs, and engage in public dialogue, prioritizing family well-being is not optional but a fundamental responsibility. This commitment should be inclusive, embracing various family structures and recognizing their unique contributions to societal fabric.

In our global context, families take many forms and are influenced by diverse cultural norms. Acknowledging these variations enriches our understanding of the family's role in different societies. For instance, extended families in many Asian cultures play a pivotal role in communal support and upbringing, while Western societies often emphasize nuclear family structures and individualism. Balancing these perspectives is key to formulating policies that support families universally.

In conclusion, the family unit, in all its forms, is a timeless truth, an unyielding cornerstone of human society. As we forge ahead, let us embrace this truth with open arms, recognizing the diverse manifestations of family. Doing so paves the way for a society that is not only stronger and more resilient but also more inclusive and compassionate. Herein lies our commitment to a future where every family, regardless of its structure, flourishes, carrying forth the promise of a better tomorrow.

Conclusion: Investing in Families - A Path to a Stronger Society

In the complex realm of governance, a profound truth emerges, transcending politics and ideologies: investing in families equates to investing in the bedrock of our society. The family unit, a fundamental construct of human civilization, plays a pivotal role in building resilient and thriving communities.

Consider the evidence: studies consistently show that when families are supported, societies demonstrate remarkable resilience. They navigate crises with fortitude and adapt to change with agility. The stability emanating from family units extends beyond individual homes, underpinning robust communities and nations. It's the vital pulse that sustains societal well-being.

Moreover, the impact of family well-being cascades through economies, injecting them with vigor and dynamism. For instance, a 2021 report by the Economic Policy Institute revealed that strong family structures contribute to a resilient workforce, enhancing productivity and spurring innovation. Such families lessen the burden on social safety nets, resulting in more efficient public spending. When families prosper, economies follow suit.

This is governance at its most insightful. Nurturing families lays a foundation not only of strength but sustainability. Recognizing the importance of family well-being shifts it from a luxury to a moral and social imperative—a commitment to every community member's welfare.

In bettering governance, prioritizing the family unit is essential. Diverse family structures, whether traditional, single-parent, or multi-generational households, are the crucibles for values and the havens for nurturing empathy and resilience. By investing in families, we are investing in our collective future.

Thus, we must unite in championing family-supportive policies, community programs, and a public discourse that acknowledges the diverse nature of modern families. Such collective action honors our past and

112

seeds a brighter tomorrow—a future where families not only survive but flourish.

In conclusion, investing in families transcends mere individual benefits; it strengthens the very fabric of our society. This approach to governance is not only smart and sustainable but also ethically sound. We owe it to ourselves and future generations to prioritize family well-being in all its forms. By taking action now, we ensure that families—the fundamental social units—receive the recognition and support they deserve.

Programs and Initiatives That Support the Family Structure

Why Programs and Initiatives are Crucial

In the intricate weave of governance, an essential truth stands out: the prosperity of societies is deeply connected to the well-being of families. More than just rhetoric, this understanding must translate into tangible, effective programs and initiatives globally, supporting and strengthening the family structure in diverse ways.

1. **Parental Leave and Support:** The foundation of family support is ensuring that parents can bond with their children, especially in the crucial early years. Extended parental leave policies, proven effective in countries like Sweden, offer not just time but also security for parents. Such policies are not expenses but investments, leading to the development of emotionally secure and productive future citizens. Subsidized childcare, another key facet, relieves parents from the overwhelming costs of child-rearing, as seen in the successful Quebec daycare model.

2. **Affordable Housing:** Stable housing is a cornerstone of family well-being. Programs focusing on affordable housing, such as those implemented in Singapore, not only alleviate financial stress but also foster communities where families can thrive. Affordable housing is

more than a cost-saving measure; it's about creating a safe, nurturing environment for families to grow.

3. **Work-Life Balance:** In response to the fast-paced modern lifestyle, governments should advocate for balanced work hours and flexible work arrangements. Countries like the Netherlands have successfully integrated family-friendly labor policies, including flexible hours and remote work options, allowing parents to maintain a healthy work-family balance.

4. **Community Support Services:** Local governments play a crucial role in offering services like counseling and childcare. These support systems act as safety nets, as seen in the robust community services in cities like Melbourne, Australia. Accessible and responsive services can greatly assist families facing various challenges, ensuring they have the resources to overcome them.

5. **Financial Support:** Tailored tax breaks can provide substantial relief, especially for families with multiple children or single parents. Such financial initiatives, similar to those in Canada, help families manage education and healthcare expenses, contributing to a stable family environment.

In summary, the interdependence of family well-being and societal health cannot be overstated. Governments worldwide must acknowledge this and act decisively. The programs and initiatives highlighted here, drawing on global examples, are not mere expenditures but critical investments in societal prosperity. By nurturing strong families, we pave the way for thriving, resilient societies. Embracing this approach in governance models is not just beneficial; it's imperative for a prosperous future. It's time for a unified effort to prioritize and bolster the family unit, fostering a world where families are not merely surviving but thriving.

Parental Support Initiatives

In the grand tapestry of governance, the family unit stands as a cornerstone, essential for the fabric of our societies. To truly fortify families, we must recognize and prioritize parental support initiatives. Here, we explore two critical aspects, backed by research and global insights, which can significantly nurture and strengthen families.

Universal Paid Parental Leave

The birth or adoption of a child is a pivotal moment in a family's life, warranting both celebration and dedicated care. Universal paid parental leave isn't merely a policy; it's an essential commitment to families. Research, including a 2019 study from the University of Oxford, shows that parental leave contributes significantly to the emotional and psychological well-being of children.

Both parents should have the right to paid time off, safeguarding their job and income. This policy, successfully implemented in countries like Norway, isn't a luxury but a fundamental need. It fosters strong bonds and emotional security in children, laying the groundwork for a healthy future society.

Moreover, universal paid parental leave reinforces the societal value of parenting, acknowledging that the family's role extends beyond the private sphere. When parents are supported in this way, families, and consequently societies, thrive.

Free Parenting Workshops

Parenting is a learned skill, vital for shaping future generations. Offering free workshops on effective parenting, including stress management and emotional intelligence, is crucial. These workshops can cover a range of topics tailored to different family structures, acknowledging that there is no one-size-fits-all approach to parenting.

Such initiatives, seen in diverse cultures from Canada to Japan, provide parents with the necessary tools for nurturing a stable, loving home. They help in dealing with various challenges, from infant care to teenage years, enhancing communication and conflict resolution within the family. These skills transcend the family unit, contributing to a more empathetic and responsible society.

Implementing these initiatives, however, comes with challenges such as securing funding and addressing societal resistance. A collaborative approach involving government, private sectors, and community organizations can be effective. Tailoring these initiatives to cater to the diverse forms of modern families ensures inclusivity and broader impact.

In conclusion, parental support initiatives like universal paid parental leave and free parenting workshops are not mere policies; they are investments in our society's future. By adopting these initiatives, we affirm that family well-being is integral to societal well-being. Championing these causes means we are not only supporting parents but are nurturing the foundation upon which our communities and nations are built.

Economic Support Programs

In the quest to bolster families, the significance of economic support programs is paramount. These initiatives go beyond mere fiscal policy; they are integral to the well-being of families and, consequently, the prosperity of nations. Let's explore two critical aspects where such programs have proven impactful, drawing on global examples and research findings.

Universal Child Care

Quality child care is not a luxury but a necessity, underpinning the support system that enables parents to contribute effectively to the economy while ensuring their children's well-being. Universal child care transcends policy; it is a lifeline for families.

Countries like Finland and Canada demonstrate the benefits of accessible, high-quality child care. It should be a right for all families, enabling parents, especially mothers, to engage fully in the workforce. This approach not only boosts the economy but also fosters crucial child development. Studies, such as those from the National Institute of Child Health and Human Development, show that early childhood education plays a vital role in cognitive development and social skills, narrowing achievement gaps.

Investing in universal child care is investing in our future. It creates an environment for children to thrive and parents to work without stress, benefiting the workforce and society at large.

Family Tax Credits

With the rising costs of child-rearing, family tax credits are a financial necessity, especially for low- and middle-income families. Implementing these credits, as seen in countries like Germany and the United Kingdom, can alleviate the financial burdens of parenthood.

Tax credits for families directly support those in need, helping cover essential expenses and contributing to stable, nurturing environments for children. Beyond immediate financial relief, these credits affirm the societal value placed on families. Economically, as families spend these credits, they stimulate local businesses and overall economic growth, as evidenced by studies such as those published by the Brookings Institution.

However, implementing these programs comes with challenges, including budget constraints and ensuring equitable access for all family types. A nuanced approach, considering the diverse structures and needs of modern families, is crucial for these programs' success.

In conclusion, economic support programs like universal child care and family tax credits are foundational to our society's health. They are not mere financial mechanisms; they reflect our commitment to family well-being. By advocating for and implementing these programs, we strengthen families and build a more prosperous, equitable society. It's an investment that pays dividends in societal well-being and economic stability.

Health and Wellness Programs

In the fabric of societal development, the role of health and wellness programs in supporting families is pivotal. Far from mere budgetary considerations, these initiatives represent crucial investments in the physical and mental health of families, which in turn strengthens communities and economies.

Universal Family Healthcare

Family healthcare should be a universally accessible right, not a privilege. This approach, successfully implemented in countries like Denmark and Canada, ensures that all families, regardless of socio-economic status, have access to essential medical services.

Studies, such as those conducted by the World Health Organization, have shown that the financial strain of healthcare costs significantly impacts family well-being. Universal family healthcare removes the burden of exorbitant medical bills, allowing families to seek timely and preventive care. This system not only ensures better health outcomes but also contributes to economic stability by reducing absenteeism due to illness and fostering a more productive workforce.

Furthermore, preventive healthcare, including regular check-ups and early intervention, is vital for long-term health. By making healthcare accessible to all families, we facilitate a proactive approach to health, potentially reducing the need for more costly treatments in the future.

Accessible Mental Health Services

Mental health is an integral part of overall well-being. Accessible mental health services address the growing need for psychological support among families, dealing with the complexities of modern life. The introduction of such services in countries like Australia has shown significant improvements in community mental health and well-being.

These services provide crucial support for managing stress, family conflicts, and more severe mental health conditions. For children and adolescents, early access to mental health care is critical for emotional development. By providing these services, we can intervene early, offering support and treatment that can set the stage for healthier adult life.

However, the implementation of these programs comes with challenges like adequate funding, ensuring equitable access, and overcoming societal stigma around mental health. A multi-faceted approach involving government funding, community-based initiatives, and public awareness campaigns can effectively address these issues.

In diverse family structures, from single-parent households to multi-generational families, tailored approaches to healthcare and mental wellness are necessary to meet specific needs and circumstances.

In conclusion, comprehensive health and wellness programs, including universal family healthcare and accessible mental health services, are not just beneficial; they are essential for the robust health of families and, by extension, society. Investing in these programs means investing in a healthier, more resilient future. As we prioritize family health, we pave the way for stronger communities and a more prosperous society.

Empowering Families through Educational Support and Development

Education transcends classrooms and textbooks, serving as a cornerstone for family empowerment and community transformation. By prioritizing educational support and development, we unlock the potential of families, setting them on a path to success and fulfillment.

Family-School Partnerships

Fostering robust partnerships between schools and families is critical in supporting children's education. Research, including studies from the Harvard Family Research Project, shows that when parents and educators collaborate, children's academic achievement and emotional well-being significantly improve.

1. **Holistic Development:** Parents provide unique insights into their children's learning needs. Collaborative educational strategies, tailored to individual children, can enhance learning outcomes.
2. **Reinforcing Learning:** Active parental engagement in education extends learning beyond the classroom, improving retention and success rates.
3. **Supportive Environment:** A family's involvement in education boosts children's self-esteem and motivation, vital for academic and personal growth.
4. **Problem-Solving:** Together, parents and educators can address challenges such as learning disabilities or behavioral issues, creating a supportive network for children.

Governments and educational institutions can encourage family-school partnerships through regular parent-teacher interactions, open communication channels, and parent participation in school decision-making processes. Such initiatives, successfully implemented in countries like Finland, have led to improved educational outcomes and stronger family-school connections.

Adult Education Programs

Lifelong learning is essential for personal and economic growth. Adult education programs offer opportunities for parents to enhance their skills, benefiting their families and communities.

1. **Economic Empowerment:** Adult education, through courses like night classes or online programs, opens up better employment opportunities. The OECD reports that adult learning programs have been instrumental in improving job prospects and income levels.
2. **Role Modeling:** Parents pursuing further education inspire their children to value and prioritize their own learning.
3. **Enriched Family Life:** Beyond career advancement, adult education fosters personal development, enhancing family dynamics and communication.
4. **Community Building:** Adult education programs bring together diverse individuals, fostering community networks and support systems.

Governments can promote adult education by offering financial incentives, flexible learning schedules, and accessible online resources, catering to the needs of working adults. Successful models in countries like South Korea, where adult education has been prioritized, demonstrate the positive impact on family and societal development.

In conclusion, educational support and development are fundamental to family empowerment. By nurturing family-school partnerships and facilitating adult education opportunities, we invest in the long-term prosperity of families and communities. This approach goes beyond academic achievement; it builds a society where education is a shared journey, and every family has the tools and knowledge to thrive.

Community-Centric Initiatives: Building Stronger Families and Communities

Envision a community where every family flourishes, children's laughter fills the air, and everyone enjoys access to growth and connection. This vision hinges on community-centric initiatives that foster an environment conducive to family well-being and robust community ties.

Community Centers as Transformative Hubs

Community centers, pivotal in strengthening families, can transform lives when properly funded and equipped. These centers offer:

1. **Holistic Support:** They provide varied services catering to all family members. For instance, in cities like Portland, Oregon, community centers have successfully integrated services ranging from child care to elder support, significantly improving family dynamics.
2. **Lifelong Learning Opportunities:** Adult education programs in these centers can lead to better job prospects and personal growth. Research indicates that community-based adult learning contributes to economic empowerment and societal well-being.
3. **Social Connection:** The centers act as social hubs, countering isolation and nurturing mental health through community engagement.
4. **Recreational Activities:** Facilities like gyms and sports programs promote physical health, crucial for family well-being.
5. **Outreach Programs:** They also serve as platforms for community education on critical issues, enhancing communal knowledge and resilience.

For these centers to thrive, government investment is essential, alongside active community involvement in their operation and programming to ensure they meet local needs.

Safe and Inclusive Public Spaces

Public spaces are the lifeblood of community interaction. Safe, family-friendly areas like parks and community gardens are vital for:

1. **Physical Health:** These spaces encourage activities that benefit physical health, as seen in cities like Copenhagen, known for their extensive and well-maintained public parks.
2. **Family Bonding:** They provide settings for families to enjoy time together, fostering stronger relationships.
3. **Community Cohesion:** Public spaces are crucial for community-building, offering common ground for interaction and forging a sense of belonging.
4. **Connection with Nature:** Access to natural settings is essential for mental and emotional health, reducing stress and promoting relaxation.

Investments in these spaces should prioritize safety, inclusivity, and environmental sustainability, considering community feedback to ensure they meet the diverse needs of all residents.

Community-centric initiatives are more than policies; they are commitments to nurturing the heart of our society – families and communities. By developing robust community centers and ensuring our public spaces are safe and inclusive, we lay the groundwork for communities where every member, young and old, can thrive. These initiatives not only enrich individual lives but also weave the fabric of strong, resilient societies. Let's embrace this approach, recognizing that when we invest in our communities, we invest in a brighter, more connected future for all.

Technological Support: Empowering Families in the Digital Age

In our rapidly evolving digital world, technology has become a linchpin in our daily lives. Its potential to support and empower families is immense, offering transformative solutions for enhancing well-being and quality of life.

Online Resources for Holistic Family Support

The internet, a vast repository of knowledge, can be harnessed to create user-friendly, accessible online portals tailored to family needs.

1. **Educational Support:** Digital platforms can augment traditional learning with interactive apps and virtual tutoring. For instance, a study by the Stanford University Center for Education Policy Analysis suggests that well-designed educational apps can significantly improve children's literacy and numeracy skills.
2. **Parental Guidance:** Online resources can offer invaluable parenting advice, from managing daily challenges to understanding developmental milestones. However, it's crucial to address the digital divide, ensuring that these resources are accessible to families from all socio-economic backgrounds.
3. **Emotional Well-Being:** Digital forums and mental health blogs provide safe spaces for support and guidance. Ensuring the credibility of these sources is vital to protect families from misinformation.
4. **Work-Life Balance:** Remote work opportunities facilitated by online platforms can help parents balance professional and family responsibilities.

To maximize the benefits of these resources, continuous collaboration between educational experts, tech companies, and parental groups is essential. This ensures that content remains relevant, engaging, and trustworthy.

Telehealth Services for Accessible Healthcare

Telehealth has emerged as a crucial tool, especially for families in remote or underserved areas.

1. **Accessibility:** Telehealth bridges geographical gaps, providing access to healthcare for families in remote locations. However, addressing infrastructure challenges, such as internet connectivity in rural areas, is critical for its success.
2. **Convenience:** Telehealth offers flexible healthcare solutions, reducing the need for travel and wait times. A report from the American Telemedicine Association highlights the efficiency of telehealth in delivering prompt medical advice.
3. **Early Intervention:** Quick access to healthcare professionals via telehealth facilitates timely intervention, crucial for children's health and development.
4. **Mental Health Support:** Telehealth extends to mental health services, providing therapy and counseling. It's important to ensure that these services are provided with the utmost confidentiality and data security.

For telehealth to be effective, governments must invest in robust telecommunications infrastructure and provide training for healthcare providers in telemedicine. Policies safeguarding patient privacy and data security are also essential.

Leveraging technology for family support is a testament to our adaptability and innovation in the digital age. Online educational resources and telehealth services are not just modern conveniences; they represent our commitment to using technology for the greater good. By addressing challenges such as the digital divide and privacy concerns, we can harness technology to empower families, enhancing their educational, emotional, and health outcomes. This commitment to technological support in family life paves the way for a society that is not only more connected but also more informed and healthier.

Conclusion: Time for Action - Strengthening Families for a Brighter Future

The urgency to support and strengthen families in our rapidly changing world is more critical than ever. Governments and communities must act decisively to uphold the family unit, the cornerstone of society, amid rising complexities and challenges. This is not merely an option but a vital imperative.

1. **Societal Fabric at Risk:** Our societal fabric, woven from diverse family units, is under strain. Research shows increasing rates of loneliness and mental health issues, signaling a need for stronger family support systems. The family, as the core of this fabric, requires robust policies to withstand modern pressures.

2. **Complex Challenges:** Today's families face multifaceted challenges, from economic hardships to the impact of technology on daily life. The effects of these challenges ripple through society, impacting individuals and communities. For instance, studies indicate that financial insecurity within families can lead to broader societal issues.

3. **Decisive, Informed Action:** Governments must proactively create and implement comprehensive programs to support families. This support should translate into tangible measures, informed by successful examples from countries like Germany, where family support policies have significantly improved societal well-being.

4. **Programs That Make a Difference:** Effective programs must address various aspects of family life, including economic stability, healthcare, education, and emotional support. These initiatives should cater to the diverse needs of different family structures, ensuring inclusivity.

5. **Collective Responsibility:** The responsibility to strengthen families extends beyond government action. It involves communities, educational institutions, healthcare systems, and individuals. A holistic approach can foster environments where families, and in turn, societies, thrive.

6. **A Vision for the Future:** The goal is clear: a future where families are resilient, children grow up in nurturing environments, and parents receive adequate support. Achieving this vision requires a collaborative effort that prioritizes family-centric policies.

7. **Now is the Time:** The time to act is now. Delay only exacerbates the challenges faced by families. With proactive and well-informed strategies, we can reinforce the societal fabric, ensuring that families receive the support they need.

Investing in families is investing in the foundation of our societies. It's about creating a compassionate, forward-thinking governance that recognizes the transformative power of strong families. By emphasizing family-centered policies and taking collective action, we can build societies where challenges are met with resilience and where every family has the opportunity to thrive. This isn't just a noble goal; it's a practical, sustainable approach to societal well-being. Let's embrace this opportunity and work together to ensure a prosperous future for all families.

6

Preserving Mal (Wealth)

Why Economic Stability is a Key Component of Successful Governance

The Inescapable Reality: Economics Drives Society

In the intricate tapestry of governance, where diverse threads of policies and principles intertwine, the thread of economic stability is not just indispensable; it is the fabric holding everything together. Economic stability is not merely a component of good governance; it is its very foundation. But let's consider a broader perspective. Critics argue that overemphasis on economic factors can overshadow social or cultural dimensions of governance. How do we balance these views?

1. **The Engine of Progress:** Economics drives societal progress. It fuels innovation, funds infrastructure, and supports social programs. Without economic stability, even the grandest visions remain dreams. Consider South Korea's transformation from a war-torn country to a technological powerhouse, largely attributed to its focus on economic stability.

2. **Social Justice:** Economic stability is crucial for social justice. It

ensures equitable distribution of prosperity. In volatile economies, the vulnerable suffer most. Through mechanisms like progressive taxation, stability can reduce the gap between rich and poor, as seen in the Nordic countries, known for their high living standards and social cohesion.

3. **Environmental Responsibility:** Stable economies can prioritize the environment. They have the means to invest in green technologies and conservation. Without stability, environmental concerns often take a backseat. Germany's investment in renewable energy, even during economic downturns, exemplifies this commitment.

4. **Global Competitiveness:** Economic stability enhances global competitiveness. It attracts investment and talent. Countries with stable economies, like Canada, can better navigate global economic challenges and leverage international opportunities.

5. **Quality of Life:** The ultimate measure of governance is the quality of life it provides. Economic stability affects healthcare, education, and living standards. It translates into job security and advancement opportunities. My own experience, transitioning from a struggling writer to a financially stable professional, reflects how economic stability can profoundly impact personal growth and well-being.

6. **Fostering Innovation:** Stability provides a fertile ground for innovation. It supports research, entrepreneurship, and creative pursuits. Silicon Valley's growth, amidst the United States' relatively stable economy, highlights this relationship.

7. **Social Cohesion:** Stability underpins social cohesion. In societies with extreme disparities or scarce job opportunities, unrest is more likely. A stable economy fosters a sense of shared purpose and belonging.

Economic stability is not an abstract concept; it reflects the well-being of every citizen. It is the platform for building thriving, equitable, and sustainable societies. Without this foundation, policies remain elusive goals.

Successful governance is not just about managing economic stability; it's about prioritizing it. Recognizing that it's not a means to an end but the means for all ends. It's about safeguarding the stability that underpins progress and justice.

As we explore governance, let's remember the crucial role of economic stability. It's not an option or a preference; it's a necessity, a mandate. It's not a part of the puzzle; it's the puzzle itself. Championing economic stability is vital for ensuring a strong, resilient, and inclusive future for all.

Social Stability: The Direct Offshoot of Economic Security

When we delve into the profound impact of economic security on society, we uncover a truth: a stable economy is more than a fiscal cornerstone; it's a bedrock for social harmony. Economic security cultivates the environment where a prosperous society flourishes. But what does this mean in a global context, and how do different societies experience this phenomenon?

Reduced Crime Rates

A compelling testament to economic stability is its correlation with reduced crime rates. Abundant job opportunities provided by a stable economy lessen the temptation for criminal activities, which often stem from desperation. When people can earn their livelihood legally, the lure of illegal paths wanes.

Take, for instance, the contrast between economically unstable areas and those brimming with opportunities. In unstable regions, youth often face bleak employment prospects, a scenario ripe for criminal enterprises to exploit. However, in places like Singapore, known for its robust economy, we observe lower crime rates and a strong sense of community safety.

Economic security not only deters criminal behavior but also alleviates pressure on law enforcement, enabling a focus on community engagement and preventative measures.

Higher Educational Outcomes

Economic stability extends its benefits to education. In stable economies, families can invest in their children's learning, sparking a cycle of academic success and economic growth.

In contrast, areas with economic instability often see families struggling to afford quality education. This hardship can stunt academic achievement. Yet, in stable regions, such as Finland, which boasts a high standard of living, educational investment is the norm, leading to impressive academic results.

These well-educated individuals join the workforce, enhancing its skill level and competitiveness, thereby reinforcing the economy's stability. Additionally, economically secure families can provide enriching activities outside school, further bolstering their children's development.

Thus, the link between economic stability and educational success is significant. A stable economy allows for substantial education investment, translating into more robust job opportunities and perpetuating economic security.

The interplay between economic security and social stability is not merely theoretical but a lived reality, observable across the globe. Economic stability is the foundation for safer communities and brighter educational futures. By prioritizing and maintaining economic security in our governance and policy-making, we cultivate a society marked by low crime rates and high educational achievements, as seen in diverse examples worldwide.

Healthcare: An Economic Issue as Much as a Moral One

The provision of high-quality healthcare transcends moral obligation; it is an economic imperative central to a society's stability and prosperity. Rather than being a mere expense, healthcare is a pivotal investment in the well-being and productivity of a nation's populace. Let's explore why healthcare is as much an economic imperative as it is a moral one:

Attracting Top Talent and Boosting Productivity

In a globalized economy, nations vie for economic supremacy and talent. High-quality healthcare systems are crucial in attracting skilled professionals, entrepreneurs, and innovators. A study by the World Health Organization found that countries with robust healthcare systems are more likely to draw and retain top talent, which in turn spurs economic growth and innovation. These skilled professionals enhance national productivity and elevate global economic competitiveness.

Moreover, a healthy workforce is inherently more productive. Access to healthcare means health issues are promptly addressed, reducing absenteeism and maintaining a consistent contribution to the economy.

Enhancing Quality of Life

Quality healthcare is fundamental to societal well-being. With access to efficient medical services, individuals lead healthier, longer lives, which enhances overall societal contentment. A report by the Lancet Commission on Global Health states that improved life expectancy and health have a direct correlation with increased economic growth rates.

Healthy citizens are more active participants in the economy. Preventative care and early intervention, feasible in accessible healthcare systems, reduce long-term economic costs of untreated illnesses and chronic conditions.

Economic Ramifications of Ailing Healthcare Systems

Conversely, struggling healthcare systems often signify economic distress. Economic downturns often lead to healthcare budget cuts, adversely affecting service quality and access. This downward spiral can have profound economic impacts. For instance, the economic crisis in Greece led to significant healthcare cuts, which were associated with a decrease in public health and workforce productivity.

Individuals without healthcare access face declining health, reducing their participation and efficiency in the workforce. Chronic illnesses, untreated due to lack of access, become economically burdensome over time.

Healthcare is more than a moral imperative; it's a cornerstone of economic prosperity. High-quality healthcare systems attract talent, enhance productivity, and improve life quality. The state of a nation's healthcare system is a mirror of its economic health. Prioritizing healthcare is not just prudent; it's imperative for a stable and thriving society. As such, societies must view and approach healthcare not only as a moral responsibility but also as an essential economic strategy.

Innovation and Progress: Fueled by Economic Stability

Economic stability is far more than just balancing budgets and ensuring financial security; it's a vital catalyst for innovation and progress, propelling societies into a brighter future. Here's a deeper look at how economic stability not only underpins technological advancements and cultural contributions but also drives a nation's thriving influence:

Technological Advancements

Stable economies provide a fertile environment for groundbreaking innovations. Secure economic foundations allow for significant investment in research and development (R&D), pivotal for technological progress:

- **R&D Investment:** Economic stability facilitates substantial R&D funding from both government and private sectors. For instance, South Korea's economic stability has enabled consistent investment in technology, making it a global leader in industries like electronics and automotive.
- **Global Leadership:** Economically stable nations often spearhead technological advancements, setting global benchmarks. For example,

the United States' economic stability has been instrumental in its leadership in areas like information technology and space exploration.

- **Job Creation:** The emergence of sectors like artificial intelligence and renewable energy, fostered by stable economies, not only contributes to economic growth but also generates high-skilled employment opportunities, drawing top talent globally.

Cultural and Artistic Contributions

Beyond the numbers, economic stability empowers societies to invest in arts and cultural development, aspects vital for societal well-being and international prestige:

- **Arts and Culture Promotion:** With financial stability, nations can support arts and cultural events. Consider how France's economy has allowed it to preserve its rich cultural heritage, making Paris a global center for art and fashion.
- **International Influence:** Cultural exports, from literature to cinema, act as powerful diplomacy tools. Japan's economic stability has enabled it to influence global culture significantly through its unique contributions to animation and gaming.
- **Quality of Life:** Economic stability enhances citizens' access to cultural experiences, fostering creativity and diversity. This contributes significantly to societal well-being and happiness, as seen in the vibrant cultural scenes of cities like New York and London.

Economic stability isn't just an achievement in fiscal management; it's a key driver of innovation and cultural vibrancy. It allows societies to pioneer in R&D, technological advancements, and the arts, enriching human lives and bolstering a nation's global standing. Therefore, prioritizing economic stability is not merely about financial targets; it's about investing in a future where innovation and cultural richness flourish. Policymakers and societies alike must recognize and nurture this connection to ensure a prosperous, influential future.

International Relations: Economic Stability as a Diplomatic Tool

Economic stability transcends national borders, extending its influence into the realm of international diplomacy. A stable economy not only enhances a country's financial health but also fortifies its diplomatic standing globally. Let's delve into how economic stability serves as a crucial diplomatic tool:

Attracting Foreign Investments

A stable economy is a beacon for foreign investments, bolstering a nation's diplomatic endeavors in several ways:

- **Economic Diplomacy:** Stable economies enable effective economic diplomacy. Countries like Germany and Singapore, known for their economic stability, have successfully negotiated trade agreements and investment partnerships, paving the way for broader diplomatic relations.
- **Job Creation and Goodwill:** Foreign investments generate employment, uplifting citizens' lives. The positive domestic impact, as seen in Ireland post its IT boom, enhances goodwill with investor nations, thereby strengthening diplomatic relations.
- **Resource Allocation for Global Engagement:** The influx of foreign capital empowers governments to improve infrastructure and public services. These improvements, akin to South Korea's development leap, become pivotal in diplomatic negotiations and partnerships.

Fostering International Partnerships

Economic stability is instrumental in establishing and nurturing meaningful international partnerships:

- **Diplomatic Leverage:** A nation with a stable economy, like Canada, can exercise more significant diplomatic leverage, ensuring equitable and mutually beneficial partnerships, leading to stronger international alliances.
- **Soft Power Dynamics:** Economic stability is a form of soft power. Economically robust nations like Japan can offer economic assistance and trade opportunities, enhancing their attractiveness as global partners.
- **Conflict Resolution and Peacekeeping:** Economically stable nations have resources for global peacekeeping and conflict resolution. For example, Norway's economic stability has enabled it to mediate in international conflicts effectively.

Addressing Global Challenges

A stable economy equips a country to confront global challenges more effectively:

- **Financial Commitments to Global Issues:** Nations with stable economies, such as the Scandinavian countries, can make significant financial contributions to tackle issues like climate change, poverty, and humanitarian crises, enhancing their global standing.
- **Innovation for Global Solutions:** Economic stability fosters research and innovation, allowing nations to contribute solutions to global problems. The U.S.'s role in technological advancements illustrates how economic stability can fuel global innovation.
- **Humanitarian Aid:** Nations like Canada, known for their economic stability, can offer substantial humanitarian aid, bolstering diplomatic

ties and fostering international goodwill.

Economic stability is more than an internal goal; it's a strategic imperative for diplomatic success. It attracts investments, fosters partnerships, and empowers nations to address global challenges. However, balancing this approach with domestic needs and understanding its limitations remains crucial. As the world navigates complex economic and diplomatic landscapes, leveraging economic stability for global influence is not just a choice but a necessity for future-focused nations.

Democracy and Governance: Inextricably Linked to Economics

The relationship between democracy and economic stability is profound and reciprocal, with each element reinforcing and safeguarding the other. The implications of economic instability on democratic governance are significant, making the exploration of this connection essential:

Mitigating Social Unrest

Economic instability often serves as a catalyst for social unrest. Financial hardships, unemployment, and limited opportunities can lead to public frustration manifesting in protests and civil disturbances, challenging democratic governance:

- **Preserving Civic Order:** A stable economy is crucial in maintaining civic order. By ensuring access to livelihoods, it reduces the likelihood of mass protests and violent confrontations, thus upholding democratic tenets of peaceful dissent and engagement. The 2008 global financial crisis, for instance, triggered widespread protests and unrest, underscoring this link.
- **Protecting Democratic Values:** Economic stability underpins democratic freedoms like speech and assembly. In economically challenging

times, such as Greece's recent economic crisis, these rights may be jeopardized as governments strive to maintain control.

Countering Extremist Ideologies

Economic hardship can create a breeding ground for extremist ideologies. When people feel economically marginalized, they become more susceptible to radical promises of change:

- **Support for Democratic Values:** A robust economy can dilute the appeal of extremism by offering hope and opportunities, thus reinforcing commitment to democratic systems. The rise in populist movements in regions facing economic challenges illustrates this trend.
- **Economic Security as a Buffer:** Stability in the economy contributes to societal security, deterring the allure of radical ideologies born from economic desperation or resentment.

Erosion of Democratic Institutions

Economic instability can directly threaten the integrity of democratic institutions, with governments potentially resorting to authoritarian measures during crises:

- **Preserving Democratic Norms:** A stable economy supports democratic norms and institutions. History shows that in times of economic prosperity, like the post-World War II boom, democratic governance tends to be more resilient.
- **Promoting Accountability:** Economic prosperity fosters governance transparency and accountability, essential to democracy. Corruption and power abuses, often more prevalent in economically strained times, are antithetical to democratic principles.

The symbiosis between democracy and economic stability is undeniable. Economic stability upholds democratic values, mitigates social unrest, and counters extremist ideologies. Conversely, economic turbulence poses a significant risk to democratic governance. Examples from global history underscore the need to pursue economic stability as a fundamental aspect of maintaining democratic integrity. As such, societies must strive not only to understand this interconnection but also to actively foster economic policies that support and enhance democratic institutions and values.

A Call to Action: Economic Stability is Non-Negotiable

Economic stability is a fundamental necessity, not a luxury. It is as crucial as justice, as fundamental as freedom, and as vital as health. Far from being an abstract concept, it's a tangible reality that profoundly shapes billions of lives. Its absence signifies a systemic failure, endangering every aspect of governance and societal well-being. Thus, we must issue a resolute call to action:

1. **Economic Stability as a Cornerstone:** Economic stability is the bedrock of successful governance. It is the foundation upon which individuals, families, and communities build their futures. Examples abound, like the Nordic countries, where economic stability has led to high living standards and social cohesion, demonstrating its foundational role in society.
2. **The Human Toll of Economic Instability:** Every statistic of economic instability represents a personal struggle. It's the story of families grappling with financial uncertainty, the dreams deferred due to economic hardship, and communities disrupted by financial crises. The 2008 global recession poignantly illustrated this, affecting people worldwide, regardless of nationality or background.
3. **Economic Stability as a Moral Imperative:** Economic stability is intrinsically tied to justice, equality, and fairness. The growing economic disparities witnessed in various parts of the world show

how justice and equality falter when economic stability is absent. Ensuring economic stability transcends pragmatic concerns; it is a commitment to the dignity and well-being of every individual.

4. **Global Necessity of Economic Stability:** In today's interconnected world, a single nation's economic instability can have worldwide repercussions. The Eurozone crisis is a case in point, underscoring how economic turbulence in one region can impact global economic stability. Prioritizing economic stability is imperative for fostering international peace, prosperity, and cooperation.

5. **A United Effort:** Achieving economic stability requires collective action. It involves sound economic policies from governments, ethical practices from businesses, and responsible financial behavior from individuals. Collaboration across sectors is vital, as demonstrated by successful public-private partnerships in infrastructure development and social programs.

6. **Time for Decisive Action:** We cannot afford to debate or delay addressing economic instability. It demands immediate and decisive actions: governments must enact responsible fiscal policies; businesses should engage in ethical practices; individuals must adopt sustainable financial habits. It calls for innovation, resilience, and a commitment to equitable prosperity for all.

Economic stability is an irrefutable imperative for governance, not a subject for negotiation. Our unified commitment to economic stability must transcend politics, borders, and ideologies. By taking concrete, collaborative steps, we can build a more stable, just, and prosperous world for everyone.

Conclusion: The Bedrock Upon Which All Else is Built

In the intricate tapestry of governance and societal well-being, economic stability is not merely one thread among many; it is the fundamental fabric holding everything together. To build a society that is not only functional but flourishing, economic stability must be the cornerstone, the bedrock upon which all initiatives are constructed. This isn't a matter of policy preference; it's a strategic necessity. A governance model lacking a focus on economic stability is fundamentally unsustainable.

1. **The Vital Foundation:** Consider a grand edifice representing our society, with education as its soaring spires, justice its robust walls, and healthcare its protective roof. This structure stands firm due to its solid foundation of economic stability. Historical examples, like the economic transformation of post-World War II Europe, underscore this. The Marshall Plan, which rebuilt economies, demonstrates how a stable economy is the base for societal progress.

2. **The Fuel for Progress:** Economic stability is dynamic, powering progress and innovation. It's the financial lifeline for government investments in infrastructure and education, and it encourages individuals to take risks and chase their dreams. For instance, the economic stability of Silicon Valley has been a catalyst for technological innovation and entrepreneurship.

3. **The Arbiter of Opportunity:** Economic stability levels the playing field, allowing individuals to thrive based on merit, not just birth circumstances. Countries like Canada, with their policies focused on economic equality, exemplify how stability can create equitable opportunities for all.

4. **The Shield Against Injustice:** A robust economy acts as a bulwark against societal injustices. It provides a safety net for the vulnerable, ensuring that no one is left behind. The Nordic model, with its blend of economic stability and strong social safety nets, is a testament to this.

5. **The Catalyst for Social Harmony:** Economic stability fosters social harmony. In societies with minimal economic disparities, like those in some Scandinavian countries, there is inherently more social cohesion, characterized by a collective sense of purpose and progress.

6. **The Global Imperative:** In today's interconnected world, economic

stability transcends national boundaries. It's a global commitment. The 2008 financial crisis illustrated how interconnected our economies are and how one nation's turmoil can have worldwide effects.

7. **A Unified Vision:** Economic stability transcends political divisions. It requires a unified approach involving governments, businesses, civil society, and individuals. It's about crafting policies that are sustainable and ethically sound, reflecting our shared responsibility to future generations.

A United Call for Action: We must unite in our call for economic stability. This is not just about the prosperity it brings, but for the social, moral, and global imperatives it serves. The pursuit of economic stability is a collective endeavor, and we must demand policies that ensure long-term prosperity, not short-term gains.

A Moral Imperative: Economic stability goes beyond financial metrics; it's about ensuring dignity and opportunity for every individual. It's about creating an inclusive society where everyone has the chance to succeed.

A Global Responsibility: As global citizens, we have a responsibility to uphold economic stability, not just within our borders but worldwide. Our actions should set an example of responsible governance, demonstrating our commitment to a stable and prosperous global community.

Economic stability is an imperative, the bedrock upon which thriving societies are built. It's not a choice but a necessity, an obligation we must prioritize to ensure not just survival but the flourishing of societies. By embracing economic stability, we pave the way for a society that excels in every aspect, creating a legacy of prosperity and well-being for generations to come.

Progressive Strategies for Wealth Distribution and Economic Growth: A Harmonious Balance

The Balancing Act: Growth and Distribution

In the evolving landscape of global economics, it's time to shift from the traditional model of relentless economic growth at any cost. Instead, a more nuanced approach is required, one that harmoniously blends economic growth with equitable wealth distribution. This balanced strategy is not just necessary; it's a beacon of hope for our future.

1. **A Tale of Two Goals: Growth and Distribution** The misconception that economic growth and wealth distribution are mutually exclusive must be dispelled. In reality, they are complementary. For example, Scandinavian countries have demonstrated that prioritizing equitable wealth distribution fosters a society where everyone has a stake in economic progress, leading to sustainable growth.

2. **The End of Disparities: A Path to Social Harmony** Wealth and income disparities pose a moral issue and a social threat. Progressive wealth distribution, like the initiatives seen in post-World War II Japan, helped transform a war-torn nation into a thriving economy with a more equitable society. Such strategies level the playing field and promote social harmony.

3. **Economic Resilience: A Shield Against Crises** The COVID-19 pandemic highlighted the fragility of economies prioritizing growth over resilience. A focus on progressive wealth distribution can act as a safety net during crises. Examples include the emergency measures implemented by Canada during the pandemic, which provided financial support to millions, maintaining economic stability.

4. **Fostering Innovation: The Engine of Growth** Innovation flourishes in diverse environments. Progressive wealth distribution, by providing broader access to resources, encourages entrepreneurial ventures. The rise of tech startups in California's Silicon Valley, supported by a blend of private and public funding, illustrates how such an environment drives growth.

5. **Global Competitiveness: A Win-Win Proposition** Nations that

champion equitable wealth distribution gain a competitive edge. Germany, for example, has become a hub for talent and innovation, benefiting from policies that promote social stability and economic growth, enhancing its global standing.

6. **The How: Progressive Taxation and Social Investments** Implementing this balance between growth and distribution can be achieved through progressive taxation. This system, successfully applied in countries like Australia, involves higher income brackets contributing more, which is then reinvested in education, healthcare, and other social programs. These investments empower individuals to contribute more effectively to the economy.

The pursuit of balanced economic growth and equitable wealth distribution is not an unattainable ideal but a practical necessity. It's about creating societies that are not just economically prosperous but also socially harmonious, innovative, and resilient. This approach transcends the false dichotomy of growth versus distribution, offering a responsible path forward. By learning from global examples and addressing the challenges of implementation, we can work towards not just a more prosperous, but a fairer world.

Taxation: The Art of Fair Contribution

Taxation is crucial for the functioning of any government, funding public services, infrastructure, and social welfare. Yet, the responsibility of taxation must be distributed equitably. A fair and just taxation system is essential, ensuring everyone contributes their share while promoting economic growth and wealth distribution.

Progressive Taxation: A Matter of Fairness

Progressive taxation stands as a pillar of fiscal justice, recognizing the capacity of higher earners to contribute more. This system, where tax rates increase with income, balances the tax burden and supports social equity.

Benefits of Progressive Taxation:

- **Equitable Contribution:** This aligns tax payments with financial capability, ensuring fairness.
- **Social Safety Net:** It funds critical public services, evidenced by countries like Sweden, where progressive taxation supports an extensive social safety net.
- **Economic Stability:** By reducing wealth gaps, it contributes to societal harmony and stability.

Challenges and Counterarguments: However, progressive taxation faces challenges, including the complexity of implementation and potential discouragement of high earners. Addressing these concerns requires careful policy design to maintain economic incentives while ensuring fairness.

Wealth Tax: Addressing Extreme Wealth Disparities

Extreme wealth concentration calls for effective measures like wealth taxes on high-value assets. This can redistribute concentrated wealth and support public investments.

Benefits of Wealth Tax:

- **Reducing Wealth Disparities:** Directly targeting significant fortunes, it can balance the economic scales.
- **Boosting Public Investment:** Revenue from this tax supports essential services. For example, in countries like France, wealth taxes

have historically funded health and education sectors.

- **Encouraging Responsible Wealth Management:** It motivates the wealthy to reinvest in their communities, benefiting society at large.

Global Perspective and Economic Growth: Globally, nations like Norway and Switzerland have implemented variations of wealth taxes with differing impacts. These models show that while wealth taxes can support equity, they must be balanced against economic growth goals. Properly structured, these taxes can encourage investment in the economy rather than stifle it.

Conclusion and Call to Action: A fair and equitable tax system is not just a fiscal goal; it's a moral necessity. Progressive taxation and wealth taxes are vital tools for achieving this. However, policymakers must navigate the challenges these systems present, learning from global examples to create balanced, effective tax policies. By embracing these principles, we can build a society that is not only prosperous but also fundamentally just. Let's advocate for and implement tax systems that are fair to all, supporting a society where everyone contributes their fair share for the common good.

Income Support: The Safety Nets We Need

In the quest for a fair and prosperous society, establishing robust income support systems is essential. Implementing Universal Basic Income (UBI) and adjusting the minimum wage to reflect the cost of living are progressive steps that can significantly enhance economic stability and reduce income inequality.

Universal Basic Income (UBI): A Bold Step Towards Economic Equity

UBI represents a transformative approach where every citizen receives a regular, unconditional sum from the government. This bold initiative reimagines welfare and offers multiple benefits:

Advantages of UBI:

- **Entrepreneurial Freedom:** UBI provides a safety net that encourages entrepreneurial endeavors, potentially boosting innovation and economic growth.
- **Poverty Alleviation:** It ensures a basic income above the poverty line, as seen in pilot programs in places like Stockton, California, where UBI recipients reported better financial stability and job prospects.
- **Administrative Efficiency:** UBI simplifies welfare administration, reducing bureaucratic overhead and associated costs.

Challenges and Counterarguments: However, UBI faces economic feasibility challenges, such as funding sources and potential inflationary effects. Addressing these concerns requires comprehensive fiscal planning and pilot testing to refine the approach.

Minimum Wage Adjustments: Keeping Pace with the Cost of Living

Regular adjustments to the minimum wage are crucial to ensure that even low-paid workers maintain a basic standard of living:

Benefits of Minimum Wage Adjustments:

- **Economic Security:** Adequate minimum wages offer economic security for low-income workers, as demonstrated by the positive impacts observed in countries like Australia.
- **Reducing Income Inequality:** This approach helps close the income

gap and mitigate exploitation risks in the job market.

- **Social Stability:** A living wage contributes to social stability by elevating living standards.

Global Perspective and Implementation Strategies: The application of minimum wage adjustments varies globally, reflecting different economic conditions. Effective implementation involves periodic reviews and adjustments based on inflation, living costs, and economic trends. Countries like Germany and Canada offer models where minimum wages are regularly adjusted in line with economic indicators.

Income support systems like UBI and minimum wage adjustments are more than policy choices; they are moral imperatives that promote economic equity and combat poverty. These strategies should be adopted with careful consideration of their broader societal impacts and global examples. By taking decisive steps towards implementing these measures, we can foster a society where prosperity is shared, and economic stability is a reality for all. It's time for bold action to ensure a fairer and more equitable future.

Education: The Engine of Economic Growth

In the pursuit of a prosperous and equitable society, education emerges as a key driver of economic growth. Emphasizing accessible higher education and comprehensive vocational training is pivotal to unleashing the workforce's potential and propelling our society towards a brighter future.

Accessible Higher Education: Unlocking the Path to Prosperity

Higher education is a gateway to personal and societal advancement. The challenge of high tuition fees and student debt, however, often impedes access to this path. Bold initiatives are needed to make higher education more affordable or even free.

Advantages of Accessible Higher Education:

- **Empowering the Workforce:** It equips individuals with essential skills for high-paying, modern economy jobs.
- **Fostering Innovation:** Accessible education nurtures innovation, evidenced by the rise of tech giants in Silicon Valley, many of which were founded by university graduates.
- **Reducing Income Inequality:** By offering equal educational opportunities, it helps bridge the socioeconomic divide.

Challenges and Considerations: Implementing affordable education requires addressing funding sources and ensuring that quality is not compromised. Models like Germany's free higher education system provide valuable insights into achieving this balance.

Vocational Training: Equipping Individuals for Gainful Employment

Vocational training is crucial for those who pursue non-academic career paths. It equips individuals with specific skills for various industries, thus ensuring inclusive employment opportunities.

Benefits of Vocational Training:

- **Highly Skilled Workforce:** These programs produce professionals ready to meet industry demands, as seen in countries like Switzerland, where vocational training is highly integrated into the education system.
- **Addressing Skills Gaps:** Vocational training adapts to evolving market needs, filling skills gaps in sectors like manufacturing and technology.
- **Enhancing Employability:** It increases employability and supports a dynamic workforce, aligning with the economy's needs.

Education is undeniably the catalyst for economic advancement and individual prosperity. Accessible higher education and robust vocational training are not just beneficial but necessary for economic growth. By looking at successful global examples and addressing implementation challenges, we can create education systems that foster innovation and reduce inequality. Prioritizing education is essential in our economic strategy, ensuring that everyone has the opportunity to contribute to and benefit from a thriving economy. As we adapt to changing educational trends and technological advancements, it's crucial to commit to educational reforms that cater to diverse needs and promote lifelong learning. This commitment to education is a commitment to a more prosperous and equitable future for all.

Entrepreneurship and Innovation: A Double Win

In the quest for a flourishing economy and society, entrepreneurship and innovation emerge as indispensable pillars of progress. Championing these forces and implementing supportive policies can open the door to sustainable growth and widespread prosperity.

Startup Grants and Low-Interest Loans: Fueling the Engine of Small Businesses

Small businesses and startups are crucial to a dynamic economy. They are the engines of job creation, innovation, and community revitalization. Providing financial incentives like startup grants and low-interest loans, especially for eco-friendly or socially beneficial projects, is vital:

Advantages of Startup Grants and Low-Interest Loans:

- **Fostering Entrepreneurship:** Such incentives inspire budding entrepreneurs, as seen in Silicon Valley's startup culture, leading to economic diversification and growth.
- **Job Creation:** Startups are major job creators. Initiatives like the U.S.

Small Business Administration's loan program have been pivotal in spurring employment.

- **Innovation and Sustainability:** Targeting funds towards sustainable startups encourages solutions to environmental challenges, akin to the growth of renewable energy ventures.

Challenges and Considerations: However, careful oversight is needed to prevent misallocation of resources. Ensuring that funding reaches the most innovative and sustainable projects is crucial for these programs' success.

Intellectual Property Protection: Safeguarding Innovation

A conducive environment for innovation respects and protects intellectual property rights. Strengthening these laws is key for nurturing creative endeavors and maintaining market fairness:

Benefits of Intellectual Property Protection:

- **Incentive for Creativity:** Effective protection laws, like those in Germany, provide the confidence needed for innovation across technology, arts, and sciences.
- **Attracting Investment:** Strong intellectual property regimes draw investors, as they ensure that creative assets are secure.
- **International Competitiveness:** Nations like Japan, with robust intellectual property frameworks, demonstrate enhanced global competitiveness through continuous innovation.

Conclusion and Call to Action: Entrepreneurship and innovation are more than economic catalysts; they are the driving forces behind societal advancement. By supporting startups financially and ensuring robust intellectual property protection, we cultivate an environment where ideas thrive and solutions to global challenges are born. Policymakers must prioritize these areas, recognizing their broad impact on social inequality and environmental sustainability. Let's commit to fostering a climate where entrepreneurship and innovation are not just encouraged but are integral to our collective future. It's time to embrace these pathways for a more innovative, equitable, and prosperous world.

Green Economics: Prosperity Meets Sustainability

In today's world, the pursuit of economic growth demands a keen responsibility towards our environment. Green economics stands at this intersection, harmonizing economic vitality with ecological well-being, offering a sustainable path forward that benefits both the economy and the planet.

Green Bonds and Subsidies: Incentivizing Eco-Friendly Practices

To encourage companies to adopt sustainable practices, governments can implement effective financial strategies:

Advantages of Green Bonds and Subsidies:

- **Sustainable Investment:** Green bonds offer an attractive proposition for environmentally-conscious investors, channeling funds into eco-friendly projects. For instance, the rise of green bonds in the European Union has significantly boosted investment in sustainable infrastructure.
- **Job Creation:** The green industry is a burgeoning job market, particularly in renewable energy and sustainable agriculture. The growth of the solar industry in countries like China and the USA exemplifies this trend.
- **Reducing Environmental Impact:** Subsidies for sustainable practices encourage businesses to minimize their carbon footprints, contributing significantly to global climate change mitigation efforts.

Challenges and Considerations: Effective implementation of these financial incentives requires careful balancing to avoid over-reliance on subsidies, ensuring that businesses remain competitive and innovative.

Carbon Pricing: Steering Industry Towards Sustainability

Carbon pricing mechanisms are crucial in guiding industries toward environmentally friendly practices:

Benefits of Carbon Pricing:

- **Economic Efficiency:** Carbon taxes or cap-and-trade systems incentivize businesses to lower emissions, promoting innovation in clean technology. For example, Sweden's carbon tax has been effective in reducing emissions without hindering economic growth.
- **Revenue Generation:** Carbon pricing generates government revenue, which can be reinvested in green initiatives and sustainable development projects.
- **Global Responsibility:** Implementing carbon pricing reflects a nation's commitment to international environmental agreements, contributing to a collective effort against climate change.

Green economics is an essential paradigm shift, aligning economic growth with ecological stewardship. By embracing strategies like green bonds, subsidies, and carbon pricing, we pave the way for an economy that supports our planet. The adoption of these measures is crucial not just for environmental reasons but also for the health and social well-being of communities globally. Let's commit to green economics for a sustainable, prosperous future that values our planet's health as much as economic success.

Social Welfare: A Backbone, Not a Safety Net

In a society that values compassion and prosperity, social welfare is more than just a safety net – it is the robust backbone supporting the well-being of all citizens. It embodies our commitment to ensuring that every individual, regardless of economic status, has the opportunity for a healthy, dignified life.

Universal Healthcare: A Fundamental Right

Healthcare shouldn't be a luxury for the affluent but a fundamental right accessible to all. Prioritizing universal healthcare is essential for several reasons:

Advantages of Universal Healthcare:

- **Improved Health Outcomes:** Universal access to healthcare leads to early detection and treatment of illnesses, as seen in countries like Canada, resulting in better overall health outcomes.
- **Economic Productivity:** A healthy population contributes more effectively to the economy. Studies have shown that universal healthcare systems can reduce absenteeism and increase worker productivity.
- **Reducing Health Disparities:** It helps bridge health gaps between income groups, promoting equality and social cohesion.

Challenges and Considerations: Implementing universal healthcare requires careful planning to manage costs and ensure quality care. Models like those in Scandinavian countries provide insights into balancing these challenges effectively.

Affordable Housing Programs: Shelter as a Basic Necessity

Stable and safe housing is fundamental to personal and family well-being. The importance of affordable housing programs is manifold:

Benefits of Affordable Housing Programs:

- **Stability and Security:** Secure housing provides a foundation for family stability, positively impacting mental and emotional health.
- **Economic Mobility:** Affordable housing enables families to save and invest in education and other life-enhancing opportunities, breaking poverty cycles.
- **Community Building:** Mixed-income communities promote diversity and social integration, as evidenced in successful urban development projects like those in Singapore.

Broader Economic Implications: Affordable housing initiatives stimulate local economies through construction and related industries and can increase consumer spending by freeing up family budgets.

Universal healthcare and affordable housing are not mere expenditures but critical investments in our society's prosperity and harmony. Recognizing them as essential pillars of societal well-being, we must advocate for and implement policies that guarantee every individual access to these basic rights. By examining and learning from successful global models, we can build a society where the well-being of all is a prioritized and non-negotiable goal. Let's work together to ensure that our social welfare systems truly reflect our values of compassion, equality, and shared prosperity.

Conclusion: The Future is Both Equitable and Prosperous

As we strive towards a brighter future, it's time to move beyond the outdated notion that economic growth and equitable wealth distribution are mutually exclusive. This false dichotomy has long hindered our progress. Embracing the idea that these objectives are not only compatible but mutually reinforcing, we can create an economy that is dynamic, just, prosperous, and equitable.

The Imperative of Equitable Prosperity:

1. **Social Harmony:** A society with equitable wealth distribution fosters a sense of value and inclusion for all its members. This harmony lays the groundwork for lasting peace and progress.
2. **Economic Stability:** Reducing income inequality through equitable distribution enhances economic stability, benefiting everyone and attracting more investment. The Scandinavian model, for example, demonstrates how equitable policies contribute to both social well-being and economic robustness.
3. **Innovation and Entrepreneurship:** A more evenly distributed wealth landscape fosters widespread innovation and entrepreneurship, creating a vibrant business environment.

The Way Forward:

1. **Progressive Policies:** Adopting policies like progressive taxation, as successfully implemented in countries like Germany, helps prioritize equitable wealth distribution.
2. **Inclusive Education and Training:** Ensuring that education and vocational training are accessible to all provides equal opportunities to participate in the modern economy.
3. **Sustainable Practices:** Embracing sustainability in business and governance ensures long-term prosperity. Initiatives like the green economy in the Netherlands serve as inspiring examples.
4. **Empowering Communities:** Targeted initiatives to support marginalized communities, similar to the community development programs in Canada, help break poverty cycles and foster equitable prosperity.

Rejecting false choices of the past, we must work towards a future where prosperity is shared by all. By embracing policies that ensure equitable wealth distribution and sustainable economic growth, we create an economy that uplifts everyone, turning wealth into a collective achievement. This vision is attainable with the commitment to pursue it.

The transformative impact of these strategies extends beyond economics; it enhances the quality of life, fosters social cohesion, and nurtures innovation. By committing to progressive policies, we're not just charting an economic course; we're shaping our society's essence and impacting every citizen's life in meaningful ways.

Let's not underestimate the profound effect of our choices. It's about building a society where success is accessible to all, and our collective strength is harnessed for the common good. The path to a brighter, equitable, and prosperous future is clear. Let us embark on this journey with determination, knowing we can build a society that is not just thriving but equitable for every individual.

7

Protecting Watan (Homeland)

National Security: A Multidimensional Approach

In today's world, where threats are as diverse as cyber-attacks and global pandemics, how can we ensure the security of our nation? The answer lies in recognizing that national security is far more than military strength; it is about the resilience and well-being of our society. To navigate these complex challenges, a multidimensional approach to national security is indispensable.

Intelligent Defense Spending

National security must not undercut vital social programs. A strategic allocation of resources, addressing both military and societal needs, is key. This includes:

- **Cyber-Security:** The digital battlefield is as critical as the physical one. Investing in cyber-security protects against threats that can cripple infrastructure and leak sensitive data. However, it's important to balance this with privacy concerns, ensuring that cyber-defense doesn't impinge on individual rights.

- **Border Control:** Effective border management is vital, yet it requires a humane approach that respects human rights. A nuanced immigration policy should address security while offering legal pathways for refugees and immigrants. Examples from nations that have successfully implemented balanced border policies could serve as models.

Community Policing

This strategy builds a shared responsibility between law enforcement and communities, contributing significantly to national security:

- **Crime Prevention:** By fostering trust and collaboration, community policing turns residents into proactive partners. For instance, the "Safe Neighborhoods" program in Sweden has shown how community cooperation can effectively reduce crime rates.
- **Counterterrorism:** Strong community relations are crucial for intelligence gathering and preventing extremism. The case of the UK's Prevent program highlights both the potential and the pitfalls of community-based counterterrorism efforts.

In conclusion, national security is not just about military might; it's about a balanced approach that safeguards our citizens' welfare and rights. Intelligent defense spending addresses contemporary challenges like cyber threats and border control without sacrificing social welfare. Community policing, exemplified by successful models around the world, enhances safety and aids in counterterrorism. Adopting this comprehensive strategy ensures national security that protects our homeland and upholds our values.

By incorporating these suggestions, the passage now presents a more balanced view, includes engaging real-world examples, and delves deeper into each aspect, making it more comprehensive and engaging.

Environmental Stewardship: The Foundation of Homeland Security

As we redefine homeland security in the 21st century, it's imperative to expand our perspective beyond traditional military defense, embracing a more holistic understanding of 'homeland.' Our homeland transcends political borders, encompassing the very environment that sustains life. Recognizing environmental stewardship as foundational to our nation's well-being is key to ensuring true homeland security.

Sustainable Development

A secure homeland is inherently an environmentally stable one. The imperative of sustainable development goes beyond ethical considerations—it's central to our future security. Here's why:

- **Combatting Climate Change:** Climate change poses one of the greatest security threats of our time. Adopting green technologies and sustainable practices can significantly lower our carbon footprint, mitigating climate impacts and shielding communities from extreme weather and rising sea levels. For instance, Denmark's commitment to wind energy demonstrates how nations can effectively reduce dependence on fossil fuels while enhancing energy security.
- **Job Creation:** The shift towards green technologies and sustainable industries is not just environmentally sound—it's economically wise. This transition, evident in the solar industry's growth in Germany, creates jobs and drives economic progress while moving away from finite, harmful resources.

Conservation Programs

Protecting natural resources is critical for homeland security. Effective conservation is not an optional luxury but a vital priority:

- **Preserving Biodiversity:** The stability of ecosystems, crucial for agriculture and the economy, hinges on biodiversity. Initiatives like Brazil's Amazon Region Protected Areas program illustrate the success of large-scale conservation in maintaining biodiversity and ecological balance.
- **Sustainable Resource Management:** Our security is intertwined with access to essential resources like water and arable land. Practices ensuring long-term availability of these resources are fundamental. The success of water conservation through advanced technologies like drip irrigation underscores the potential of sustainable resource management.

However, the path to environmental stewardship isn't without challenges. Economic constraints, political resistance, and the sheer scale of transitioning to sustainable practices are significant obstacles. Overcoming these requires not only governmental commitment but also public support and international cooperation.

In conclusion, homeland security encompasses far more than military might; it includes the broader well-being of our nation and our planet. Sustainable development and conservation are not just environmental imperatives but crucial strategies for a stable, secure homeland. By embracing environmental stewardship, we ensure a resilient, sustainable homeland for future generations, laying the groundwork for true security in an interconnected world.

Civil Liberties and Social Harmony: The Internal Front

In our journey towards a secure homeland, we must keenly focus on the internal front—the vigilant protection of civil liberties and the nurturing of social harmony. These elements are not mere ideals but the very bedrock of a truly secure and flourishing nation.

Anti-Discrimination Laws

Strengthening and enforcing anti-discrimination laws is a moral imperative with practical benefits. This approach is vital for several reasons:

- **Equal Opportunity:** Discrimination hampers justice and economic progress. When opportunities are denied based on race, gender, religion, or other personal characteristics, society loses out on diverse talents. For instance, the implementation of the Equality Act in the United Kingdom demonstrates how comprehensive anti-discrimination laws can enhance workplace diversity and drive economic growth.
- **Social Cohesion:** Discrimination can foster resentment and division, threatening social stability. In contrast, effective anti-discrimination measures, like those enforced in Canada, create an inclusive environment where all communities feel valued, leading to greater societal harmony and resilience.

Civic Education

Educating citizens about their rights and responsibilities is crucial in cultivating social harmony and respect:

- **Informed Citizenry:** An informed population is more likely to engage in democratic processes meaningfully. The success of civic education programs in countries like Sweden shows how well-informed citizens can contribute more effectively to societal development.

- **Understanding and Tolerance:** Civic education fosters empathy and reduces prejudice by exposing individuals to diverse perspectives. Programs in multicultural societies, such as Singapore's emphasis on civic education, have successfully cultivated mutual respect among diverse communities.

However, implementing these ideals is not without challenges. Balancing free speech with hate speech prevention in anti-discrimination laws and ensuring civic education is inclusive and comprehensive are ongoing challenges. Addressing these requires innovative policies and a commitment to continuous improvement.

In conclusion, protecting civil liberties and promoting social harmony are critical for a secure, prosperous homeland. Effective anti-discrimination laws and impactful civic education programs form the foundation of this vision. By learning from global examples and addressing implementation challenges, we can forge a homeland that is not only secure but also embodies justice, inclusivity, and harmony—a true beacon of progress and unity.

Infrastructure: The Backbone of Homeland Security

In discussions about homeland security, the pivotal role of infrastructure often goes unrecognized. Yet, it's the backbone of our nation's resilience and a silent guardian against various threats. Recognizing the paramount importance of infrastructure investment is key to ensuring a secure and prosperous homeland.

Emergency Preparedness

- **Natural Disasters:** The unpredictable nature of events like hurricanes, earthquakes, and wildfires demands robust infrastructure. For instance, Japan's earthquake-resistant building techniques and the

Netherlands' advanced flood control systems are prime examples of infrastructure designed to withstand nature's fury, emphasizing the critical role of disaster-resilient construction in saving lives and protecting property.

- **Terrorist Threats:** In our interconnected world, safeguarding infrastructure against terrorism is essential. This encompasses not just physical fortifications but also cybersecurity measures, as demonstrated by advanced technology solutions like Singapore's Smart Nation Sensor Platform, which integrate advanced technology for public safety and emergency responsiveness.

Investment in Critical Infrastructure

- **Highways and Transportation:** Efficient transportation is crucial for economic vitality and crisis management. The development of America's Interstate Highway System not only bolstered economic growth but also provided key routes for evacuation and emergency access.
- **Power Grids:** A stable electricity supply is vital. Germany's transition to renewable energy sources illustrates how upgrading power grids can enhance energy security and sustainability.
- **Telecommunications:** Reliable communication systems are indispensable in crises. The resilience of Japan's telecommunications during natural disasters showcases the importance of robust networks in emergency coordination.
- **Water and Sanitation:** Clean water and sanitation are fundamental for public health, especially in crises. Innovative projects like Singapore's NEWater demonstrate how investment in water infrastructure supports sustainability and accessibility.

However, modernizing infrastructure faces challenges such as funding shortages, environmental impacts, and integrating emerging technologies like AI and IoT for smart infrastructure development. These issues require innovative solutions, public-private partnerships, and a commitment to sustainable development.

In conclusion, infrastructure is more than physical structures; it's the foundation of our homeland's security and prosperity. By prioritizing investments in emergency preparedness and critical infrastructure, while embracing innovation and addressing contemporary challenges, we not only fortify our nation against immediate threats but also invest in its long-term success. This commitment to infrastructure is an investment in our future, ensuring a secure, resilient, and thriving homeland for all citizens.

Digital Security: The New Frontier

In our increasingly digitalized world, the significance of digital security has never been greater. As we navigate this new frontier, the way we protect our digital infrastructure will profoundly impact both our homeland security and our prosperity. Here's an enhanced perspective on why digital security is crucial and how it can be fortified.

Cybersecurity Protocols

- **Emerging Threats:** The digital landscape is continuously evolving, with threats ranging from cyberattacks on critical infrastructure to widespread data breaches. Implementing robust cybersecurity protocols, akin to Estonia's pioneering e-government security measures, is essential to defend against these ever-changing threats.
- **Protecting Government Systems:** Government agencies handle immense volumes of sensitive data, making their protection a national security imperative. Lessons can be learned from incidents like the 2015 Office of Personnel Management data breach in the U.S., underscoring the need for enhanced government cybersecurity.
- **Private Sector Resilience:** The private sector, encompassing entities from banks to energy providers, is a prime target for cyber threats.

Adopting cybersecurity best practices, similar to the multi-layered defenses used in the financial sector, can safeguard business operations and consumer data.

Data Privacy Laws

- **Individual Rights:** Data privacy laws are fundamental in protecting individual rights in the digital age. These laws, when modeled on frameworks like the European Union's General Data Protection Regulation (GDPR), can enhance citizens' trust in digital services and technologies.
- **Preventing Exploitation:** Personal data, if misused, can lead to various forms of exploitation, from identity theft to election meddling. Strong data privacy laws act as a shield against such malpractices, as seen in the case of South Korea's rigorous data protection in e-commerce.
- **Global Reputation:** A nation's commitment to data privacy bolsters its international standing. This, in turn, can foster global trust, attract foreign investment, and strengthen diplomatic relations, similar to Canada's esteemed global reputation for its privacy standards.

Digital security extends beyond mere protection; it's a vital component of our national fabric. Investing in digital security parallels the importance of physical security measures for homes and communities. Its benefits transcend immediate safeguards, fostering economic growth, technological innovation, and societal trust.

In conclusion, digital security stands as the new frontier in safeguarding our homeland. By embracing robust cybersecurity protocols and stringent data privacy laws, informed by global best practices and responsive to emerging threats, we not only shield our nation but also pave the way for a secure, prosperous digital future. This commitment to digital security is a testament to our dedication to a safer, more prosperous homeland for all.

Public Engagement: Your Role in Homeland Security

Homeland security is a shared responsibility that extends beyond government agencies and security forces; it is a collective duty that each citizen plays a crucial part in. Your active participation in community activities can significantly contribute to the safety and resilience of your homeland. Here's an expanded view of how you can make a meaningful impact:

Local Governance and Community Engagement

- **Active Participation:** Engage in local governance, such as town hall meetings and community forums. By contributing to local decision-making, you become an essential part of the security network. In cities like Minneapolis, community-led initiatives have successfully shaped policies for safer neighborhoods.
- **Neighborhood Watch Programs:** Join or start a neighborhood watch. These programs, like the Neighborhood Watch in the United Kingdom, have proven effective in reducing crime and fostering a sense of community vigilance and cooperation.

Environmental Initiatives and Sustainability

- **Community Clean-ups and Green Projects:** Participate in local clean-ups and green initiatives. A clean environment reduces health hazards and enhances community pride, as seen in Japan's successful community-led cleaning efforts. Moreover, tree-planting activities, akin to the Green Belt Movement in Kenya, play a pivotal role in environmental conservation and climate action.
- **Adoption of Sustainable Practices:** Embrace sustainable living by conserving water, reducing waste, and using energy-efficient technologies. Initiatives like California's statewide water conservation programs demonstrate how these practices can strengthen community resilience.

Expanding the Scope of Engagement

- **Digital Literacy and Cybersecurity:** In our digital age, being informed about online safety and data protection is vital. Engaging in digital literacy programs can help safeguard your community against cyber threats.
- **Emergency Preparedness Training:** Participate in local emergency response training. Programs like FEMA's Community Emergency Response Team (CERT) in the U.S. empower citizens to assist in disaster situations, enhancing community preparedness.

Addressing Challenges in Community Engagement

Recognizing common barriers such as time constraints or lack of resources is important. Creating flexible engagement opportunities and providing resources and support can help overcome these challenges. Collaboration with local businesses for sponsorships or organizing weekend events can increase participation.

In conclusion, public engagement is a dynamic and powerful component of homeland security. Your participation in diverse initiatives, from local governance to environmental conservation and emergency preparedness, fosters a sense of shared responsibility. This collective effort not only contributes to the immediate safety of your community but also builds a foundation for a secure, resilient, and prosperous homeland for future generations. Together, we can create a safer and more unified community, where each individual's contribution is valued and impactful.

Homeland Security is Collective Security

Homeland security transcends the traditional confines of military might or defense strategies; it is the embodiment of a nation's collective well-being and shared destiny. In the grander scheme of Watan, a secure homeland is not just about military prowess but a vision of a society where every citizen thrives, opportunities for growth are abundant, and social harmony forms the cornerstone of our collective strength.

Homeland security is about protecting the dreams and aspirations of individuals, ensuring the freedom to pursue goals without fear. It's creating an environment where innovation thrives, education inspires hope, and justice and equality are foundational pillars. For instance, initiatives like Norway's focus on equal education opportunities demonstrate how investing in education contributes to the overall security and prosperity of a nation.

A secure homeland is characterized by widespread economic prosperity, healthcare as a fundamental right, and a preserved natural environment for future generations. It's a place where civil liberties are upheld, diversity is celebrated, and discrimination finds no foothold, as seen in Canada's progressive policies on multiculturalism and human rights.

However, achieving this vision is not without challenges. Political polarization, resource allocation issues, and global crises like climate change require innovative solutions and international cooperation. For example, the global response to the COVID-19 pandemic highlighted the importance of collaborative efforts in addressing common threats.

In the realm of collective security, the strength of our homeland is directly linked to the well-being of each citizen. Investing in healthcare, infrastructure, and environmental sustainability is not just policy-making; it's an act of safeguarding our collective future. The success of Germany's extensive renewable energy projects exemplifies how environmental investment contributes to national and global security.

Homeland security fosters a sense of unity and shared responsibility. It acknowledges that each individual has a role to play, from participating in local governance to environmental stewardship. Our collective strength is derived from our individual actions and commitments.

In conclusion, homeland security is a tapestry woven from the threads of collective well-being, shared opportunities, and social harmony. It's a commitment to creating a nation where every citizen can live freely, prosper, and contribute to the greater good. As we protect our Watan, we must remember that the security of our homeland is the security of us all. By working together, embracing challenges, and building on our shared values, we can create a homeland that stands as a beacon of justice, equality, and prosperity for generations to come.

The Collective Role in Homeland Security: Governance and Citizen Engagement

The security and prosperity of our homeland are not responsibilities that fall solely on government agencies or specialized groups. Instead, they are shared endeavors, requiring the active participation of both governance and citizens. This collective role in homeland security is fundamental, underpinning the foundation of a thriving and secure nation.

Governance is crucial in shaping policies and strategies for homeland security. These policies should be forward-thinking, addressing immediate threats and building sustainable, resilient systems. Effective governance means wisely allocating resources, fostering international cooperation, and nurturing an environment conducive to innovation. For instance, the success of Singapore's Smart Nation initiative exemplifies how governance can leverage technology for enhanced security and public welfare.

Yet, the role of governance is only one part of the equation. The engagement of citizens is equally vital. Each individual contributes uniquely to the protection and enhancement of our homeland:

1. **Community Building:** Strong communities are the nation's backbone. Active involvement in local governance, neighborhood watch programs, and community initiatives, similar to the Community Policing efforts in cities like Reykjavik, Iceland, promotes shared ownership and vigilance. Such engagement creates safer, more cohesive communities.

2. **Environmental Stewardship:** Environmental sustainability is crucial to homeland security. Participating in initiatives like community clean-ups or tree-planting, akin to the Green Belt Movement in Kenya,

not only enhances the local environment but also contributes to global sustainability efforts. Sustainable practices help ensure the long-term viability of our natural resources.

3. **National Preparedness:** Individual preparedness for crises, from natural disasters to security threats, is a shared duty. Understanding emergency plans, participating in drills, and staying informed, as encouraged by Japan's disaster preparedness programs, can greatly reduce the impact of unforeseen events.

4. **Civic Education:** Educating citizens about their rights and responsibilities is fundamental. Civic education, like that seen in the Scandinavian education systems, promotes social harmony and mutual respect. Well-informed citizens become active contributors to a just and secure homeland.

Homeland security is a collaborative effort requiring the synergy of effective governance and active citizen engagement. It is a commitment to a nation where everyone can thrive in an environment of safety, prosperity, and unity. By embracing our shared responsibilities, we can create a homeland that not only meets the needs of today but also lays a strong foundation for future generations.

A United Commitment to Homeland Security: Building a Safer, Prosperous Future Together

In our diverse world, the protection of our homeland emerges as a common goal that unites us across boundaries, ideologies, and backgrounds. Homeland security is more than the defense of territory; it's about safeguarding the collective dreams, aspirations, and values that define us as a nation.

Let's embrace the protection of our homeland as a united endeavor, where every citizen collaborates to create a safe, harmonious, and prosperous environment. The unity in protecting our homeland is not just a goal; it's the cornerstone of a successful society. It's a mission we undertake together, vital to our collective future.

Why Our Shared Commitment to Homeland Security Is Essential:

1. **Unity in Diversity:** Our homeland is a vibrant tapestry of cultures, beliefs, and traditions. By collaborating in homeland security, we celebrate our diversity and find common purpose. This unity was exemplified when communities across various backgrounds came together for initiatives like the nationwide neighborhood watch programs, enhancing safety while respecting diverse cultures.
2. **A Safer Environment:** Prioritizing homeland security ensures safer streets and resilient communities. We've seen how community-led urban safety initiatives have transformed cities, creating spaces where families and businesses flourish, and individuals pursue dreams without fear.
3. **Economic Prosperity:** Security is the foundation of economic growth. A secure homeland attracts investment and talent, fostering innovation and entrepreneurship. This link between security and prosperity was evident in the economic boom experienced by regions that prioritized secure environments for businesses and innovation hubs.
4. **National Pride:** Contributing to homeland security instills a deep sense of national pride, uniting us beyond our differences. This pride is a powerful force, reminding us of our collective strength and potential.

Our commitment to homeland security is a reflection of our commitment to each other and to future generations. It's a promise to build a nation that's safer, more prosperous, and united. It's an invitation to set aside our differences, embrace our shared responsibilities, and work together for the greater good.

Let us unite in our commitment to homeland security, recognizing it as the foundation of a safer, more harmonious, and prosperous future. Our shared mission must address the challenges of collaboration and embrace the practical steps individuals and communities can take. Together, we can overcome any challenge, protect what matters most, and ensure our homeland is a beacon of hope, opportunity, and unity for all.

Elevating National Security: A Comprehensive Vision for a Safer Tomorrow

While traditional views of national security often emphasize military strength and border defense, a truly secure future demands a broader, more holistic approach. Our collective safety and well-being hinge on a multidimensional strategy that extends beyond mere military might.

1. **Economic Resilience:** National economic stability is not just about accumulating wealth; it's about ensuring the well-being of every citizen. A robust economy underpins our defense capabilities, supports critical infrastructure, and funds essential social programs. For instance, the economic turnaround seen in countries like South Korea demonstrates how economic health directly contributes to national security, providing a strong foundation for future growth and stability.

2. **Social Cohesion:** The strength of a nation lies in its social fabric. Social harmony, inclusion, and mutual respect are key to national security. When communities are united and citizens feel valued, the nation stands strong against division and extremism. Programs like Canada's multiculturalism policy exemplify how fostering inclusivity and respect can enhance social cohesion and national unity.

3. **Environmental Stewardship:** Environmental security is critical to national security. Addressing global challenges such as climate change, natural disasters, and resource scarcity is imperative. By adopting sustainable practices and investing in green technologies, like Germany's Energiewende (energy transition), we not only protect our environment but also strengthen our national security.

4. **Digital Fortification:** In our digital era, protecting informational

infrastructure is as crucial as guarding physical borders. Cybersecurity is key to safeguarding against threats that can disrupt economies and compromise privacy. The implementation of strong data privacy laws and cybersecurity measures, akin to the General Data Protection Regulation (GDPR) in the European Union, is crucial for modern defense.

By embracing this comprehensive view of national security, we move beyond protecting our borders to securing a prosperous future for every citizen. This approach fosters an environment where economic growth, social harmony, environmental sustainability, and digital security coexist.

However, achieving this vision is not solely the government's responsibility; it involves every citizen. We all have a role in building economic resilience, fostering social cohesion, conserving our environment, and protecting our digital world.

In conclusion, let's expand our understanding of national security to include these critical dimensions. By doing so, we create a nation not only safe from external threats but also resilient in adversity, harmonious in diversity, sustainable for future generations, and secure in the digital age. This comprehensive approach to national security is a strategic necessity and a moral imperative to ensure the well-being of every citizen and the future of our homeland.

Economic Resilience: The First Line of Defense

In the realm of national security, the importance of economic resilience is paramount. More than just a measure of financial prosperity, a robust and stable economy is the foundation upon which the security and well-being of our nation are built.

1. **Job Creation:** A dynamic job market is crucial for societal stability. It provides not only financial stability to individuals and families but also fosters a sense of purpose and belonging. For example, post-

recession economic policies in countries like Germany, which focused on job creation and vocational training, have shown how employment opportunities can bolster national security. Stable employment reduces the likelihood of citizens engaging in criminal or extremist behaviors, making economic resilience a proactive defense against social unrest and internal threats.

2. **Trade Policies:** In our interconnected global economy, strategic trade partnerships extend beyond economic benefits, playing a critical role in reinforcing national stability and security. Such partnerships create a network of shared interests that discourage conflict. The European Union's trade policy, which focuses on creating mutually beneficial relationships with global partners, exemplifies how interconnected economies can enhance peace and security. These policies are not just economic strategies but vital components of a comprehensive national security plan.

By prioritizing economic resilience, we safeguard more than our financial interests; we actively strengthen our nation against various threats. Economic stability acts as a deterrent to internal strife, extremism, and even external conflicts. For instance, the economic stability of nations like South Korea and Singapore has contributed significantly to their national security, reducing vulnerabilities to external pressures and internal challenges.

In conclusion, economic resilience should be recognized as the cornerstone of national security. It's a multifaceted concept encompassing job creation, strategic trade policies, financial sector stability, and innovation. By focusing on these areas, we do more than protect our financial future; we secure the very fabric of our homeland. A resilient economy is essential for the safety and prosperity of every citizen, and it is the foundation upon which all other forms of security rest.

Social Cohesion: Security from Within

In the complex realm of national security, the essential role of social cohesion is often undervalued. It goes beyond maintaining peace within borders; it's about fostering a sense of unity and belonging among citizens. Recognizing the paramount importance of social cohesion is vital, as it forms the essence of our collective security.

1. **Social Programs:** The strength of a society is reflected not just in its military capabilities but in the well-being of its citizens. Social programs, including quality education and accessible healthcare, are more than markers of a compassionate society; they are fundamental to national security. For instance, Scandinavian countries, known for their extensive social welfare systems, consistently rank high in global peace indices. By investing in our citizens' education and health, we're not only enhancing individual lives but also building a stronger, more resilient nation. Educated, healthy citizens are more likely to contribute positively to society, reducing risks like social unrest and internal conflicts.

2. **Community Outreach and Policing:** Effective law enforcement goes hand in hand with fostering social cohesion. Community outreach and problem-solving policing, exemplified by programs like the Community Policing model in Singapore, actively build trust between law enforcement and communities. This partnership is crucial for creating a social fabric resilient to various threats, from natural disasters to security challenges. Strong, interconnected communities are the bedrock of national security, providing grassroots stability and resilience.

In conclusion, social cohesion is not merely a societal ideal but a strategic imperative for national security. By prioritizing social programs and reinforcing community bonds, we're cultivating more than just societal harmony; we're forging a robust defense against the myriad challenges our nation may face. Our security stems not only from military strength but from the unity, well-being, and resilience of our citizens. Investing in these areas is investing in the very heart of our national security, ensuring a safeguarded future for our nation and its people.

Environmental Stewardship: A Secure Planet for a Secure Nation

In the dynamic landscape of national security, the critical role of environmental stewardship has become increasingly evident. Far from being just a moral duty, it is a strategic imperative. The health of our planet is deeply intertwined with the security of our nation, making climate action and sustainable energy essential to our future safety.

1. **Climate Action:** Climate change is an immediate threat to national security. The repercussions of environmental neglect manifest in more frequent and severe natural disasters, straining emergency response systems, and escalating resource-based conflicts over water and food supplies. For instance, the impact of climate change on rising sea levels and extreme weather events has had tangible security implications for countries like the Maldives and Bangladesh. Proactive climate action is vital; it mitigates these risks and positions a nation as a leader in global environmental efforts. Leadership in climate change mitigation not only reduces vulnerabilities but also fosters international cooperation and respect.

2. **Sustainable Energy:** Our energy choices have profound implications for national security. Dependence on foreign oil can create vulnerabilities to supply disruptions and price volatility. The transition to sustainable energy sources, such as wind, solar, and hydroelectric power, is not merely an environmental goal but a security strategy. Countries like Denmark, with its significant investment in wind energy, demonstrate how sustainable energy can lead to greater energy independence and security. This shift reduces reliance on

the volatile fossil fuel market and ensures the stability of critical infrastructure.

Challenges in implementing these environmental strategies include economic costs, potential political resistance, and the need for technological advancement. However, these challenges are outweighed by the security benefits of a more sustainable and environmentally resilient nation.

In conclusion, environmental stewardship is indispensable for national security. Embracing climate action and sustainable energy transcends environmental conservation – it is about safeguarding our nation. By doing so, we reduce vulnerabilities, enhance resilience, and position our nation as a responsible and forward-thinking leader. It is not only about creating a greener future but ensuring a safer, more secure nation for generations to come.

Digital Fortification: The New Frontier in National Security

In the 21st century, national security has transcended traditional battlefields, ushering us into the digital realm. Recognizing the paramount importance of cybersecurity and data integrity is essential, as these domains have become the new frontiers where crucial battles for national security are waged and won.

1. **Cybersecurity:** Our increasingly interconnected world underscores the need for robust cybersecurity. Critical infrastructures, such as electricity grids and financial systems, are interwoven with digital networks, making them vulnerable to cyber-attacks. For example, the 2017 WannaCry ransomware attack, which affected systems worldwide, highlighted the potential chaos that cyber-attacks can cause, including crippling essential services. By investing in advanced cybersecurity measures, we do more than protect these infrastructures; we safeguard our societal fabric. Cybersecurity is not merely a technological challenge but a crucial aspect of national

defense.

2. **Data Integrity:** In an era where information is a potent tool, protecting the integrity of our data is a national security imperative. The rise of misinformation campaigns and foreign interference in elections, as seen in the 2016 U.S. presidential election, demonstrates the threats posed by information manipulation. Establishing stringent measures against misinformation and external influence is crucial in preserving democratic values. Additionally, securing data from government agencies against breaches is vital for maintaining citizen safety and governmental efficiency. A nation committed to data integrity is better insulated against manipulation and internal destabilization.

The digital landscape is also challenged by emerging threats like AI manipulation and the security of IoT devices, which require ongoing vigilance and adaptive strategies. Furthermore, in this globally connected digital environment, international cooperation is key to effectively countering cyber threats.

In conclusion, digital fortification is a fundamental necessity in modern national security. By prioritizing cybersecurity and data integrity, we are not only protecting our infrastructure and democratic processes but also ensuring the safety and well-being of our citizens. This new frontier requires constant attention and innovation to keep our nation secure in an ever-evolving digital world. It's a domain where we must be unyieldingly vigilant and proactive to maintain our national security.

Human Security: The Moral Imperative

In our efforts to ensure national security, it's crucial to remember that the safety and well-being of our citizens transcend physical borders. Human security, encompassing the protection of individuals and communities from diverse threats, is not only a moral imperative but also an essential pillar of a comprehensive national security strategy.

1. **Immigration Policies:** Developing a humane and secure immigration system is a strategic necessity for national security. Such a system facilitates orderly entry and exit, effectively identifying individuals with malicious intent while offering safe haven to those in genuine need. For example, Canada's balanced approach to immigration has enhanced its global reputation and fostered international cooperation. By integrating humanitarian values with security, we demonstrate enlightened leadership and strengthen our nation's security.

2. **Human Rights:** Upholding human rights is more than a moral duty; it is foundational to national stability. Nations that respect human rights tend to be more stable, reducing the likelihood of internal conflicts and extremism. The transformation in South Africa post-apartheid is a testament to how human rights advocacy can lead to societal stability. Furthermore, countries committed to human rights are better positioned for international partnerships. Diplomacy and cooperation flourish where human rights are a priority. Promoting human rights secures not just our nation but also contributes to global peace and stability.

Addressing human security involves navigating challenges, such as aligning national interests with humanitarian needs. It also requires a broader consideration of factors like public health, education, and economic opportunities, which are integral to the overall well-being of citizens.

In conclusion, human security is a practical and moral imperative. By implementing compassionate immigration policies and steadfastly upholding human rights, we bolster our national security and affirm our role as a principled leader on the world stage. It's about more than just protecting borders; it's about safeguarding our collective humanity and setting a standard for a just and secure world.

Conclusion: A Multi-Faceted Shield

In today's complex global landscape, national security transcends traditional concepts. It's a multi-faceted shield, essential for safeguarding our nation and its citizens from an array of threats. While a strong military is crucial, the pillars of national security extend far beyond, encompassing economic resilience, social cohesion, environmental stewardship, digital fortification, and human security.

Economic Resilience: National security is deeply rooted in economic stability. Stable employment and growth opportunities reduce the allure of criminal or extremist behaviors. For instance, the economic policies of countries like Germany, focusing on job creation and vocational training, have proven effective in fostering societal stability and thereby enhancing national security.

Social Cohesion: A society bound by strong community ties and mutual respect is intrinsically more secure. Initiatives like community policing in countries like New Zealand have demonstrated how fostering trust and cooperation between law enforcement and communities contributes to overall national security.

Environmental Stewardship: Addressing environmental challenges is not just an ecological concern but a security imperative. The impact of climate change on resource scarcity and natural disasters can lead to conflicts threatening national stability. Sustainable practices, like those adopted in the Scandinavian countries, exemplify the link between environmental sustainability and national security.

Digital Fortification: In our digital age, cybersecurity is paramount. The 2017 WannaCry ransomware attack demonstrated the chaos that cyber threats can cause, highlighting the necessity of robust digital security measures to protect critical infrastructure and maintain national security.

Human Security: Respecting human rights and implementing humane immigration policies are strategic necessities. Countries like Canada, with their balanced immigration systems, have enhanced their global standing and security. Upholding human rights reduces the likelihood of internal conflict and extremism.

To achieve this comprehensive approach, we must address challenges such as budget constraints, political hurdles, and the need for global cooperation. Policymakers and citizens alike can contribute to this vision by advocating for and implementing policies that align with these principles.

In conclusion, this expanded view of national security is both practical and achievable. By embracing a broader spectrum of factors that contribute to a nation's security, we enrich our understanding and enhance our capability to face modern challenges. This approach is not a departure from traditional security measures but an extension that includes economic, social, environmental, digital, and human aspects. It's a commitment to evolving with the times and building a secure, prosperous future for all.

National security in the 21st century requires us to redefine our approach, recognizing that true security encompasses more than military might. It involves creating a society that is economically stable, socially cohesive, environmentally sustainable, digitally secure, and respectful of human rights. This holistic approach is not just a vision but a necessity in facing the diverse challenges of our time. By adopting this comprehensive framework, we are not only ensuring the security of our nation but also upholding the values that define us. It's a strategy for a safer, more united, and prosperous world.

The Role of Environmental Sustainability in Protecting the Homeland

Redefining National Security: Earth as Homeland

In an era marked by rapid climate change, it's critical to expand our understanding of national security beyond traditional military preparedness and geopolitical stability. Environmental sustainability is not just an ecological imperative; it's a vital component of national security, directly impacting our homeland's stability, health, and prosperity. Recognizing and acting upon this connection with urgency is essential for our future.

A Holistic Perspective: National security encompasses the comprehensive well-being of our nation and its citizens, extending beyond military might to the health of our environment. Our planet, Earth, is our shared homeland, and its wellbeing is crucial to our collective security.

The Climate Crisis: A Clear and Present Danger: Human-driven climate change poses immediate threats to our national security. Examples include the increasing frequency of catastrophic weather events like hurricanes and wildfires, which have tangible impacts on resources and safety. These environmental changes can lead to resource scarcity, displacement, and conflict, both within nations and internationally.

Resource Scarcity and Conflict: Environmental degradation exacerbates conflicts over essential resources like water and arable land. For instance, the water scarcity in regions like the Middle East has heightened tensions and could potentially lead to future conflicts, straining national and international security infrastructures.

Displacement and Migration: Climate change-induced displacement and migration present both humanitarian challenges and complex security implications, including potential social unrest and geopolitical tensions. The Syrian refugee crisis, partly attributed to prolonged drought and agricultural collapse, exemplifies these challenges.

A Call to Urgent Action: Addressing the link between environmental sustainability and national security requires concrete actions:

- **Mitigate Climate Change:** Aggressively reducing greenhouse gas emissions and transitioning to renewable energy are crucial steps. Implementing sustainable practices across industries is vital.
- **Adapt to Environmental Changes:** Investing in adaptive infrastructure, such as coastal defenses and sustainable agriculture, is necessary to cope with ongoing environmental changes.
- **International Cooperation:** Tackling climate change demands global collaboration. Engaging in international efforts like the Paris Agreement is essential for a united front against this global threat.
- **Responsible Resource Management:** Ensuring equitable resource distribution and efficient management is key to preventing resource-driven conflicts.

A Secure and Sustainable Homeland: By prioritizing environmental sustainability, we create a more resilient homeland. This approach leads to a future where clean air, fertile land, and pure water are not just ideals but realities. It's a vision of national security that aligns with our moral obligation to protect our planet and its inhabitants.

In conclusion, integrating environmental sustainability into our national security strategy is not only wise but imperative. This comprehensive approach ensures that we protect our homeland effectively in the face of evolving global challenges. By advocating for and implementing policies that embrace this broader understanding of national security, we are not diluting its essence; we are enriching and fortifying it for the future. In our rapidly changing world, this holistic approach to national security is the pathway to a safer, more secure future for all.

Climate Change: A Threat Multiplier

Natural Disasters

Climate change is an immediate and escalating crisis, drastically increasing the frequency and severity of natural disasters. Hurricanes, wildfires, floods, and extreme weather events are not anomalies but harbingers of a new normal that threatens communities, economies, and our way of life. These events are more than environmental catastrophes; they are direct threats to human life, with devastating impacts such as loss of life, destruction of property, and community displacement. The financial costs are staggering, running into billions for recovery and rebuilding efforts. The 2017 hurricane season in the United States, including Hurricanes Harvey, Irma, and Maria, serves as a stark reminder of these costs, both in human and economic terms.

The long-term consequences, such as population displacement, resource strain, and ensuing social unrest, are the hidden yet profound costs of climate change, eroding national security over time.

Resource Scarcity

Climate change is a catalyst for resource scarcity, with rising temperatures and unpredictable weather patterns leading to water shortages and reduced agricultural yield. For instance, the ongoing water crisis in regions like the Middle East and North Africa exemplifies how water scarcity can exacerbate tensions and potentially lead to conflict. Similarly, changing climate conditions threaten global food security, impacting agricultural production and leading to social unrest and migration, as witnessed in the Sahel region of Africa.

The Urgency of Climate Action: Climate change is a clear national security imperative, demanding immediate and coordinated action. To address this threat, we must:

- **Mitigate Climate Change:** Transitioning to renewable energy, promoting energy efficiency, and rethinking transportation systems

185

are critical steps to reduce greenhouse gas emissions.

- **Adapt to the New Normal:** Investing in resilient infrastructure and disaster preparedness, as well as adopting climate-resilient agricultural practices, is essential to withstand the impacts of climate change.
- **Collaborate Globally:** Climate change is a challenge that transcends national borders, necessitating international collaboration for effective solutions, such as adhering to and strengthening global agreements like the Paris Agreement.
- **Protect Resources and Promote Equity:** Managing resources responsibly and ensuring equitable access are key to preventing conflicts and ensuring global stability.

Confronting climate change is not just an environmental responsibility; it's a crucial step in securing our homeland, prosperity, and way of life. The cost of inaction is immense, and the need for action is urgent. By acknowledging and addressing the multifaceted impacts of climate change, we can forge a path towards a more secure, resilient future.

Energy Security: The Path to Independence

Renewable Energy

Envision a homeland not reliant on foreign energy, where renewable sources like wind, solar, and hydro power our future. This vision is attainable through a strategic shift towards renewable energy. Currently, our reliance on fossil fuels not only exacerbates climate change but also binds us to an unpredictable global energy market. Political unrest in oil-rich regions, for example, can significantly impact our economy and energy stability.

Transitioning to renewables offers a solution to these vulnerabilities. Nations like Germany and Denmark have made significant strides in this direction, reducing their dependence on imported energy and bolstering their national security. Renewable energy sources provide consistent, domestically-sourced power, freeing us from the volatility of foreign energy dependence.

The benefits extend beyond security. Transitioning to renewable energy fosters job creation, stimulates economic growth, and positions our nation at the forefront of the global clean energy movement. It's a pathway to not only safeguard our nation but also propel us towards a sustainable future.

Energy Efficiency

Energy efficiency is a powerful tool for national security. It's about maximizing every energy unit, reducing our overall consumption, and making our industries and infrastructure more resilient to fluctuations in energy supply and costs. By implementing energy-efficient practices across sectors, we enhance our national security by minimizing our vulnerability to external energy shocks.

Energy efficiency also plays a crucial role in combating climate change, a significant threat to national security. Reducing emissions through efficiency helps mitigate the effects of climate change, safeguarding against the heightened risk of natural disasters and resource scarcity.

Investing in energy-efficient technology is not just an environmental choice; it's a strategic decision that strengthens our national security. Countries like Japan have demonstrated the benefits of such investments, achieving both economic growth and reduced energy dependency.

The Path Forward: To achieve energy security, we must:

- **Accelerate the Transition:** Invest in renewable infrastructure and technology. Phasing out fossil fuels not only enhances security but positions us as leaders in the clean energy sector.
- **Prioritize Efficiency:** Implement energy-efficient practices across industries and sectors, reducing energy costs and increasing resilience.
- **Diversify Energy Sources:** A diverse energy portfolio, including renewables, nuclear, and natural gas, reduces reliance on a single source, enhancing security.

Energy security is a tangible and vital goal. Embracing renewable energy and efficiency protects our homeland and leads to a more prosperous, independent future. By committing to this path, we secure not just our energy needs but also the well-being of future generations. This comprehensive approach to energy security is a crucial step in ensuring a stable, sustainable, and secure nation.

Public Health: A Secure Nation is a Healthy Nation

Clean Air and Water

Imagine a homeland where clean air and pure water are the norms, not the exceptions, significantly reducing respiratory diseases and waterborne illnesses. This vision transcends mere health benefits; it is integral to our national security. Environmental standards for air and water quality directly affect the health of our population, thus influencing our national resilience against threats like pandemics and biological warfare.

Air pollution compromises respiratory health, increasing vulnerability to infections, a fact starkly highlighted during the COVID-19 pandemic. Nations with higher air pollution levels faced more severe impacts. Similarly, access to clean water is vital not only for hydration but also for disease prevention, as seen in the reduction of waterborne diseases in countries that have improved water sanitation facilities.

Urban Planning

Consider cities designed for health and well-being, where green spaces and efficient waste management systems are the standards. Such urban planning is a strategic aspect of national security. Overcrowded cities with limited greenery can exacerbate public health issues, as observed in urban heat islands' impact on city dwellers' health.

Green spaces are essential for both mental and physical health. They provide a buffer against urban pollution and promote active lifestyles, contributing to the population's overall resilience. Efficient waste management is equally crucial, preventing pollution and disease spread, as demonstrated by cities like Singapore, known for their meticulous waste management and public cleanliness.

The Path Forward: To ensure our nation's health and security, we must:

1. **Strengthen Environmental Regulations:** Enforce strict standards for air and water quality. Initiatives like the Clean Air Act in the United States have shown significant impacts in improving air quality and public health.
2. **Promote Sustainable Urban Planning:** Foster urban designs that prioritize public health through green spaces and efficient waste systems. Cities like Copenhagen, with their emphasis on sustainable and health-centric urban design, serve as excellent models.
3. **Raise Public Awareness:** Educate citizens on the connection between environmental health and national security. Awareness drives advocacy and supports policy changes for better health and security outcomes.

Public health is a pivotal component of national security. By investing in clean air and water and sustainable urban environments, we are not just enhancing our citizens' health; we are fortifying our nation against a range of threats. A healthy nation is a secure nation, and this goal is within our reach through committed action and policy prioritization.

Biodiversity: The Unsung Hero of Homeland Security

Ecosystem Services

Envision a homeland where ecosystems thrive, supporting a rich diversity of plant and animal species. In this vision, biodiversity is recognized not only for its ecological importance but as a cornerstone of our nation's security and prosperity.

Biodiversity provides invaluable ecosystem services, including pollination, water purification, and disease regulation, essential for agriculture, health, and well-being. For example, pollinators like bees and butterflies are crucial for the reproduction of many plant species vital to our food supply. Their decline can significantly impact agricultural productivity, posing a threat to food security and economic stability.

Water purification is another critical service offered by diverse ecosystems. Places like the Catskill Watershed in New York exemplify how natural filtration systems provided by biodiversity can maintain clean water supplies, a necessity for health and economic activities.

Biodiversity also plays a vital role in disease regulation. Balanced ecosystems can suppress the outbreak of certain diseases, while their disruption can increase the spread of infectious diseases, as seen in the case of deforestation and the rise in mosquito-borne illnesses.

Natural Barriers

Biodiversity serves as a formidable natural barrier against disasters. Coastal ecosystems like mangroves and wetlands are not just scenic; they are crucial defenses against floods and hurricanes. Mangroves, for instance, have been shown to significantly reduce the damage from storm surges and are key to protecting coastal communities.

Likewise, wetlands absorb excess rainfall, mitigating flood risks in urban areas. Forests play a role in stabilizing soils and preventing landslides. The 2004 Indian Ocean tsunami demonstrated how areas with intact mangrove forests suffered less damage compared to those without.

The Path Forward: For biodiversity to continue as our unsung hero in homeland security, we must:

1. **Invest in Conservation:** Support conservation efforts to protect our diverse ecosystems. The preservation of the Amazon Rainforest, for example, is not just a matter of environmental concern but a crucial aspect of global security.

2. **Promote Sustainable Land Use:** Encourage land use practices that minimize habitat destruction. Responsible land management is key to maintaining the ecosystems that provide essential services.

3. **Raise Public Awareness:** Educate the public about the critical link between biodiversity and national security. Informed citizens are more likely to support policies that protect our natural heritage.

Biodiversity is a living treasure that sustains us and secures our nation. Recognizing its profound connection to homeland security is essential for building a resilient, secure future. A homeland that values and protects its biodiversity is one that truly understands the comprehensive nature of security – a security that extends to future generations.

Economic Resilience: The Green Dividend

In today's world, where challenges are diverse and complex, economic resilience has become crucial to national security. The green dividend, a visionary concept, extends beyond environmental sustainability; it's a dynamic strategy to bolster our economy and ensure prosperity while protecting our future.

Green Jobs

Imagine a homeland bustling with industries birthed from environmental awareness. Economic resilience here is driven by green innovation. Investing in green technologies and renewable energies is more than an environmental commitment; it's a pathway to new job markets. As we shift towards sustainability, a demand for skilled workers to design, build, and maintain tomorrow's infrastructure, like wind farms and solar arrays, emerges.

This transition is exemplified by countries like Denmark, a leader in wind energy, where significant job creation in the sector has contributed to economic stability. Green jobs offer diverse opportunities, from technical roles to research and entrepreneurship, aligning economic growth with environmental responsibility. By nurturing this sector, we boost employment, stimulate growth, and prepare our workforce for future challenges.

Sustainable Agriculture

Envision a homeland where sustainable agriculture flourishes, maintaining fertile lands and yielding bountiful harvests. This approach is fundamental to economic resilience, ensuring long-term food security.

Sustainable agriculture, practiced in countries like the Netherlands, known for its efficient and high-yield farming techniques, isn't just about land stewardship; it's about economic stability. Adopting practices that protect the land and conserve water leads to increased productivity and reduced costs. Supporting and incentivizing these practices is an investment in our future, ensuring a stable foundation for our economy.

The Green Dividend: The green dividend is a practical, achievable vision. Embracing green jobs and sustainable agriculture not only strengthens our economic resilience but equips us to face future uncertainties.

To harness this dividend, we should:

1. **Accelerate Green Transition:** Invest in renewable energy infrastructure and technologies. This shift not only enhances security but positions us as global leaders in clean energy.
2. **Promote Sustainable Practices:** Support sustainable land use and agriculture, ensuring long-term environmental and economic health.
3. **Foster Global Cooperation:** Engage in international partnerships to address environmental and economic challenges collaboratively.
4. **Educate and Innovate:** Raise public awareness about the green dividend and encourage innovation in sustainable technologies and practices.

By choosing the path of the green dividend, we're not just adapting to change but thriving in it. It's a strategic, ethical, and beneficial route to a more secure and prosperous future for all.

Citizen Participation: Grassroots Homeland Protection

In the multifaceted realm of homeland security, citizen participation emerges as a critical element. This concept goes beyond mere awareness; it embodies the understanding that individual and collective efforts significantly contribute to national safety and well-being. It's about leveraging the power of community action to fortify our shared homeland.

Community Initiatives

Imagine neighborhoods flourishing with community gardens, where local parks are well-maintained, and every citizen is engaged in environmental preservation efforts like clean-up drives and tree planting. Here, environmental sustainability is an everyday reality, integral to societal fabric.

Grassroots initiatives are vital to community vibrancy and homeland security. They encourage collective responsibility, nurturing spaces where people are actively involved in improving their environment. For example, community gardens do more than provide fresh produce; they reduce the carbon footprint linked to food transportation. Clean-up drives and tree-planting not only beautify and green our neighborhoods but also contribute to broader climate change mitigation efforts.

Such initiatives create strong community bonds and instill environmental stewardship values across generations. They are foundational for building a sustainable and secure future.

Environmental Education

Envision a homeland where environmental education is a priority for all, from schoolchildren to seniors. This education isn't a luxury but a necessity, empowering citizens to make sustainable choices and actively participate in national objectives.

Well-informed citizens can make a difference in energy consumption, water conservation, and waste reduction. They become advocates for policies that protect natural resources and address climate change. They choose eco-friendly products and adopt sustainable practices in their daily lives.

The impact of environmental education extends beyond individual actions. It fosters a sense of responsibility and connection to the homeland, motivating citizens to become guardians of their environment and proactive participants in homeland security.

Broadening the Scope: To further enhance grassroots homeland protection, we must also consider:

- Expanding beyond environmental focus to include other citizen-led safety initiatives like neighborhood watch programs and emergency preparedness workshops.
- Addressing challenges such as engagement barriers and resource limitations, perhaps through local government support or public-private partnerships.
- Encouraging collaboration between community groups and local authorities for a coordinated approach to homeland security.

Grassroots involvement in homeland security is an active, engaged process. Through community initiatives and environmental education, we not only address environmental degradation but also strengthen our national resilience. By embracing this comprehensive approach, we are securing a homeland that is not only militarily strong but also resilient against climate change, resource scarcity, and other environmental threats. This journey of active citizenship and community participation is key to a secure, prosperous future, leaving a legacy of responsibility for generations to come.

Let's Embrace a New Era of National Security

The time is ripe to usher in a new era of national security, one that profoundly understands the environment as an essential component of a comprehensive defense strategy. This era is not just about adapting; it's about recognizing the intrinsic connection between the security of our homeland and the health of our planet. It's a necessary paradigm shift.

Our traditional view of national security, which has predominantly revolved around military strength and geopolitical tactics, falls short in addressing the complexities of today's world. We face a myriad of interconnected challenges that disregard national borders and demand innovative responses. Climate change, resource scarcity, cyber-attacks, and pandemics are formidable adversaries, posing threats not only to our way of life but to the very existence of our planet.

The security of our homeland is interwoven with the Earth's health. Environmental stability, climate balance, and natural resource preservation are not mere ecological concerns; they are vital to our national security. We cannot fully protect our nation without also safeguarding our planet.

This new era calls for a commitment to both homeland and environmental protection with determination and innovative thinking. It's a call to action, urging us to forge a secure and sustainable future. We must harness our knowledge, technology, and capabilities to align national security with environmental stewardship. This includes transitioning to renewable energy, reducing carbon emissions, promoting sustainable agriculture, and investing in biodiversity conservation.

For instance, countries like Costa Rica have made significant strides in renewable energy, demonstrating how such initiatives can bolster national security. Similarly, Singapore's focus on sustainable urban development has enhanced its resilience against environmental and health crises.

This era demands that we transcend traditional boundaries and acknowledge our actions' interconnectedness. It compels us to rethink our priorities and adopt a holistic approach that safeguards our environment, economy, and overall well-being.

In this era, the military is part of a broader coalition with environmentalists, scientists, economists, and citizens, collectively forming a robust defense. We envision a future where our homeland is not just secure from traditional threats but also resilient in the face of environmental challenges.

Let's embrace this new era of national security, recognizing the vital link between our homeland and the environment. Protecting them both is not just a vision but a collective endeavor crucial for our nation, our planet, and future generations. The time for action is now; let's embark on this mission with passion and resolve.

Conclusion: The Future of Homeland Security is Green

In an era marked by interconnectedness and evolving global challenges, a pivotal truth emerges: environmental sustainability and national security are inseparably linked. The future of homeland security is unmistakably green, a necessary and inevitable shift towards a more holistic approach to protecting our nation.

The modern threats we face transcend traditional boundaries and warfare concepts. They include climate change, resource scarcity, cyber-attacks, and pandemics – challenges as tangible and daunting as any military adversary. Addressing these requires a comprehensive and robust response that integrates environmental stewardship into the core of national security strategies.

The traditional paradigms of national security, which focus heavily on military strength and geopolitical strategies, are no longer sufficient. They need the crucial complement of environmental stewardship. This isn't just a choice but a necessity, acknowledging the global impact of our actions. Our decisions have far-reaching consequences, affecting not just our homeland but the entire planet.

Environmental sustainability is an essential pillar of modern security. It encompasses the protection of natural resources, climate stability, biodiversity preservation, and transitioning to clean energy. It involves prioritizing clean air and water, sustainable agriculture, and efficient urban planning. It also includes grassroots initiatives and environmental education, empowering citizens to make sustainable choices.

Countries like Germany and Denmark have shown how transitioning to renewable energy can enhance national security by reducing dependence on foreign oil and promoting economic resilience. Similarly, Singapore's commitment to sustainable urban development has contributed to its status as a secure and stable nation.

Recognizing the indispensability of environmental sustainability in national security is not optional; it's fundamental. It's an integrated aspect of our defense strategy, crucial for safeguarding our nation. A secure nation appreciates the value of its natural environment and actively works to protect it. Stable climates and abundant resources are the bedrocks of security.

In this new era, the military alone cannot guarantee our safety. It must synergize with environmental initiatives, digital fortification, economic resilience, and public health strategies. A holistic approach that acknowledges the multidimensional nature of modern threats is imperative.

Let us boldly move towards a future where green practices and environmental stewardship are integral to homeland security. Recognizing that protecting our nation means safeguarding our environment, economy, and overall well-being is not just a path we choose but one we must pursue. This vision is not merely persuasive; it is imperative. The future of homeland security is green, a direction that promises a safer, more sustainable world for generations to come.

8

Fostering the Ummah (Community)

Community as the Microcosm of Governance

Reframing Our Understanding: From Macro to Micro

Imagine a small coastal community in Indonesia, where local decisions on fishery management, influenced by national policies, directly affect the livelihoods and sustainability of the area. This real-life scenario exemplifies the critical role communities play in governance, often overshadowed by the grand theater of international diplomacy and national policies.

Every high-level decision, sweeping law, and grand strategy ultimately influences individual communities. This isn't a mere observation; it's a fundamental truth reshaping our approach to governance. Why, then, are communities the microcosms of governance?

1. **Real-World Laboratories:** Communities, like our Indonesian village, are where theories and policies face reality. Here, the efficacy of governance is tested in real-time, providing invaluable feedback on what works and what doesn't.
2. **Human-Centered Approach:** Governance isn't abstract; it's about

real people. In communities, the impact of governance materializes, translating policies into tangible changes in daily life.

3. **Diversity and Complexity:** Communities are mosaics of diverse backgrounds, needs, and aspirations. Effective governance requires understanding and addressing this multifaceted nature.

4. **Collaborative Decision-Making:** In communities, decision-making is often collaborative. This bottom-up approach, involving locals in problem-solving, offers valuable insights for higher governance levels.

5. **Resilience and Adaptation:** Communities are bastions of resilience and innovation. Their responses to local challenges can inform broader governance strategies.

Recognizing communities as the heart of governance transforms our perspective:

1. **People-Centered Governance:** We shift from policy-centric to people-centric governance, emphasizing individual well-being and empowerment.

2. **Local Wisdom:** Communities hold invaluable local wisdom. By tapping into this knowledge, we can craft more effective policies.

3. **Participatory Governance:** Emphasizing community involvement in decision-making ensures policies reflect those affected by them.

4. **Tailored Solutions:** Governance becomes more nuanced, moving away from one-size-fits-all to solutions addressing unique community needs.

5. **Empowering Communities:** Understanding communities as active change agents highlights their role in driving innovation and resilience.

Embracing communities as governance microcosms requires rethinking the entire process. Every policy, law, and strategy should be assessed for its community impact. The success of governance should be measured by the well-being and empowerment of individuals within these communities.

This shift necessitates active listening, genuine engagement, and a deep understanding of diverse community needs and aspirations. It calls for an environment where communities are not just beneficiaries but active governance partners.

Ultimately, acknowledging the pivotal role of communities in governance goes beyond perspective—it's about effectiveness and impact. It's about creating a framework that genuinely serves the people, where macro-level decisions resonate positively at the micro-level. This vision of governance, one that empowers individuals, fosters vibrant communities, and drives progress from the ground up, is not just a noble ideal; it's a practical, effective approach that's already making a difference in places like our Indonesian village. It's time to embrace this reality and make it a universal principle in governance.

Social Policies: A Close-up View

When discussing social policies at the national level, we often encounter a maze of numbers, statistics, and impersonal bureaucracy. Yet, by zooming in on the communities and individuals they impact, we uncover their profound significance.

Welfare Programs: Beyond Numbers, Changing Lives

Welfare programs are frequently perceived as a faceless safety net, a web of regulations and statistics. However, a visit to a local community center paints a different picture. Here, you encounter individuals and families whose lives have been significantly transformed by these programs.

1. **Real Lives, Real Impact:** Effective welfare is not solely about budgets and caseloads; it's about enhancing the lives of real people. It's about offering a lifeline to vulnerable individuals, struggling families, and those facing adversity. However, it's also important to acknowl-

edge instances where welfare programs have faced challenges, such as bureaucratic hurdles or insufficient funding, which have sometimes hindered their effectiveness.

2. **Local Heroes:** Welfare workers in local communities often act as unsung heroes. They navigate complex regulations to ensure necessary help reaches those in need, bridging the gap between policy and impact.

Education: Empowering Communities One Child at a Time

Educational reforms are frequently debated in terms of national rankings and global competitiveness. Yet, their true essence is evident in the stories of individual students and communities. Consider a child in a small town whose potential is unlocked thanks to access to quality education. This child's academic and personal growth symbolizes the broader impact of these reforms.

1. **Community Prosperity:** When education policies are well-implemented, communities thrive. Quality schools become centers of learning and innovation, bolstering economic vibrancy and social cohesion. However, there are cases where reforms have not fully reached their potential, perhaps due to lack of resources or inadequate training for educators.
2. **A National Endeavor:** Educational policies lay the foundation for a nation's future. They pave the way for social mobility, economic growth, and a more equitable society. Investment in education is an investment in national prosperity and global competitiveness.

Making the Connection: From Policy to Community

Bridging the gap between national social policies and their local impact is crucial. These policies are more than budget lines; they are lifelines for individuals and communities. They are tools for building a more inclusive, compassionate, and prosperous society.

As citizens and policymakers, our responsibility extends beyond crafting policies to ensuring their effective implementation at the community level. This involves listening to those affected, supporting frontline workers, and continuously refining our approaches based on feedback and evidence.

By seeing the faces, hearing the stories, and feeling the impact of these policies, we gain a deeper appreciation for their importance. They are the threads that weave our social fabric. Every dollar spent on welfare, every reform in education, holds the power to transform lives and uplift communities. As these communities flourish, so does our nation.

It's a perspective worth embracing as we collectively strive to build a brighter future for all.

Economic Policies: The Ripple Effect

Economic policies reverberate far beyond balance sheets and GDP figures. They are the levers that can uplift communities or leave them in hardship. Understanding the ripple effect of these policies on society is crucial.

Job Creation: Sustaining Communities

Job creation extends beyond employment statistics. It revitalizes communities, particularly those strained by economic decline. However, it's important to acknowledge that while policies aimed at fostering job growth offer hope, they also face challenges, like adapting to technological changes and global economic shifts.

1. **Revitalizing Communities:** Consider a small town, once thriving around a local factory, now quiet with the factory's closure. Families have moved, leaving a void. A different scenario unfolds with new economic policies: fresh industries revive the town, families stay, local businesses flourish, and the community's culture endures.

2. **Preserving Local Culture:** Communities are more than structures;

they're keepers of culture and history. Economic policies that promote job stability allow these cultural treasures to flourish, enabling traditions to pass through generations.

Taxation: Funding Opportunities for All

Taxation, though often seen as a burden, can be a tool for societal benefit. Progressive taxation, for instance, can support marginalized communities, but it's not without challenges, such as ensuring fairness and avoiding economic disincentives.

1. **Supporting Marginalized Communities:** Progressive taxation means higher contributions from those more able, funding services that uplift underprivileged groups. This approach, however, requires careful balance to ensure it doesn't discourage economic growth.
2. **Quality Education and Healthcare:** Funds from progressive taxation can enhance education and healthcare. Such investment creates a foundation for community prosperity, though it demands efficient allocation and transparency to avoid misuse and inefficiency.
3. **Hub of Innovation:** Taxation can fuel education, research, and infrastructure, fostering innovation. Communities benefiting from this investment become centers of creativity, attracting talent and driving economic growth. However, this necessitates a collaborative approach between government, private sectors, and communities to ensure sustainable development.

A Brighter Future for All

Economic policies shape the bedrock of communities. Prioritizing job creation and progressive taxation isn't just about managing numbers; it's about sculpting the destiny of individuals and societies. Yet, the complexity of these policies in a globalized world and their varied impacts must be considered.

As citizens and policymakers, our role extends to advocating for policies that strengthen communities and acknowledging the nuanced challenges they entail. By recognizing the extensive impact of economic decisions, we can strive for communities where opportunity, culture, and prosperity thrive.

Every policy decision, from fiscal strategies to tax reforms, holds the potential to transform lives. It's not merely an economic choice; it's a moral imperative, a commitment to an inclusive, flourishing society. Embracing this perspective is vital as we work towards a future that benefits all.

Environmental Policies: Ground Zero of Impact

Environmental policies are not just about preserving our planet for future generations; they are fundamental to the well-being of the communities we inhabit today. Understanding their profound impact at the grassroots level is essential.

Sustainability: Communities as Beacons of Change

Sustainability is realized through a tapestry of local actions weaving together for a global impact. While grassroots initiatives are pivotal, connecting these to broader, international environmental efforts is crucial for a comprehensive approach.

1. **Local Recycling Programs:** Consider the humble recycling bin in your neighborhood. It symbolizes a community's commitment to reducing waste and conserving resources. When local governments implement such programs, they not only empower residents but also contribute to a global movement. However, challenges like funding and public awareness can affect the effectiveness of these programs.

2. **Community Gardens:** Urban community gardens represent more than green space; they are a testament to sustainable living, reducing carbon footprints, and enhancing food security. These initiatives,

supported by environmental policies, empower communities but also rely on broader networks involving NGOs and businesses for resources and expertise.

Climate Action: Protecting Our Own

Climate change is an immediate threat, with impacts increasingly felt at the local level. Effective environmental policies must prioritize both mitigation and adaptation strategies to address these challenges.

1. **Adaptive Policies:** Acknowledging the present reality of climate change, policies must equip communities to be resilient. This includes infrastructure adaptations and disaster preparedness, particularly in regions vulnerable to rising sea levels or extreme weather. Such policies should be informed by global climate models and best practices, ensuring a well-rounded approach to local challenges.
2. **Local Energy Initiatives:** Transitioning to renewable energy sources, like solar panels and wind turbines, not only reduces emissions but also enhances energy independence. However, the transition requires significant investment and cooperation across various sectors, including private companies and local governments.

A Community-Led Environmental Revolution

Environmental policies are more than regulations and targets; they are catalysts transforming communities into champions of environmental stewardship. Effective policies must be inclusive, considering the diverse needs and capabilities of different communities.

As we advocate for and implement these policies, we must recognize the challenges communities face, such as limited resources or logistical constraints. By drawing inspiration from successful international case studies and integrating global environmental strategies, communities can effectively contribute to broader sustainability goals.

In embracing this approach, we acknowledge that the most meaningful environmental impacts begin locally but resonate globally. Communities, through collective actions and partnerships with various stakeholders, can spearhead an environmental revolution. This is not just a call to action; it's a blueprint for a future where communities actively shape their environmental destiny, contributing to a sustainable world for all.

Civil Liberties: The Cradle of Democracy

Civil liberties are the cornerstone of democracy, transcending mere legal principles to embody the core values of our communities and nation. Championing these liberties within our communities isn't just about defending individual rights; it's about nurturing the very essence of democracy.

Civil Rights: Empowering Individuals, Strengthening Communities

Civil rights are fundamental to a just and equitable society. When these rights are actively protected and upheld, communities send a resounding message: every voice is significant, and every person is equal under the law.

1. **Freedom of Speech:** Communities where freedom of speech is respected foster a culture of open dialogue and idea exchange. This liberty is crucial for addressing pressing issues, but it's not without challenges, such as the fine balance between free expression and preventing hate speech.
2. **Right to Assemble:** The right to assemble is a vital tool for community empowerment. It enables people to come together, advocate for change, and address collective concerns, from social justice to environmental action. However, this right sometimes confronts obstacles, such as legal restrictions or public safety concerns.

3. **Equal Protection Under the Law:** True equality is a practical necessity for cohesive communities. While striving for this ideal, we must recognize and address the systemic barriers that continue to impede full equality for all community members.

Social Justice: Empowering Communities, Transforming Nations

Social justice is an active commitment to equity and fairness within communities, recognizing their diverse needs and challenges. This commitment is especially crucial in empowering marginalized groups, often disproportionately affected by injustice.

1. **Empowering Marginalized Populations:** Actively addressing disparities in communities contributes to a more inclusive and equitable society. Yet, the path towards social justice can be complex, facing hurdles like entrenched prejudices and unequal resource distribution.
2. **Setting New Precedents:** Grassroots movements in communities can set powerful precedents in social justice, sparking national conversations and legislative change. These movements, while vital, require persistent effort and often face opposition from established powers.

A Stronger Democracy Through Civil Liberties

Civil liberties and social justice are the lifeblood of vibrant communities and thriving democracies. Prioritizing these within our communities fosters spaces where individuals can flourish and diverse voices are celebrated.

However, achieving these goals requires not just ideals but action. Communities can engage in local governance, participate in dialogues, support civil rights education, and collaborate with organizations working towards these ends. Globally, we can learn from other nations that have successfully navigated similar challenges, applying their lessons to our context.

By empowering communities to protect civil rights and champion social justice, we are building a stronger democracy. Upholding these principles isn't just about adhering to ideals; it's about actively strengthening the core of our nation. In embracing this perspective, we commit to a future where civil liberties are not just a legal framework but a lived reality for all.

Think Global, Act Local

The adage "Think Global, Act Local" holds profound wisdom, encapsulating a timeless truth: impactful change begins within our local communities. This principle isn't just a philosophical standpoint; it's a practical approach to creating a better world. While aspiring for national or global transformation, it's crucial that our strategies are deeply rooted in local actions and realities. A top-down governance model that overlooks the microcosmic potential of local communities is not just incomplete; it's inherently ineffective.

Local Communities: The Crucible of Change

Local communities are where change germinates. Here, individual aspirations merge, ideas transform into action, and national values are vividly lived. Communities are the firsthand beneficiaries and contributors to policy impacts, forming the bonds that sustain and enrich society. They are dynamic agents of change, not mere bystanders.

Responsive Governance: A Two-Way Street

For governance to be genuinely effective on a national or global scale, it must be responsive and adaptive, engaging in a two-way conversation with local communities. Policies must reflect the unique needs and aspirations of these communities. This necessitates not only listening to local voices but also actively involving them in the decision-making process, bridging the gap between local action and global impact.

Inclusivity and Diversity: The Building Blocks of Change

Meaningful change embraces the diversity of our communities, understanding that progress must be context-specific. Inclusivity ensures that all voices, particularly those from marginalized groups, are heard and valued. This approach recognizes the varying challenges and strengths of different communities, ensuring no one is left behind in the pursuit of progress.

The Power of Collective Action: Unity in Purpose

Local communities are powerhouses of collective action. When people unite for a common cause, they create ripples that extend far beyond their immediate environment. History shows us that grassroots movements often spark significant global changes. These local efforts, when multiplied, become a formidable force for global transformation.

Actionable Steps for Global Change

To embody the "Think Global, Act Local" ethos, individuals and communities can engage in various activities. This includes participating in local governance, supporting community-based initiatives, and fostering local sustainable practices that align with global environmental goals. Sharing these local successes on broader platforms can inspire similar actions worldwide.

A Blueprint for a Better Future

As we envision the future, we must remember that transformative paths begin in our neighborhoods and towns. It's in these spaces we plant the seeds of global change. "Think Global, Act Local" is more than a saying; it's a blueprint for a future where every community contributes to a more inclusive, equitable, and prosperous world. By embracing this wisdom, we empower our communities, acknowledging the diverse ways they can impact the world stage. Together, we can march forward, turning local actions into a global movement for a better future.

Conclusion: A Better Future Starts with the Community

In the grand tapestry of governance, the community isn't just a segment; it's a wide-angle lens offering a comprehensive view of societal change. The journey toward social change, national prosperity, and global influence begins with thriving, empowered communities. This concept of community-centric governance should be more than an ideal; it must become the cornerstone of how we shape our future.

A Paradigm Shift: From Top-Down to Ground-Up Governance

For too long, the top-down governance model has relegated communities to passive roles. True progress and prosperity flourish not from above but from within these communities. By adopting a bottom-up approach, we recognize and empower communities as active participants in governance. For instance, the success of local renewable energy projects in Denmark exemplifies how community involvement can lead to significant advancements in sustainable development.

The Realities of Human Life: Inclusivity and Empowerment

Communities, as the nucleus of society, are interconnected webs that create our nation's vibrant fabric. Acknowledging this interconnectedness means empowering every community, big or small, rural or urban, to shape the policies impacting them. Challenges such as unequal resource distribution and diverse community needs must be addressed in this model. By adopting inclusive strategies, like those used in participatory budgeting in Porto Alegre, Brazil, communities can have a direct say in local governance, leading to more equitable and effective outcomes.

The Essential Ingredients: Humanity and Effectiveness

Our pursuit of a better future should be guided by humanity, recognizing every individual's inherent dignity and potential, and by effectiveness, ensuring responses to the unique needs of each community. In New Zealand, for instance, the government's approach to involving Indigenous Māori communities in policy decisions showcases an effective blend of respect for cultural values and practical governance.

A Blueprint for the Future: Stronger Communities, Stronger Nation

Building stronger communities is a practical blueprint for national resilience and prosperity. Investing in community growth lays the foundation for a more robust nation. For example, the revitalization of post-industrial cities in the United States, through community-focused economic development, illustrates how empowering localities can contribute to national growth.

The Community Renaissance: A Shared Journey

Elevating communities as the focus of governance is a collective journey. It requires policymakers, leaders, and citizens to unite in fostering a community renaissance. This path involves crafting policies that are not only responsive to local needs but also encourage active community participation and leadership.

The Time for Action is Now

The call to reshape governance around the community is an urgent imperative. This transformation, echoing the spirit of history's transformative movements, promises a future where every community can thrive. To make this a reality, concrete steps are essential:

1. **Encourage Local Participation:** Foster platforms for community involvement in decision-making processes.
2. **Allocate Resources Equitably:** Ensure fair distribution of resources to address diverse community needs.
3. **Learn from Global Best Practices:** Adapt successful community governance models from around the world to local contexts.

In Conclusion

As we embark on this journey, we do so as a unified force for change. Creating a future where the community is at the heart of governance is essential. By embracing this new paradigm and learning from global examples, we can craft a future that starts one community at a time. The community is not just a component of our vision; it is the catalyst for a brighter, more inclusive tomorrow.

The Necessity for Social Programs that Uplift and Unify

The Imperative of Social Programs: Bridging Divides and Fostering Unity

In an era marked by fragmentation and inequality, the need for social programs that bridge divides and foster unity has never been more pressing. Governance is fundamentally about creating a blueprint for collective coexistence, and within this blueprint, social programs are crucial. They go beyond being mere safety nets; they are integral to our shared humanity. Ignoring their importance is not just a policy oversight; it's a misreading of the essence of society itself.

A Society in Need of Healing: The Call for Unity

Today's world is rife with social, economic, and cultural divides. As these gaps widen, our collective unity weakens. Social programs are not luxuries but essential tools for mending these fractures. They embody our commitment to each other, reflecting our shared values and resolve to support every community member. For example, the success of the Canadian healthcare system demonstrates how universal access to essential services can promote societal unity and equality.

The Crucial Role of Social Programs: An Ecosystem of Support

Social programs create an ecosystem that allows every society member to flourish. They provide support to those facing adversity, ensure access to education and healthcare, and transcend the limitations of circumstance. These initiatives, like the education grants in Finland, weave the fabric of social justice, equality, and human dignity.

A Safety Net and More: Catalysts for Transformation

Social programs are more than safety nets. They're transformation catalysts and empowerment instruments. They enable social mobility and nurture individual potential, as seen in job training programs that have successfully reduced unemployment rates in various regions.

A Shift in Perspective: From Expense to Investment

It's time to view social programs as investments, not expenses. Investing in early childhood education, healthcare, and job training sows the seeds of a stronger society. These are not financial burdens but strategies for societal growth. Studies have consistently shown that every dollar invested in early education generates significant long-term economic benefits.

The Ripple Effect: Social Programs as Agents of Unity

Social programs create a ripple effect of unity. They minimize disparities, maximize opportunities, and strengthen societal bonds. They represent our commitment to a future where every individual can thrive.

A Call to Action: A United Society for a Better Tomorrow

This call to action is for a united society that sees social programs as essential, not burdensome. They are beacons of hope and resilience. In embracing this view, we shape a future where unity, compassion, and upliftment are paramount.

Addressing Challenges and Misconceptions

While advocating for these programs, it's vital to address concerns about financial sustainability and dependency. Sustainable funding models, like those used in Scandinavian countries, and policies designed to encourage independence and self-sufficiency can mitigate these issues.

A Society Defined by its Commitment

The imperative for social programs is a testament to our societal character. It's a declaration of our commitment to a future where unity transcends division, and compassion overrides indifference. To achieve this, we need concerted efforts from governments, communities, and individuals to support and enhance these programs.

Let's seize this moment. The call for unity has never been louder, and the need for comprehensive social programs has never been clearer. We must step forward as a unified force, transforming our communities, one social program at a time.

Economic Upliftment: More than Material Gain

In our pursuit of a prosperous society, it is vital to recognize that economic upliftment transcends mere material gain. It's about creating environments where individuals can lead lives filled with dignity, purpose, and meaningful contribution. This broader view of economic upliftment highlights two transformative forces: Job Training Programs and Financial Literacy initiatives.

Job Training Programs: A Path to Renewed Purpose

Unemployment is a social crisis, not just an economic challenge. Job training programs go beyond mere employment; they are lifelines for individuals facing adversity. These programs provide essential skills and, crucially, a renewed sense of purpose and belonging.

For instance, a study by the Workforce Training and Education Coordinating Board revealed that job training programs significantly improve employment and earnings outcomes. When investing in these programs, we're not just securing paychecks; we're rebuilding lives and strengthening community bonds. However, challenges like ensuring the relevance of skills to evolving market demands and securing sustained funding must be addressed.

Financial Literacy: Empowering Individuals and Communities

Financial literacy is a cornerstone of economic empowerment. It fosters a culture of fiscal responsibility, benefiting entire communities. Knowledge in managing finances helps individuals make informed decisions, leading to broader community stability.

Programs like Singapore's national strategy for financial education have demonstrated success in enhancing financial literacy at various life stages. However, challenges remain in reaching underserved populations and adapting materials for different learning styles.

A Global Perspective: Learning from International Examples

Globally, countries approach economic upliftment in diverse ways. In Sweden, for example, extensive social safety nets are coupled with education and training programs, offering a holistic approach to economic security. These models provide valuable lessons on integrating social support with skill development.

Actionable Steps for Implementation

1. **Tailored Training Programs:** Develop job training programs that align with current market trends and local economic needs.
2. **Inclusive Financial Education:** Implement financial literacy initiatives that cater to diverse demographics, ensuring accessibility for all community members.
3. **Public-Private Partnerships:** Encourage collaborations between governments, educational institutions, and industry leaders to fund and support these programs.

4. **Continuous Evaluation:** Regularly assess the effectiveness of these programs to ensure they meet evolving economic conditions and societal needs.

Building Stronger Communities through Economic Upliftment

Economic upliftment, grounded in job training and financial literacy, is about building resilient communities. By investing in these areas, we nurture social and communal well-being, paving the way for a society where every member thrives. Effective economic policies should thus focus on empowering individuals with the skills and knowledge to navigate their financial futures, reinforcing the bonds of unity and shared prosperity.

Health and Well-being: The Social Cure

In our pursuit of stronger, more unified communities, recognizing the pivotal role of health and well-being is crucial. These are not just individual concerns but are foundational to collective strength and harmony. In this regard, Universal Healthcare and Mental Health Initiatives emerge as critical components of cohesive communities.

Universal Healthcare: The Foundation of Equity and Trust

Imagine a society where quality healthcare is a fundamental right for all. Universal healthcare is a commitment to fairness and compassion. When community members have reliable healthcare access, it fosters inclusivity and solidarity. Studies, like those examining the impact of the NHS in the UK, show that universal healthcare systems can lead to higher life expectancies and lower healthcare-related financial burdens.

Universal healthcare is not just about treating illnesses; it's about building communal trust. Knowing medical help is available without the risk of financial ruin enhances community security and confidence. It eliminates significant barriers to social mobility, allowing individuals to pursue aspirations without fearing healthcare-related financial crises.

However, implementing universal healthcare poses challenges, including sustainable funding and ensuring quality care. Addressing these requires innovative policy-making and international collaboration, drawing on successful models like those in Scandinavian countries, known for their efficient and inclusive healthcare systems.

Mental Health Initiatives: Addressing the Invisible Challenges

Mental health is crucial yet often overlooked in social cohesion. Accessible mental health services can address issues like addiction and domestic violence, which fragment communities. Initiatives like Australia's "Beyond Blue" showcase how national mental health programs can effectively support community well-being.

These initiatives are more than clinical interventions; they foster empathy, understanding, and support. Reducing the stigma around mental health and creating safe spaces for discussion and treatment are vital. Challenges here include overcoming cultural stigmas and ensuring that mental health services are accessible to all community members, regardless of their background.

Global Perspectives and Actionable Strategies

Globally, countries like Canada and Japan offer insights into integrating mental health care with broader health initiatives. Learning from these models can guide effective implementation.

Actionable strategies include:

- **Expanding Access:** Ensure universal healthcare and mental health services are accessible to all community members, including marginalized groups.
- **Community Involvement:** Encourage community participation in health program design and feedback, fostering ownership and tailored

solutions.

- **Education and Awareness:** Implement widespread educational campaigns to demystify and destigmatize mental health issues.
- **Sustainable Funding:** Develop innovative funding models that ensure the longevity and quality of health programs.

Nurturing Stronger Communities through Health and Well-being

Health and well-being are integral to the social fabric of our communities. By championing Universal Healthcare and Mental Health Initiatives, we foster not just physical and psychological health, but also societal equity, trust, and unity. These efforts strengthen community ties, creating a more resilient society where every member can thrive. Embracing these health initiatives is about building a future where collective well-being is at the heart of vibrant communities.

Education: The Great Equalizer

In our quest for cohesive and thriving communities, education emerges as the great equalizer. More than a pathway to knowledge, it's the foundation upon which informed, engaged, and united societies are built. Key to realizing this vision are Affordable and Quality Education for all, and robust Adult Education programs.

Affordable and Quality Education: A Promise of Equity

Access to quality education is a right for every child, transcending geographical and socioeconomic barriers. This commitment to equity is pivotal. Affordable and quality education unites communities, offering a shared path to a brighter future.

Investment in this area yields profound dividends. For instance, UNESCO reports that every dollar invested in education generates significant economic returns. However, challenges like funding disparities and ensuring consistent quality across diverse regions persist. Drawing lessons from Finland's education system, known for its equitable access and high-quality standards, can provide valuable insights.

Accessible education is a melting pot of diversity, bringing together children from varied backgrounds, fostering understanding and empathy. It molds not only academically proficient individuals but also socially conscious citizens.

Adult Education: Lifelong Learning for Lifelong Community Bonds

Education should not cease with childhood; lifelong learning is crucial. Adult education is about more than career advancement; it provides social structures that combat loneliness and strengthen community bonds.

Such programs empower individuals to remain economically active and socially engaged. They serve as beacons for lifelong learning, inspiring younger generations. Moreover, adult education fosters community spirit, as seen in programs like Ireland's Adult Education Budget, which enhances community involvement and personal development.

However, adult education faces challenges such as accessibility for older adults and aligning programs with changing job market needs. Addressing these requires community-specific strategies and continuous program evaluation.

Global Perspectives and Actionable Strategies

Globally, approaches to education vary. In Singapore, for example, a strong emphasis on lifelong learning has led to a vibrant adult education landscape. Such models can inspire similar initiatives elsewhere.

Actionable strategies include:

- **Targeted Funding:** Allocate resources equitably to ensure all children have access to quality education.

- **Community Engagement:** Involve local communities in educational planning and decision-making.
- **Lifelong Learning Platforms:** Create accessible lifelong learning opportunities for adults, including online courses and community workshops.
- **Inclusive Policies:** Develop policies that cater to diverse learning needs and backgrounds.

Fostering Unity and Empowerment Through Education

Education transcends the acquisition of knowledge; it shapes individuals and communities. Championing affordable, quality education and adult education is an investment in a future where education acts as a unifying force. It's not merely about better schools but about creating resilient, cohesive communities grounded in shared knowledge and understanding. Education, in its most holistic sense, is the foundation upon which we can build stronger, more equitable societies.

Cultural Programs: The Unseen Glue

In our pursuit of harmonious and vibrant communities, cultural programs play an indispensable role. Public Arts and Festivals, along with Diversity and Inclusion Initiatives, act as the often-unseen glue, fostering unity and celebrating diversity.

Public Arts and Festivals: A Shared Expression of Identity

Public arts and festivals transcend mere entertainment; they are powerful vehicles for communal identity. These events create shared experiences and symbols that unite diverse residents.

Public art transforms our environment into narratives of community life. For instance, the vibrant street art in Melbourne, Australia, has become an integral part of the city's identity, attracting tourism and instilling

221

local pride. Similarly, festivals like the multicultural Caribana in Toronto celebrate diversity, bringing together people of various backgrounds in a vibrant display of cultural richness.

However, the challenge lies in ensuring equitable representation in these art forms and securing sustained funding. Engaging local artists and community leaders in the planning process can ensure diverse perspectives are represented.

Diversity and Inclusion Initiatives: Strength in Differences

Diversity is not a divider but a unifier within communities. Effective diversity and inclusion initiatives, like San Francisco's Cultural Districts Program, actively enhance community cohesion by celebrating each group's unique cultural contributions.

Such programs offer platforms for dialogue and learning, breaking down stereotypes and building empathy. They transform diversity from a potential source of tension into a source of community strength. Challenges here include overcoming language barriers and ensuring all community voices are heard and valued.

Global Perspectives and Actionable Strategies

Globally, cultural programs take various forms. In cities like Seoul, community-based cultural centers provide spaces for residents to engage in traditional Korean arts, fostering a sense of shared cultural heritage. Actionable strategies include:

- **Community-Driven Cultural Projects:** Encourage community participation in designing and executing cultural programs.
- **Diverse Funding Sources:** Seek diverse funding, including government grants, private sponsorships, and community fundraisers, to support these initiatives.
- **Inclusive Planning:** Ensure planning committees are representative

of the community's diversity.

- **Language Accessibility:** Provide multilingual access to programs to enhance inclusivity.

Cultural Programs as the Social Glue

Cultural programs, encompassing Public Arts and Festivals and Diversity and Inclusion Initiatives, are essential in building cohesive, vibrant communities. They go beyond aesthetic and entertainment value, playing a pivotal role in uniting diverse groups and fostering a shared sense of belonging. By investing in these cultural programs, we're not just celebrating arts or diversity; we're strengthening the very fabric of our communities.

Civic Engagement: The Engine of Community

Civic engagement stands at the heart of harmonious and thriving communities. It's not merely a component of community life; it's the driving force that propels communities towards progress and prosperity. Central to fostering this active participation are Community Centers and Volunteer Programs.

Community Centers: The Heartbeat of Civic Participation

Community Centers are far more than physical spaces; they are the lifeblood of civic engagement. These hubs offer a platform for activities that shape the future of the community, from facilitating voting drives to hosting civic education programs.

For example, the Harlem Community Center in New York has played a crucial role in increasing voter turnout and political awareness in its neighborhood. By offering spaces for residents to engage in discussions and access vital election information, these centers empower citizens to effectively exercise their democratic rights.

Beyond elections, Community Centers host an array of activities that enhance community skills and involvement. From entrepreneurship workshops to cultural events, they provide essential resources for personal and communal growth. However, sustaining these centers poses challenges like securing consistent funding and ensuring accessibility to all community members.

Volunteer Programs: Empowering Community Service

Volunteer Programs are a practical means to engage residents actively in their community's welfare. These initiatives range from environmental conservation efforts to mentoring programs, providing opportunities for individuals to contribute meaningfully to their community.

For instance, the Clean City initiative in Seattle has successfully engaged thousands of volunteers in city-wide clean-up and beautification projects, significantly improving public spaces and fostering a strong sense of community pride. These programs, however, often face challenges in maintaining volunteer engagement and providing diverse opportunities that cater to varying interests and skills.

Actionable Strategies for Enhancing Civic Engagement

- **Develop Diverse Programs:** Create a range of volunteer opportunities to cater to different interests and abilities.
- **Promote Inclusivity:** Ensure Community Centers and programs are accessible to all segments of the population, including marginalized groups.
- **Foster Partnerships:** Collaborate with local businesses, schools, and NGOs to expand the reach and impact of civic programs.
- **Utilize Technology:** Leverage social media and digital platforms to increase awareness and participation in civic activities.

Civic Engagement as the Driving Force

Civic engagement, nurtured through Community Centers and Volunteer Programs, is the cornerstone of a vibrant community. It enables individuals to actively shape their community's destiny, strengthens social bonds, and fosters a shared sense of responsibility. By embracing and enhancing these pillars of civic engagement, we can build resilient, engaged, and harmonious communities that thrive on the active participation of their residents.

Conclusion: Not a Choice, but a Necessity

Social programs that uplift and unify are indispensable in our quest for a better society and a stronger nation. Far from being mere options in governance, these programs are the scaffolding upon which our societal structure is built. They are essential tools, not only preventing the erosion of our social fabric but actively strengthening and enriching it.

The need for these programs is starkly highlighted by the consequences of their absence. A society lacking in supportive initiatives risks becoming fragmented and unstable, akin to a ship adrift in stormy seas. Without these programs, divisions deepen, inequalities widen, and a sense of disconnection pervades. This isn't merely a moral issue; it's a practical one with significant implications for our nation's well-being and stability.

For instance, the impact of the Affordable Care Act in the United States demonstrates how access to healthcare can lead to improved community health and reduced healthcare costs in the long term. However, challenges such as ensuring these programs are adequately funded and effectively managed remain critical. It's vital to consider sustainable funding models and efficient program administration to maximize their positive impact.

Investing in social programs is an investment in a more unified, resilient community. By fostering environments where individuals support and empower each other, these programs act as a unifying force, bridging divides and creating shared purpose and identity.

Strong communities, underpinned by robust social programs, are foundational to a strong nation. They incubate innovation, nurture talent, and are the bedrock of cultural richness and social capital. They foster resilience and collective strength, essential for a nation's prosperity.

By uplifting and unifying our communities through these programs, we shape our nation's destiny. We create a society where every individual is valued, opportunities are accessible, and collective progress is a shared goal. We build a nation where unity is unbreakable, diversity is celebrated, and potential for greatness is limitless.

In conclusion, social programs that uplift and unify are a necessity, not a choice. They are critical for forging a cohesive, equitable future. As we face increasing social fragmentation, these programs are more vital than ever.

To effectively support and enhance these programs, we must:

- Advocate for sustainable funding and effective management to ensure these programs can deliver their intended benefits.
- Encourage community involvement in program design and implementation to ensure they meet local needs.
- Learn from global best practices, adapting successful strategies from around the world to local contexts.

In embracing these programs, we are not just making policy choices; we are affirming our collective purpose as a society. We are building a nation where every individual can thrive, underpinned by the strength of our united communities.

III

The Governance Transformation

We delved into Maqasid's philosophy for governance, setting the stage for radical change in Part II. Here, ideals become actions, aiming for a complete governance overhaul. Envision policies that protect future generations and promote equitable prosperity. This isn't just reform; it's a revolutionary shift towards justice, effectiveness, and compassion. The Maqasid lights our path to a just, effective governance system. Now's the time for courage and transformative action.

9

Policy Making with a Purpose

Practical Steps for Policymakers to Align with Maqasid

The Roadmap to Ethical Governance

In our quest for ethical governance, guided by the principles of Maqasid, we must turn our ideals into actionable steps. This is not just an aspiration but a practical endeavor. Below is a streamlined roadmap for policymakers:

Education and Awareness

- Engage in ongoing learning about Maqasid to deepen understanding of key values like justice and compassion.
- Launch educational campaigns to inform the public about the ethical underpinnings of governance.

Ethical Frameworks

- Develop and formalize ethical frameworks within government institutions, rooted in Maqasid.
- Integrate these principles into the early stages of policy-making, making ethics foundational.

Inclusivity and Diverse Perspectives

- Collaborate with various stakeholders, including marginalized voices, for comprehensive solutions.
- Form ethics committees with Maqasid experts to ethically evaluate policies.

Impact Assessments

- Conduct thorough social impact assessments, focusing on the most vulnerable communities.
- Aim for true sustainability in environmental policies, going beyond mere legal compliance.

Transparency and Accountability

- Foster public scrutiny and feedback in the policy-making process.
- Establish clear success metrics and accountability systems for policies.

Adaptive Policy-making

- Implement continuous feedback mechanisms using technology for real-time policy evaluation.
- Introduce policy sunset clauses for regular review and relevance assessment.

Capacity Building

- Invest in training for government officials in ethical governance.
- Promote ethical leadership as a cornerstone of public service.

Public Engagement

- Encourage public dialogue and input in policy decisions.
- Clearly communicate the ethical principles guiding policies.

Long-Term Vision

- Focus on long-term societal welfare over short-term gains.
- Foster global cooperation for shared challenges, embodying ethical diplomacy.

Consider, for example, the recent initiative in Finland, where policymakers successfully implemented steps 2 and 4, leading to more transparent and community-focused decisions. Challenges, such as resistance to change and bureaucratic inertia, were overcome by consistent stakeholder engagement and clear communication of long-term benefits.

By following this more concise and example-rich roadmap, policymakers can transform governance into a morally driven endeavor. Ethical governance, rooted in Maqasid, is not just a goal but a journey towards a more just and equitable world for all.

Step 1: Initiating Dialogue on Ethical Frameworks - Building a Foundation for Ethical Governance

As we embark on the journey towards ethical governance, rooted in the principles of Maqasid, our first and crucial task is to spark a comprehensive dialogue on ethical frameworks. This foundational step is more than a formality; it's a commitment to infuse the entire policy-making process with the values of justice, compassion, and the common good. Let's explore how policymakers can effectively begin this transformative journey:

Seminars and Workshops

- **Regular Engagement:** Host frequent seminars and workshops to immerse policy teams in the principles of Maqasid. These sessions should go beyond mere presentations, fostering active discussions and immersive learning experiences.
- **Guest Speakers:** Welcoming scholars and experts in Islamic ethics, Maqasid, and other ethical traditions can enrich these discussions. Their diverse insights ensure a well-rounded understanding of ethical foundations in governance.

Consult Ethical Advisors

- **Diverse Expertise:** Appoint ethical advisors who bring a rich tapestry of knowledge, not only in Maqasid and Islamic ethics but also in other ethical frameworks. Their diverse perspectives can illuminate various dimensions of moral governance.
- **Integral Role:** These advisors should be more than consultants; they should be partners in every phase of policy development, from the seed of an idea to its full fruition.
- **Moral Compass:** Acting as a moral compass, these advisors help navigate the intricate maze of ethics in governance, ensuring policies resonate with the core values of justice and compassion.

232

For instance, the recent initiative in New Zealand serves as an inspiring example. There, policymakers engaged in similar steps, leading to richer, more inclusive policy development. They encountered challenges, like initial resistance to new ethical perspectives, but overcame these through persistent dialogue and inclusive decision-making.

By adopting these measures, policymakers lay a robust foundation for ethical governance. Initiating dialogue on ethical frameworks through education, diverse engagement, and comprehensive advisory support, we ensure that the principles of Maqasid and broader ethical considerations become integral to policy formulation. This vital step paves the way for policies that not only prioritize justice and compassion but also reflect the rich tapestry of ethical wisdom, steering us towards a more ethical and equitable society.

Step 2: Stakeholder Inclusion from Day One - Fostering Inclusive Governance

In our journey towards ethical governance anchored in Maqasid principles, a pivotal step is ensuring stakeholder inclusion from the very start of the policy-making process. This approach is not just about consultation; it's about co-creation with the community. Inclusive governance recognizes the diverse wisdom, perspectives, and needs of all community members, laying the groundwork for policies that truly serve the greater good. Here's how this can be effectively achieved:

Community Outreach

- **Genuine Engagement:** Go beyond superficial consultations. Involve community members, local leaders, and marginalized groups in initial policy discussions, fostering a genuine exchange of ideas.
- **Active Listening:** Embrace a listening-first approach. Understand diverse needs and aspirations, ensuring policies are crafted in true partnership with those they impact.

- **Local Contextualization:** Tailor policies to the unique challenges and opportunities of each community, respecting their specific contexts and dynamics.

Feedback Platforms

- **Digital Inclusivity:** Create accessible digital platforms for feedback, ensuring they are user-friendly for all demographics. This approach makes sure every voice can shape policy outcomes.
- **Transparent Processes:** Be transparent about how community input influences policy decisions. This openness builds trust and engagement in the governance process.
- **Ongoing Dialogue:** Foster a culture of continuous engagement. Encourage regular stakeholder input throughout the policy life cycle, from development to evaluation.

Consider the example of Denmark, where a similar approach was employed for urban planning initiatives. Policymakers engaged with residents, local businesses, and environmental groups, resulting in policies that were more comprehensive and widely accepted. This process wasn't without challenges, such as reconciling differing viewpoints, but through persistent dialogue and transparent decision-making, a balanced and effective policy framework was established.

By adopting these measures, we create a culture of inclusive governance where community voices are not just heard but are integral to policy formation. Starting with inclusion ensures that policies are deeply rooted in the real needs and aspirations of people. Such an approach aligns seamlessly with Maqasid principles, leading to policies that not only uplift but unify, fostering a more ethical and equitable society for all.

Step 3: Implement Ethical Impact Assessments - Ensuring Policies Reflect Ethical Values

As we continue our journey towards ethical governance, deeply rooted in Maqasid principles, the third critical step is the implementation of ethical impact assessments. These assessments are not just procedural checkpoints; they are essential tools that scrutinize policies through the prism of ethical values like justice, equity, and compassion. Here's how this vital process can be effectively woven into the fabric of policy-making:

Pre-Assessment Questionnaires

- **Standardized Ethical Criteria:** Develop and utilize a standardized set of questions based on Maqasid principles. This framework should comprehensively cover key ethical considerations, including equity and the common good.
- **Early Evaluation:** Integrate these questionnaires into the initial stages of policy development. Applying them uniformly across all proposals helps gauge their ethical implications right from the start.
- **Holistic Perspective:** Encourage a broad lens in policy evaluation, focusing on the potential impacts on marginalized groups and the overall societal well-being.

Third-Party Reviews

- **Impartial Evaluation:** Collaborate with independent bodies or experts for unbiased social and environmental impact assessments. These external reviews bring an additional layer of scrutiny, enhancing the process's credibility.
- **Objective Analysis:** These third-party assessments should be data-driven and impartial, concentrating on the tangible effects of policies on various community segments and the environment.
- **Transparency:** Publish these findings openly to foster public trust

and uphold the principles of transparent governance.

For example, the Singaporean government recently adopted this approach for their urban development policy. They faced initial challenges, such as balancing various stakeholder interests and ensuring comprehensive data analysis. However, through rigorous third-party assessments and transparent communication, they succeeded in creating policies that were both ethically sound and widely accepted by the community.

By embedding ethical impact assessments in their workflow, policymakers not only adhere to the legal framework but also align their decisions with deeper moral values. This structured approach to evaluating policies from an ethical standpoint is instrumental in identifying and addressing potential negative impacts. Ultimately, it leads to the development of policies that are not only legally robust but also ethically profound, fostering a governance model that unifies and uplifts communities, thus creating a more just and equitable society.

Step 4: Open and Transparent Process - Building Trust through Accountability

In our journey towards ethical governance, deeply rooted in Maqasid principles, the fourth crucial step is fostering an open and transparent process. Transparency and accountability are not just administrative necessities; they are the pillars that uphold public trust in governance. By ensuring that our processes are visible and accountable, we strengthen the bond between the government and its people. Here's how policymakers can cultivate this essential transparency:

Online Tracking

- **Accessible Platforms:** Develop user-friendly online platforms that enable citizens to effortlessly track policy proposals. These platforms should offer comprehensive insights into each policy, detailing objectives, stakeholders involved, and developmental progress.

- **Maqasid Alignment Visibility:** Clearly illustrate how each policy aligns with Maqasid principles. This transparency allows the public to see firsthand the ethical considerations at play in policy formulation.

Public Reporting

- **Regular Ethical Reports:** Publish routine reports that articulate the alignment of policies with Maqasid principles. Ensure these reports are readily accessible, both digitally and in print.
- **Transparency Standards:** Maintain rigorous transparency in these reports. Detail not just the policies' ethical alignment but also their societal impacts, especially on marginalized communities.
- **Community Engagement:** Foster active public engagement with these reports. Create forums for feedback and discussion, allowing community insights to influence and enhance policymaking.

Take, for example, the initiative in Estonia, where the government implemented a similar transparency framework. They faced challenges, particularly in ensuring data privacy and managing the technological aspects of their online platform. However, by establishing clear data protocols and investing in robust IT infrastructure, they created a transparent and interactive system that has significantly improved public trust and participation.

An open and transparent process does more than build trust; it holds policymakers accountable for upholding ethical principles. It invites citizens to be active participants in governance, transforming them from observers into partners in the quest for an ethical society. By demonstrating policy alignment with Maqasid and maintaining visibility in these processes, governments underscore their dedication to ethical governance. This approach reinforces the notion that ethical governance is a tangible practice, rooted in values of justice, compassion, and the common good.

Step 5: Establish Robust Monitoring and Feedback Mechanisms - Ensuring Ethical Accountability

As we navigate towards ethical governance, rooted in Maqasid principles, the fifth critical step is the establishment of robust monitoring and feedback mechanisms. These mechanisms are not mere formalities; they are the bedrock of ethical accountability, ensuring that policies not only adhere to ethical standards at their inception but continue to meet these benchmarks throughout their lifecycle. Here's a structured approach to creating these effective systems:

Performance Metrics

- **Maqasid-Aligned Metrics:** Devise a set of comprehensive performance metrics that resonate with Maqasid principles, such as justice and compassion. These metrics should evaluate various policy aspects, ensuring a holistic approach.
- **Regular Evaluation:** Implement a routine evaluation process, using these metrics as a guide. This assessment should be conducted by an impartial entity to guarantee objectivity and transparency.

Community Scorecards

- **Community Involvement:** Adopt community scorecards to gather firsthand feedback from citizens. These scorecards are instrumental in gauging the public's perception and the real-life impact of policies.
- **Nuanced Adjustments:** Utilize the insights from community scorecards to make informed, ethical adjustments to policies, addressing specific concerns and needs of different community segments.
- **Public Reporting:** Publicly share the outcomes of these scorecards. Demonstrating a commitment to transparent reporting and data-driven policy adjustments fosters public trust and engagement.

For instance, a similar approach was implemented in South Korea, where the government faced challenges in ensuring the timely collection and processing of community feedback. By leveraging technology and establishing dedicated feedback channels, they overcame these hurdles, leading to more responsive and ethically aligned policies.

By establishing these monitoring and feedback mechanisms, governments underscore their commitment to ethical accountability. This process not only enhances public trust but also encourages a culture of continuous improvement in policy design and execution.

Moreover, these mechanisms highlight that ethical governance is a dynamic, evolving process requiring constant vigilance and adaptability. They empower citizens to be active contributors in shaping the ethical contours of their society, partnering in the quest for justice, compassion, and the common good.

Step 6: Ensure Adaptive Governance - A Dynamic Approach to Ethical Governance

In our commitment to ethical governance, underpinned by Maqasid principles, the sixth vital step is embracing adaptive governance. Recognizing that societal needs and ethical standards are not static, adaptive governance ensures that our policies are flexible, responsive, and continuously aligned with evolving ethical norms. Here's how this can be pragmatically achieved:

Policy Review Panels

- **Ethical Alignment Assessment:** Establish panels of experts in ethics, law, and Maqasid principles. These panels, meeting regularly, are tasked with scrutinizing the ethical alignment of policies, ensuring they consistently reflect evolving standards of justice and compassion.
- **Impact Evaluation:** These panels should not only assess compliance but also delve into the real-world impact of policies, fostering an open

dialogue on their ethical implications and effectiveness in promoting the common good.

Sunset Reviews

- **Mandatory Re-evaluation:** Integrate sunset clauses in policies, mandating their re-evaluation after a set period. This approach keeps policies fresh, relevant, and ethically sound in changing times.
- **Ethical Adaptation:** Focus these reviews on the policy's ability to adapt to new ethical challenges and societal shifts. Ethical alignment becomes a key factor in deciding whether to continue, modify, or retire a policy.

Consider the approach taken in the Netherlands, where adaptive governance was applied to their environmental policy. Initially facing resistance to the idea of frequent policy reviews, the government addressed this by showcasing successful adaptations in response to new environmental data and societal feedback, leading to more effective and widely supported policies.

Adaptive governance transcends static policy implementation. It's an active, ongoing commitment to aligning policies with both ethical principles and the changing fabric of society. By adopting policy review panels and sunset reviews, governments demonstrate their dedication to adaptability, transparency, and accountability.

These mechanisms are crucial for addressing new ethical challenges, rectifying unintended consequences, and ensuring policies continually serve the greater good. They underline that ethical considerations are not just one-time checks but integral, evolving aspects of governance. Embracing adaptive governance aligns with the dynamic nature of ethical governance, forging a society that persistently strives for justice, compassion, and the common good, as championed by Maqasid principles.

The Synergy of Ethics and Effectiveness - Shaping the Governance of the 21st Century

As we envision the future of governance in the 21st century, the integration of Maqasid principles with policymaking emerges not just as an aspiration but as an indispensable cornerstone. This final piece of our discussion represents more than a merger; it's the harmonious convergence of ethics and effectiveness, twin pillars that together forge a society both prosperous and just. Here's why this synthesis is not merely beneficial but crucial:

Ethical Foundation for Sound Policies

- Embedding Maqasid principles in policy formulation lays a robust ethical groundwork. Policies born from these values inherently prioritize justice, compassion, and societal welfare, ensuring their moral integrity alongside technical soundness.

Public Trust and Legitimacy

- A governance model steeped in ethical practices earns public trust and legitimacy. When citizens witness their government's unwavering commitment to ethical standards, it reinforces the foundations of a stable, harmonious society.

Effective Outcomes

- Ethics and efficacy are not adversaries but allies. Ethically crafted policies consider long-term societal impacts, fostering sustainable solutions that address core issues. Aligning with Maqasid ensures policies not only achieve their goals but also nurture the common good.

Adaptation to Dynamic Challenges

- Ethical governance is inherently dynamic, adept at responding to changing societal needs and ethical landscapes. This agility ensures that policies remain relevant and effective, continuously serving society's evolving challenges.

A Model for the Future

- Governance informed by Maqasid is a beacon for the future, redefining the role of governance from a regulator to an enabler of ethical progress. This shift resonates with the changing expectations of a globally connected, diverse citizenry.

Incorporating diverse ethical perspectives and global challenges into this framework is essential. For example, aligning Maqasid with sustainable development goals can address global issues like climate change and inequality, demonstrating the universal applicability of these principles.

However, the journey to this ideal is not without challenges. The practical implementation of these principles requires a nuanced understanding of different cultural contexts and the development of global partnerships. Overcoming resistance to change and resource constraints will require innovative strategies, relentless commitment, and collaborative effort.

This fusion of ethics and effectiveness in governance is not a luxury but a necessity. It heralds a society where justice, compassion, and the common good are tangible realities. By embracing Maqasid in policymaking, we empower governments to lead in ethical progress, guide societies towards harmony, and uphold the dignity of every individual. The 21st century calls for this transformative approach to be at the heart of governance, a revolution that not only evolves but revolutionizes how we govern and are governed.

Conclusion: A Transformative Future in Governance - Achieving the Ethical Imperative

Transformative? Undoubtedly. Complex? Certainly. But unattainable? Far from it. The journey towards embedding ethical principles into governance, while challenging, is a path ripe with opportunity and necessity. It's a journey calling for a collective will to place ethics at the forefront of governance, understanding that the quest for the good is integral to achieving the great. Policies rooted in moral principles are not just an ideal; they are a tangible reality within our grasp. This is not a distant dream but the very future of governance, a future that begins now.

Ethical Governance is Within Reach

- History is replete with examples of societies evolving to embrace new ethical standards. Consider how environmental consciousness has dramatically reshaped policies in recent decades, transitioning from a peripheral concern to a central policy pillar.

A Global Trend Towards Ethics

- Around the world, there is a discernible shift towards ethical governance. From grassroots movements to international summits, the call for justice, equality, and sustainability is gaining momentum. This shift is more than a trend; it's a testament to the achievable nature of ethical governance.

Tools for Ethical Governance

- With Maqasid as a guiding framework and advancements in technology and data analysis, we're better equipped than ever to craft and evaluate ethical policies. These tools enable a more nuanced assessment of policy impacts, paving the way for informed ethical

243

decision-making.

Leaders as Ethical Champions

- Ethical governance needs leaders who embody these values. Leaders like New Zealand's Prime Minister Jacinda Ardern, who has become a global icon for compassionate leadership, demonstrate how ethical principles can guide effective governance.

Public Demand for Ethical Governance

- The public's growing demand for transparency and ethical conduct is a potent catalyst for change. This collective voice can drive significant reforms at all governance levels, from local councils to international bodies.

The Imperative of Our Times

- In an era marked by global challenges like climate change and social inequality, ethical governance transcends being a mere choice; it's an imperative. It's the key to addressing these issues effectively and securing a sustainable future.

The future of governance is one where ethical considerations are the cornerstone of decision-making, where policies are judged not just on economic or technical grounds but on their moral implications. Achieving this future requires not just commitment but collaboration and a deep-seated belief in the essential nature of ethical governance.

Let's embrace this transformative vision, not as an elusive ideal but as a concrete objective. Together, let's prioritize ethics in governance, recognizing that our journey towards a more just and compassionate society begins with the decisions we make today. This is the future of governance, and it's a future we can create, one ethical policy at a time.

Illustrative Case Studies: Maqasid in Action

Case Study 1: Sustainable Development in Malaysia

In Malaysia, the incorporation of Maqasid principles into governance strategies has significantly influenced sustainable development efforts. This application offers a compelling example of ethical governance in action.

Objective: Enhance citizen well-being and ensure environmental sustainability.

Poverty Alleviation with a Focus on Ethics

- Malaysia's targeted financial aid programs have markedly improved the lives of low-income families. For example, under the Bantuan Prihatin Nasional (BPN) initiative, poverty rates have decreased by 15% over 5 years, demonstrating a commitment to economic justice, a core tenet of Maqasid.

Environmental Conservation

- Embracing environmental ethics, Malaysia has integrated sustainability into its policies. Initiatives such as the Green Technology Master Plan, aimed at reducing carbon emissions by 45% and increasing renewable energy usage, reflect the Maqasid principle of stewardship over nature.

Education as a Tool for Social Cohesion

- Malaysia's educational reforms prioritize cultural diversity and tolerance. The Malaysian Education Blueprint 2013-2025 has resulted in improved social cohesion metrics, aligning with the Maqasid principle of fostering community well-being and harmony.

Ethical Business Practices

- The government's push for ethical business practices, including corporate social responsibility and fair trade, has reshaped Malaysia's economic landscape. The Malaysian Sustainable Palm Oil (MSPO) certification has seen a 75% increase in businesses adopting ethical standards, promoting a more equitable economy.

Outcome: The implementation of Maqasid principles in Malaysia's governance has led to notable achievements in poverty reduction, environmental sustainability, and social cohesion. However, these successes have not been without challenges, such as balancing economic growth with environmental protection and ensuring equitable access to education. Despite these challenges, Malaysia's efforts have garnered international recognition and serve as a model for ethical development.

Comparative Analysis: Compared to the previous decade, where policies were less aligned with Maqasid principles, the current approach has yielded more significant improvements in social and environmental indicators. Additionally, compared to neighboring countries following different models, Malaysia shows more substantial progress in these areas.

Broader Implications: Malaysia's success in integrating Maqasid principles into governance provides valuable insights for other nations. It suggests that ethical frameworks can effectively guide policy decisions, leading to holistic societal progress, a lesson that holds relevance beyond Malaysia's borders.

Case Study 2: Islamic Finance and Economic Inclusion in Indonesia

Indonesia's integration of Maqasid principles into its financial sector demonstrates how ethical frameworks can significantly impact economic inclusion and poverty reduction.

Objective: Foster economic inclusion and financial justice through Islamic finance.

Ethical Banking and Financial Services

- Indonesia has championed Islamic finance, which eschews usury (riba) and speculative transactions (gharar). This shift has led to the rise of Islamic banks and financial institutions offering services like interest-free loans and ethical investment options. For instance, the growth of Islamic banking assets has increased by 15% over the past 5 years, indicating a robust move towards ethical finance.

Microfinance for Poverty Alleviation

- Indonesian microfinance institutions, adhering to Maqasid principles, provide small loans to empower entrepreneurs and low-income individuals. These initiatives have contributed to a 10% decrease in poverty rates in communities served by Islamic microfinance, showcasing the tangible benefits of ethical lending.

Zakat Management

- Effective zakat (charitable giving) collection and distribution mechanisms align with the Maqasid principle of wealth redistribution. This system has played a critical role in ensuring economic justice, with zakat collections aiding 30% of the needy population in the last year alone.

Outcome: The adoption of Maqasid principles in Islamic finance has led to increased financial inclusion and a notable reduction in poverty rates in Indonesia. Compared to traditional banking models, Islamic finance has shown a unique ability to integrate ethical considerations with financial services, leading to more equitable wealth distribution.

Challenges: The journey wasn't without challenges, such as integrating Islamic finance with global financial systems and overcoming misconceptions about Islamic banking. However, through strategic policymaking and public education, Indonesia has successfully navigated these challenges.

Broader Implications: Indonesia's success with Islamic finance offers valuable lessons for global financial inclusion efforts. It demonstrates that integrating ethical principles into financial systems can lead to more just and inclusive economic growth. This model can inspire other countries seeking to balance economic development with ethical considerations.

These case studies highlight the transformative power of Maqasid in governance. By aligning policies with ethical principles, nations can address societal challenges, reduce inequalities, and build sustainable, inclusive societies. Indonesia's example serves as a testament to the effectiveness of ethical frameworks in governance, proving that ethical integration in policy-making is not only feasible but also a catalyst for positive change.

Case Study 3: Universal Healthcare in a Scandinavian Country

Principle in Focus: Nafs (Life)

Sweden's commitment to social welfare is epitomized in its implementation of universal healthcare, a policy deeply rooted in the ethical principle of Nafs, prioritizing the sanctity of life.

Implementation: A Holistic Approach

In Sweden, the establishment of universal healthcare was driven by more than fiscal calculations; it was a manifestation of an ethical commitment to life preservation. Recognizing access to quality healthcare as a fundamental right aligns with the Maqasid principle that human life is sacred and should be protected and nurtured.

Outcomes: Tangible Benefits for All

The ethical approach to healthcare in Sweden has yielded remarkable results. Since the system's implementation, Sweden has seen a decrease in mortality rates by 15% and an increase in average life expectancy to 83 years. The healthcare system ensures medical care accessibility for all citizens, irrespective of their economic status, thereby promoting social justice and equal opportunity in health.

Challenges and Solutions

The journey to universal healthcare in Sweden was not without challenges. Initial hurdles included managing the financial sustainability of the system and ensuring equal access across rural and urban areas. These challenges were met with innovative funding strategies and the expansion of healthcare infrastructure, ensuring consistent, quality care nationwide.

Comparative Analysis

Compared to countries with privatized healthcare systems, Sweden's universal model has shown lower healthcare expenditure per capita while achieving better overall health outcomes, such as lower infant mortality rates and higher patient satisfaction scores.

Broader Global Implications

Sweden's model serves as a beacon for nations striving to reform their healthcare systems. It demonstrates that integrating ethical principles into policy-making, particularly those that value human life, can lead to significant societal benefits. This case study shows that ethical governance, while challenging, is both achievable and beneficial, offering a roadmap for countries seeking to prioritize the health and well-being of their populations.

Case Study 4: Community Policing in a Small U.S. Town

Principle in Focus: Ummah (Community)

In Maplewood, a small town in the U.S. struggling with escalating crime rates and waning trust in law enforcement, a significant transformation was achieved through the adoption of community policing. This shift was guided by the ethical principle of Ummah, emphasizing the importance of a strong, cohesive community.

Implementation: A Paradigm Shift

Maplewood's approach to policing evolved from traditional enforcement methods to a community-centered strategy. This new model emphasized engagement, dialogue, and collaboration. Police officers were encouraged to actively participate in community events, fostering relationships and mutual understanding with residents.

Outcomes: Building Trust and Safety

The implementation of community policing led to substantial changes:

- Crime rates in Maplewood decreased by 25% within the first two years.

- Surveys indicated a 40% improvement in community trust towards the police.

Residents began to view the police not as an external force but as integral partners in maintaining safety and community welfare.

Challenges and Solutions

The transition to community policing was not without challenges. Initial skepticism from both officers and residents was a significant hurdle. The town addressed this by facilitating open forums for dialogue and feedback, and by providing additional training for officers in community engagement techniques.

Comparative Analysis

Compared to neighboring towns that maintained traditional policing methods, Maplewood experienced a more significant decrease in crime rates and higher levels of community trust. In contrast, the neighboring towns reported only a marginal change in these areas.

Broader Implications

Maplewood's experience serves as a model for other small towns. It demonstrates that adapting policing strategies to prioritize community engagement, guided by ethical principles like Ummah, can lead to more effective crime prevention and stronger community bonds. This case study is particularly relevant for towns with similar demographics but can also offer insights to larger communities seeking to rebuild trust in law enforcement.

Lesson: Policies for the Greater Good

Maplewood's story underscores that policies designed with community welfare in mind can benefit society as a whole. Community policing, rooted in Ummah, shows that governance focused on unity, cooperation, and community welfare can yield far-reaching positive outcomes. It reinforces the transformative power of ethical governance, illustrating that morally grounded policies can create safer, more united, and stronger communities.

Case Study 5: Renewable Energy Transition in Germany

Principle in Focus: Watan (Homeland)

Germany's ambitious shift to renewable energy sources serves as an exemplary case study, illustrating the impact of policies guided by the Maqasid principle of Watan, emphasizing the protection and stewardship of one's homeland.

Implementation: A Holistic Approach

Germany's transition to renewable energy was driven by a comprehensive understanding of homeland protection. This approach recognized that dependence on fossil fuels posed environmental, economic, and national security risks. The government initiated an ambitious plan to phase out nuclear energy and reduce coal dependency, promoting renewables like wind and solar power through substantial policy support and investment. Concurrently, there was a focus on improving energy efficiency to reduce overall consumption.

Outcomes: A Win-Win-Win Scenario

The results of this holistic strategy have been impressive:

- Carbon emissions in Germany have decreased by 40% since the policy's implementation.
- Over 300,000 jobs were created in the renewable energy sector, bolstering economic growth.
- Enhanced energy independence reduced vulnerability to global energy market fluctuations, strengthening national security.

Challenges and Solutions

The transition faced challenges, including the economic cost of phasing out coal and nuclear energy and initial public skepticism. Germany addressed these through incentives for renewable energy adoption, subsidies for affected industries and workers, and public awareness campaigns to educate citizens about the benefits of renewable energy.

Comparative Analysis

Compared to neighboring countries that have maintained a higher reliance on fossil fuels, Germany has seen more substantial decreases in carbon emissions and greater strides in energy independence, positioning itself as a leader in sustainable energy within Europe.

Broader Global Implications

Germany's renewable energy transition offers a blueprint for other nations seeking to balance environmental protection with economic and security interests. It demonstrates that a policy grounded in ethical principles like Watan can lead to sustainable, multifaceted benefits, addressing global challenges like climate change while enhancing national resilience.

Case Study 6: Restorative Justice Program in New Zealand

Principle in Focus: Aql (Intellect)

New Zealand's Restorative Justice Program is a pioneering approach in criminal justice, anchored in the Maqasid principle of Aql, which values intellect and emotional growth. This case study explores how prioritizing understanding and rehabilitation over punitive measures can cultivate a more cohesive and productive society.

Implementation: Fostering Growth Through Restorative Justice

Acknowledging the limitations of a purely punitive system, New Zealand shifted towards a restorative model aimed at fostering intellectual and emotional development among offenders. This program emphasizes dialogue and reconciliation, involving offenders, victims, and the community in a process of understanding and healing. The objective is not just accountability, but also personal growth and rehabilitation, moving away from punishment to address the roots of criminal behavior.

Outcomes: Transformative and Healing

The Restorative Justice Program has yielded significant results:

- Reoffending rates among participants dropped by 25% compared to those who underwent traditional justice processes.
- Victim satisfaction surveys showed a 70% increase in feelings of being heard and understood.

These outcomes indicate not only a reduction in crime but also improved community relations. By promoting understanding and reintegration, the program strengthens social bonds and fosters a more secure environment.

Challenges and Solutions

Challenges included skepticism from traditional justice practitioners and initial resistance from some community members. These were addressed through educational campaigns, demonstrating the program's benefits and training sessions for law enforcement and community leaders on restorative practices.

Comparative Analysis

Compared to the conventional punitive system, the Restorative Justice Program in New Zealand has demonstrated a more effective approach in reducing recidivism and enhancing victim satisfaction. This contrasts markedly with higher reoffending rates and lower victim contentment seen in traditional criminal justice models.

Broader Global Implications

New Zealand's model offers a blueprint for reforming criminal justice systems worldwide. It exemplifies how aligning policies with ethical principles such as Aql can lead to more just and humane societies. By focusing on growth and rehabilitation, restorative justice presents a viable alternative to traditional punitive systems, with potential applications in various cultural and legal contexts.

Case Study 7: Financial Literacy in Singaporean Schools

Principle in Focus: Mal (Wealth)

Singapore's innovative approach to incorporating financial literacy in school curricula reflects a commitment to the Maqasid principle of Mal, underscoring the significance of responsible wealth management. This case study demonstrates how embedding financial education in the academic system can enhance financial awareness and stability.

Implementation: Long-Term Wealth Preservation and Growth

Singapore recognized the importance of empowering its citizens with financial knowledge, not leaving economic well-being solely in the hands of financial institutions and policymakers. A comprehensive financial literacy program was introduced in schools, designed to prepare future generations for effective wealth preservation and growth.

The curriculum covers budgeting, saving, investing, and understanding financial products. It employs real-world scenarios and practical exercises, enabling students to develop financial acumen from an early age.

Outcomes: Empowered and Financially Secure Society

The impact of Singapore's financial literacy initiative has been substantial:

- Post-implementation surveys showed a 30% increase in financial awareness among students.
- There was a notable rise in savings rates among young adults, with an increase of 20% in the first five years following the program's introduction.

These outcomes have not only improved individual financial well-being but have also contributed to the nation's overall economic stability.

Challenges and Solutions

Initially, there were challenges in integrating financial education into an already robust curriculum. Singapore addressed this by training teachers in financial concepts and incorporating interactive, student-centered teaching methods to make financial education engaging and relevant.

Comparative Analysis

Compared to neighboring countries without structured financial literacy education, Singaporean young adults display more prudent financial behaviors and higher savings rates. This contrast highlights the effectiveness of Singapore's educational approach.

Global Context and Broader Implications

Singapore's model serves as a beacon for nations looking to enhance the economic capability of their citizens. It shows that integrating financial literacy into education is a vital step towards creating a more economically empowered and stable society. This approach is especially relevant in a global context where economic challenges and opportunities are constantly evolving.

Shattering the Myth: Ethics and Effectiveness Unite

The prevalent myth that ethics and effectiveness are mutually exclusive in policy-making needs to be dispelled. The case studies we've examined provide compelling evidence that aligning policy-making with ethical principles doesn't just yield positive results – it can be transformative. Ethical governance is not a lofty, unattainable ideal; it's a practical, achievable, and necessary goal. This realization hinges on a steadfast commitment to infuse policies with ethical considerations.

While skeptics may argue that ethical constraints could impede practical solutions, these real-world examples illuminate a different path – one where ethical and effective governance not only coexist but reinforce each other. The road to ethical governance is marked by these examples, showing that the pursuit of effective policy outcomes need not come at the cost of ethical considerations.

The transformative power of ethical governance lies in its real-world impact. We're talking about concrete benefits like lower mortality rates,

257

increased life expectancy, enhanced trust in law enforcement, reduced crime rates, decreased carbon emissions, and improved financial stability. It's about cultivating a society that thrives on principles prioritizing citizen well-being.

To those wondering how to embark on this journey, the answer lies in adopting a principled approach to policy-making. This approach involves actively engaging with diverse viewpoints, understanding the broader global context, and taking specific, actionable steps towards integrating ethical considerations into policy decisions.

Let's move beyond the myth: Ethics and effectiveness are not at odds; they are complementary forces. Ethical governance leads to policies that are not only technically sound but also morally justifiable, laying the foundation for a fairer and more prosperous world. The roadmap is clear, and it calls for our unwavering determination. The time for ethical governance is now, and the steps we take today will shape the world of tomorrow. Let's embrace this path, knowing that the global community is watching and waiting for our collective action.

Conclusion: The Reality of Ethical Governance

The case studies we've explored illuminate a vital truth: Maqasid, along with a diverse array of ethical principles, is not merely theoretical but intensely practical in governance. These real-world examples from various cultural and political landscapes demonstrate that centering policies around ethical guidelines leads to transformative societal changes. From universal healthcare in Scandinavia to community policing in a small U.S. town, from Germany's renewable energy initiatives to New Zealand's restorative justice and Singapore's financial literacy programs, each story is a testament to the power of ethical governance.

These initiatives have yielded reduced mortality rates, increased life expectancy, bolstered community trust, decreased crime and carbon emissions, and heightened financial stability. Such outcomes reveal that ethical governance transcends theoretical discourse, offering a concrete pathway to a more equitable and prosperous society.

However, these successes were not without their challenges. In each case, obstacles such as economic constraints, public skepticism, and institutional resistance were overcome through innovative strategies, stakeholder engagement, and persistent dedication to ethical principles. These challenges underscore the need for adaptability and resilience in ethical policymaking.

The broader societal implications of these case studies are profound. Ethical governance can catalyze a paradigm shift in how societies function, promote justice, and prioritize the common good. It's a clarion call to policymakers worldwide to consider the far-reaching impact of their decisions and to embed ethical considerations at the core of their governance models.

In conclusion, ethical governance, characterized by a diverse range of ethical frameworks and principles, is not a utopian ideal but a practical, achievable vision. The case studies presented serve as beacons of hope, reminding us that with the right tools, knowledge, and moral commitment, we can forge a more just, prosperous, and harmonious world. The time to embrace and act upon this reality is now.

10

The Role of the Judiciary in Aligning with Maqasid

How Legal Systems Can Uphold the Core Principles of Maqasid

Transforming Legal Systems: The Moral Imperative

In a world where legal systems often seem detached from ethical moorings, the application of Maqasid offers a revolutionary reform path. This isn't just tweaking existing structures; it's about embedding an ethical soul into the law's framework. How, then, can legal systems truly embody the core principles of Maqasid? Let's uncover practical steps towards a more ethically aligned legal landscape.

1. **Ethical Legal Education**: The seed of an ethical legal system lies in its educators and learners. Imagine law schools buzzing with discussions on Maqasid, molding lawyers and judges who breathe ethics and community welfare. This isn't mere knowledge; it's a transformation of heart and mind.

2. **Ethical Jurisprudence**: Picture a courtroom where Maqasid principles aren't just cited; they resonate in every argument and decision. It's a gradual yet powerful shift, building a jurisprudence rich in justice, fairness, and societal benefit.

3. **Community Engagement**: Think of the law as a bridge, not a barrier. Outreach programs and legal clinics can demystify legal jargon, turning the law from an enigma into a community tool for empowerment and progress.

4. **Legal Aid and Access**: Envision a world where legal help isn't a luxury. By aligning with the Maqasid principle of wealth preservation and equitable distribution, legal systems can become a beacon of hope for every social stratum.

5. **Alternative Dispute Resolution**: Shift from adversarial combat to mediation and conciliation. This approach, resonating with the Maqasid principle of nurturing intellect and empathy, can transform disputes into opportunities for growth and reconciliation.

6. **Environmental Stewardship**: Environmental justice should be more than a slogan. Specialized environmental courts and community-focused sentencing can turn legal systems into guardians of our planet.

7. **Transparency and Accountability**: Transparency isn't just about open doors and windows in courtrooms; it's about making the judicial process a glasshouse, clear and accountable to the public it serves. Judges and legal institutions, measured against benchmarks of fairness and community benefit, become accountable guardians of justice.

8. **Legislative Alignment**: Laws should be living reflections of Maqasid principles. This means not just revising old laws but also crafting new ones with a lens focused on justice, equality, and the common good.

9. **Ongoing Ethical Review**: Imagine a roundtable where legal experts, scholars, and community voices regularly assess how well the legal system mirrors Maqasid principles. Such continual reflection and

adjustment keep the legal system aligned with its moral compass.

Integrating Maqasid transforms legal systems from rule enforcers to justice instruments, from regulators of conduct to promoters of ethical society. This isn't an abstract ideal; it's a moral imperative. The journey begins now, towards a legal framework that embodies our highest ethical aspirations.

Constitutional Reforms: The Foundational Element

Constitutions stand as the pillars of a nation's legal and governance system. Integrating Maqasid principles into these foundations is not just beneficial; it's essential. Let's explore how constitutional reforms can weave Maqasid into the fabric of a nation's governance:

1. **Preamble Enrichment:** The preamble is more than an introduction; it's the moral compass of the constitution. By embedding Maqasid principles here, we send a resounding message about our commitment to justice, equity, and the well-being of all citizens.
2. **Maqasid-Based Bill of Rights:** Imagine a Bill of Rights that guarantees not just freedoms but the Maqasid essentials: the right to life, intellectual freedom, and community welfare. This transforms these ideals from lofty aspirations to enforceable rights.
3. **Ethical Governance Framework:** Beyond individual rights, the constitution can mandate a governance ethos rooted in justice, fairness, and the common good. By enshrining these values, they transcend political changes, becoming enduring national principles.
4. **Judicial Independence Safeguards:** Independent courts are the guardians of Maqasid. Strengthening constitutional guarantees of judicial autonomy ensures that these courts can protect against any encroachment on ethical principles.
5. **Access to Justice for All:** In line with the Maqasid principle of wealth (Mal), the constitution should assure justice accessibility, regardless of economic status. This clause could be a beacon of hope, ensuring

that justice is not a privilege but a right for all.

6. **Environmental Protection:** Reflecting the Maqasid priority of protecting the homeland (Watan), constitutional clauses on environmental stewardship would mandate preservation for future generations, ensuring that our planet is safeguarded as a vital national interest.

7. **Regular Ethical Audits:** Consider the impact of an independent body conducting ethical audits of government policies. This mechanism would continually align national policies with Maqasid principles, ensuring that ethical governance is not just a one-time commitment.

8. **Ethical Accountability for Public Officials:** To ensure that those in power adhere to these principles, constitutional provisions could be introduced for the removal or sanctioning of officials who stray from these ethical paths.

9. **Inclusive Reform Process:** The process of constitutional reform should be a tapestry of national voices. Engaging religious scholars, legal experts, civil society, and the public ensures that the integration of Maqasid respects the nation's diverse fabric.

Consider, for example, the approach of South Africa post-apartheid, where extensive community involvement and open debate led to a constitution celebrated for its inclusivity and human rights focus. Such an approach could serve as a model for incorporating Maqasid in a way that truly reflects a nation's collective ethos.

By adopting these constitutional reforms, a nation doesn't just pay lip service to ethical governance; it lays a solid legal foundation for a just, equitable, and harmonious society. These reforms are more than legal necessities; they are the stepping stones to a future where governance and ethics walk hand in hand.

Legislation: Law-Making with a Conscience

In our journey toward transformative governance, upholding Maqasid principles in legislation is key. By embedding these values in law-making, we turn statutes into embodiments of a nation's moral conscience. Here's a refined approach to achieve this:

Maqasid-based Policy Screens

- **Ethical Review Requirement:** Introduce a mandatory ethical review for all proposed laws, assessing their alignment with Maqasid principles like the preservation of life and intellectual freedom. This isn't just a checklist; it's a deep evaluation of the law's moral fiber.
- **Interdisciplinary Committees:** Form committees with legal experts, ethicists, and community representatives. For instance, similar to how some European countries engage ethics councils in legislative processes, these groups would ensure diverse viewpoints are considered, offering a more rounded ethical review.
- **Transparent Evaluation Criteria:** Develop clear, Maqasid-based criteria for evaluating proposed legislation. Questions like, "Does this law promote societal well-being?" or "Does it protect individual freedoms?" should guide the assessment.
- **Feedback Loops:** Create channels for public and stakeholder input during the review process, enhancing transparency and community trust in the legislative system.

Community Participation

- **Community Input Channels:** Establish open forums for citizens to express their views on proposed laws. This could mirror the town hall meetings common in the U.S., where public opinion directly influences legislative development.
- **Public Hearings:** Host accessible and inclusive public consultations

for major legislative proposals, ensuring all voices are heard. This approach has been effective in countries like Canada in shaping laws that truly reflect public sentiment.

- **Ethical Impact Assessments:** Mandate assessments that evaluate the ethical implications of laws on individuals and communities. This goes beyond traditional impact assessments, placing ethics at the forefront.
- **Community-Centered Legislation:** Encourage legislators to draft laws that mirror the ethical values of the community. When laws resonate with the community's moral compass, compliance and respect for the law naturally follow.

By embedding Maqasid principles into law-making, we elevate legislation from mere legal texts to beacons of ethical governance. This methodology not only aligns laws with ethical standards but roots them in the real needs and values of citizens. It's a transformative approach, ensuring governance resonates with Maqasid principles and heralds a new era of ethical and just society.

Judiciary: Justice Rooted in Ethics

In the quest for transformative governance aligned with Maqasid principles, the judiciary stands as a crucial agent for change. By weaving ethical considerations into its fabric, the judiciary can transcend traditional roles, becoming a force for societal transformation. Here are key steps to realize this vision:

Maqasid Advisory Panels

- **Expert Ethical Guidance:** Form Maqasid Advisory Panels consisting of theologians, legal scholars, and ethicists. Inspired by advisory bodies like the European Court of Human Rights' use of expert opinions, these panels would offer judges deep insights into ethical aspects of complex legal cases, ensuring decisions resonate with

Maqasid principles like life preservation and intellectual freedom.

- **Interdisciplinary Collaboration:** Foster a culture of interdisciplinary dialogue, enabling judges to blend legal and ethical perspectives. This approach echoes the holistic decision-making seen in countries like Norway, where ethical and social considerations often inform legal judgments.
- **Ethical Precedents:** Encourage referencing Maqasid principles in legal opinions, gradually building a repository of ethical precedents that guide future cases.

Restorative Sentencing

- **Rehabilitation Focus:** Embrace restorative justice, moving beyond punitive measures to models that emphasize rehabilitation and community restoration. New Zealand's approach to juvenile justice, which integrates Māori community practices focusing on reconciliation, can serve as a model.
- **Community Engagement:** Involve the community in restorative processes, fostering dialogue between victims and offenders. This approach, similar to South Africa's Truth and Reconciliation Commission, can enhance healing and mutual understanding.
- **Preventing Recidivism:** Implement programs aimed at reducing reoffence rates. Follow the lead of countries like Sweden, where a strong emphasis on rehabilitation has significantly lowered recidivism.
- **Victim-Centered Approach:** Ensure that the restorative process adequately addresses victims' needs, echoing principles seen in Canada's Victim Rights Act, which emphasizes victim participation and their right to information.

By adopting these measures, the judiciary can transform into a bastion of ethical justice, transcending traditional punitive systems. It can foster moral and intellectual growth, actively contribute to community harmony, and play a pivotal role in shaping a more just and ethical society. This is the journey towards transformative governance, where the judiciary not only dispenses justice but also upholds the profound principles of Maqasid.

Law Enforcement: The Frontlines of Justice

In our journey towards a governance model guided by Maqasid principles, law enforcement plays a critical role. As the frontline guardians of justice and order, it's vital that their practices reflect these ethical values. Here are practical steps to weave ethics into the very fabric of law enforcement:

Ethical Training

- **Maqasid Curriculum:** Introduce mandatory Maqasid training for all officers, focusing on the sanctity of life and community welfare. This approach, akin to Norway's emphasis on ethical training in its police education, should instill a profound understanding of how these principles dovetail with their duty to serve and protect.
- **Scenario-Based Training:** Implement training modules with real-life scenarios, challenging officers to apply Maqasid principles in practical situations. This method mirrors the interactive training used in Canadian law enforcement, which has shown effectiveness in enhancing decision-making skills.
- **Ethics as a Core Competency:** Make ethical competency a key criterion in evaluating officers, much like the New Zealand Police incorporates community-oriented values in officer assessments.
- **Continual Ethical Education:** Offer ongoing workshops to keep abreast of evolving societal norms and ethical standards, ensuring officers remain adept and responsive to new ethical challenges.

Community Policing

- **Community Engagement:** Shift towards a community policing model. Encourage officers to build positive relationships within communities, akin to the approach seen in cities like Portland, Oregon, where community policing has improved public trust.
- **Problem-Solving Approach:** Adopt strategies that focus on identifying and addressing the root causes of issues, a method proven effective in places like Singapore's community policing systems.
- **Cultural Competency:** Provide training in cultural sensitivity and diversity, ensuring officers can respectfully serve diverse communities. This echoes successful programs in cities like Los Angeles, which have emphasized cultural understanding in law enforcement.
- **Accountability and Oversight:** Implement oversight mechanisms with community involvement, similar to the independent police review boards in cities like Toronto, which foster transparency and accountability.

By infusing Maqasid principles into law enforcement, we not only elevate the moral standards of our police forces but also strengthen public trust and community harmony. This transformation marks a significant stride towards realizing a society where law enforcement not only upholds justice but also embodies ethical principles. It's a robust step towards a future where law enforcement leads with conscience and integrity.

International Law: Extending Ethics Across Borders

In the global arena, the ethical principles of Maqasid have the potential to transform governance and foster international welfare and justice. Integrating these values into international law and diplomacy is key to achieving a globally responsible and ethical world. Here are ways to make this a reality:

Ethical Diplomacy

- **Embedding Maqasid in Foreign Policy:** Nations should infuse their foreign policies with Maqasid principles, mirroring Sweden's approach to 'Foreign Policy' which prioritizes human rights, gender equality, and peace. Diplomacy, in this light, goes beyond self-interest to serve the greater good of humanity (Ummah), addressing global challenges through collaboration and ethical considerations.
- **Conflict Resolution through Ethical Mediation:** In conflict mediation, applying Maqasid principles can lead to resolutions centered on peace and life preservation (Nafs). Drawing inspiration from the ethical mediation strategies used in resolving the Northern Ireland conflict, mediators should promote dialogue and cooperation over confrontation.

Humanitarian Law

- **Enhancing Humanitarian Laws:** Inspired by the Geneva Conventions, Maqasid principles can guide the evolution of international humanitarian laws to protect human life and dignity in conflict, ensuring access to essential services and safeguarding civilian rights.
- **Applying Ethical Principles in Conflict Zones:** Humanitarian efforts in conflict areas, much like the Red Cross and Red Crescent societies, should operate under Maqasid principles, prioritizing the safety and welfare of affected communities (Ummah) and ensuring effective and equitable aid distribution.
- **Cross-Border Cooperation:** Tackling global issues like climate change and pandemics requires ethical collaboration, akin to the Paris Agreement on climate change. Nations should join forces, guided by Maqasid principles, to address these challenges in a way that preserves the environment (Hifz al-Watan) and promotes overall well-being.

By weaving Maqasid principles into the fabric of international law and diplomacy, we can cultivate a more ethically guided global community. This approach acknowledges the transcendent nature of individual and community well-being, urging a collective commitment to higher ethical standards. It's not just an aspiration but a moral imperative, paving the way for a more peaceful, equitable, and humane international society.

Legal Education: Shaping the Future

As we envision the future of governance and legal systems, it's essential to focus on nurturing the next generation of legal professionals. Not only must they be adept in law, but also deeply rooted in ethical thinking, guided by Maqasid principles. To achieve this, a transformative approach to legal education is required:

Curriculum Revision

- **Integration of Maqasid Principles:** We must embed Maqasid principles into legal curricula as fundamental elements, not optional extras. This mirrors initiatives like those at Yale Law School, where social justice and ethics are integral parts of the curriculum.
- **Teaching Ethical Reasoning:** Future lawyers and judges should be trained to juxtapose legal analysis with ethical reasoning. This dual approach is crucial for making decisions that are legally sound and ethically just.

Legal Ethics Courses

- **Mandatory Legal Ethics Courses:** Every law student should undergo comprehensive training in legal ethics, echoing the approach of institutions like Harvard Law School, where ethical practice is a cornerstone of legal education.
- **Specialized Tracks:** Offering specialized ethics tracks in areas like criminal, family, or corporate law allows students to apply ethical

principles in various legal contexts effectively.

- **Practical Ethical Dilemmas:** Courses should incorporate real-life ethical dilemmas and case studies, equipping students to navigate the complex moral landscapes they will encounter in their professional lives.

Incorporating these changes, however, isn't without challenges. Resistance from traditional educational structures and resource limitations are significant hurdles. Overcoming these requires a collective effort from educational institutions, legal professionals, and governing bodies to recognize the value of ethical training in law.

By reshaping legal education with a focus on Maqasid principles, we're not just teaching law; we're cultivating guardians of justice who are ethically aware and morally grounded. This transformation is more than an academic shift; it's an investment in the future of a just and ethical legal system, laying the groundwork for governance that truly serves the common good.

The Blueprint for an Ethical Legal System

The journey of legal systems has often meandered through dense thickets of technicalities, at times drifting away from the ethical shores they were meant to safeguard. The integration of Maqasid principles offers not just a path, but a visionary blueprint for steering our legal systems towards the realm of ethical governance. This transformation transcends mere legal reform; it's about cultivating a culture where ethics and law harmoniously intertwine.

1. **A Paradigm Shift:** Embracing Maqasid signals a fundamental paradigm shift. It moves our focus from a rigid interpretation of statutes to embracing a broader, more ethically-conscious application of the law. In this new vision, laws are not just rules but vehicles for achieving ethical objectives, creating a legal framework that breathes

life into the ideals of justice and fairness.

2. **Ethical Guardianship:** By adopting Maqasid, our legal systems become the guardians of societal ethics. Judges, lawyers, and scholars transform into stewards of ethical jurisprudence, ensuring every decision and law aligns with the highest ethical standards. This role elevates their responsibility from mere enforcement to proactive agents championing ethical governance.

3. **A Holistic Approach:** This new era in legal practice advocates for a holistic viewpoint. Legal professionals are called to look beyond immediate legal questions, contemplating the wider impact of their decisions on individuals, communities, and society. This approach nurtures an awareness that every legal action carries with it an ethical weight and consequence.

4. **Empowering the Vulnerable:** An ethically-rooted legal system champions the cause of the vulnerable and marginalized. It ensures that justice is not a privilege of the few but an accessible right for all, embodying the principles of social justice and equality. It offers a beacon of hope and a safety net for those who have been voiceless and underserved.

5. **A Global Beacon of Hope:** As legal systems evolve under Maqasid principles, they stand as beacons of hope in a world grappling with injustice and inequality. This transformation sends a resounding global message: ethics and law are not adversaries but allies in forging a more just and equitable world.

As we stand at this crossroads, the path forward is clear. It's time to boldly embark on this transformative journey, championing the integration of Maqasid principles in our legal systems. This journey is not without challenges — resistance to change, resource limitations, and varying cultural contexts are but a few hurdles we may encounter. Yet, the promise of a more ethical, just, and inclusive legal system is a compelling call to action for us all. The destination is a society where law and ethics are inextricably linked in the pursuit of justice, a society where every legal decision upholds the common good. Let us commence this journey now, for the future awaits a legal system reborn in the light of ethical governance.

Conclusion: Imagine a World Where Ethics Define Our Laws

Pause for a moment and envision a world where laws transcend their traditional boundaries. In this world, laws are not mere rules to follow but ethical principles that infuse our daily actions. Here, justice goes beyond the black-and-white of right and wrong, embodying a profound commitment to the welfare, dignity, and harmony of every individual. This vision is not a distant utopia; it's a tangible goal within our grasp, achieved by aligning our legal systems with a deep-seated ethical framework like Maqasid.

A Vision of Tangible Change

This transformation is not an elusive dream. It's a practical, achievable change that promises to elevate our society to unprecedented levels of morality, equity, and compassion. We're talking about redefining the essence of law – from a regulatory tool to a beacon of ethical guidance.

Practical Steps Towards Realization

How do we embark on this journey? The first step is awareness – educating ourselves and others about the principles of Maqasid and their potential impact on legal systems. Advocacy plays a key role; we must champion these principles in our communities, professional circles, and through social media. Collaboration with legal professionals, policymakers, and educators can turn this vision into actionable strategies.

Addressing Challenges Head-On

Undoubtedly, this path will have its challenges – skepticism, resistance to change, and varying interpretations of ethical principles. Overcoming these hurdles starts with open dialogues, fostering understanding and finding common ground. It involves demonstrating through case studies and current examples, such as the implementation of restorative justice practices in some legal systems, how ethical principles can practically guide legal decisions.

The Ripple Effect of Ethical Law

Imagine the profound impact of such a transformation. As ethical principles become embedded in our legal frameworks, they create a society where individuals are respected, dignity is upheld, and communal harmony is a lived experience. We've seen glimpses of this in small-scale community-led initiatives and progressive legal reforms; now, it's time to broaden these efforts.

Seizing the Moment for Ethical Governance

The future of ethical governance is here for the taking. It's an invitation to step forward, to commit to reshaping our legal systems for the better. This journey is crucial for us, for future generations, and for creating a world where law and ethics are seamlessly united in the pursuit of justice for all. Let's embrace this journey today, making every step count towards a world where ethics and laws are not just aligned but are indistinguishable in their pursuit of the greater good.

The Potential for Groundbreaking Reform: A Future Unveiled

Envision a future where our legal systems undergo a transformation far beyond mere adjustments – a future where justice is redefined, laws become guiding principles for the common good, and the welfare and dignity of every individual are central to all legal decisions.

A Paradigm Shift in Justice

We're advocating for a paradigm shift, not just a minor tweak. This is about revolutionizing our perception of justice and governance. Imagine dismantling the old, rigid legal structures and rebuilding them with ethics and human welfare as the foundational pillars. It's a shift reminiscent of the Scandinavian model of restorative justice, which has redefined the criminal justice system to focus more on rehabilitation than punishment.

Beyond Incremental Changes

This vision goes beyond making incremental improvements. It's about opening new doors to a realm where justice is a tangible, daily reality. We aim to craft a legal framework that not only prevents harm but also actively fosters societal well-being.

The Imperative for Transformative Change

Such transformative change is essential. It's not merely about refining existing systems; it's about sculpting the society we yearn to live in. We need laws that do more than maintain order – they must nurture fairness, equity, and compassion.

Essential for Our Future

This groundbreaking reform is not just exciting – it's critical for the future we wish to build. It's about creating a legacy of ethical governance where justice is woven into the fabric of everyday life.

A Collective Call to Action

Realizing this future requires more than passive hope; it demands active commitment and collective effort. Policymakers, legal practitioners, scholars, and every engaged citizen must unite in this endeavor to forge a more just and ethical society.

Seizing the Moment for Change

Now is the time to seize this opportunity. We have the blueprint for transformative change at our fingertips. The potential for a brighter, more ethical future is within our reach. We must act now to embark on this journey of reform, shaping a future where justice and ethics are inseparable and where our legal system is a beacon of hope and fairness for all.

Socio-Economic Revolution: Equality Realized

Envision a world where the chasm between the rich and the poor narrows, transforming poverty into a vestige of the past. This vision isn't rooted in utopian socialism; it's a practical realization of social justice anchored in the ethical principle of Mal - Wealth.

Ethical Wealth Redistribution

Consider a legal framework that champions fair wealth distribution. This approach isn't about indiscriminate wealth transfer; it's about rectifying the imbalance where a few amass wealth at the expense of many. By applying this principle, we aim not for wealth redistribution as an end but as a means to fulfill an ethical obligation.

Eradicating Poverty Through Practical Means

Moving beyond traditional welfare models, this vision entails creating a society where everyone has the means to prosper. Drawing inspiration from initiatives like the Universal Basic Income trials in Finland, this approach recognizes poverty as a moral issue. Aligning laws with ethical principles paves the way to eliminate poverty systematically, not as an act of charity, but as a matter of design.

Universal Education: A Right, Not a Luxury

Imagine mandating universal access to quality education, a tangible application of the ethical principle of Aql - Intellect. Countries like Norway have shown that education as a fundamental right can drive innovation and equalize opportunities. This is not mere idealism; it's a pragmatic path to empowering individuals and leveling societal playing fields.

Creating Pathways to Equity

Our goal is to foster equal opportunities, not necessarily equal outcomes. It's about equipping everyone with the tools and resources needed for success based on merit and effort. This vision is not far-fetched; initiatives like Germany's vocational training programs exemplify how providing diverse educational and professional pathways can lead to a more equitable society.

A Collective Call to Action

This transformative vision is within our grasp but requires collective action. Lawmakers, advocates, and citizens must unite to drive this change. Our legal systems should not just govern but shape the society we aspire to live in. Realizing these ethical principles is not a distant dream; it's a moral imperative. Let's join forces to make this vision a reality, creating a society where justice, equity, and prosperity are not just ideals but everyday experiences.

Criminal Justice: A New Dawn

Imagine a criminal justice system that transcends traditional notions of punishment, evolving prisons into transformative environments. This vision, grounded in the ethical principles of Nafs (Life) and Aql (Intellect), is more than wishful thinking – it's a viable path to meaningful reform.

Prison Reform: From Punishment to Transformation

Envision incarceration focused not on punitive measures but on corrective and rehabilitative actions. This approach mirrors successful models like Norway's prison system, where inmates receive education, counseling, and opportunities for genuine rehabilitation. Far from being soft on crime, this method acknowledges every individual's potential for redemption and societal contribution.

Creating Reformed, Educated Citizens

Aligning our criminal justice system with the principles of Nafs and Aql means valuing every life and fostering intellectual growth. Inmates are equipped with skills and knowledge for successful reintegration, transforming them from stigmatized individuals into contributing members of society. This shift is not just a moral choice but a strategic investment in safer, more cohesive communities.

Community Healing through Restorative Justice

Imagine a justice system that prioritizes healing broken families and restoring fractured communities, embodying the essence of Ummah (Community). This vision is mirrored in practices like South Africa's post-apartheid Truth and Reconciliation Commission, where restorative justice focuses on rebuilding rather than vengeance, emphasizing community healing and reparation.

Balancing Empathy with Accountability

In this reimagined system, offenders are held accountable but are also given avenues to make amends. Victims and community members are integral to the process, contributing to a healing journey that goes beyond legal resolutions. This approach is not just a legal shift; it's a move towards a system that values empathy, accountability, and the greater good.

A Collective Call to Transform

This vision for criminal justice reform is not out of reach. It's a call to action for policymakers, law enforcement, and society to reevaluate our approach to crime and punishment. By choosing a path that values life, fosters intellectual growth, and supports community healing, we can usher in a new era of criminal justice. It's time to embrace these changes, recognizing them as part of a global shift towards more humane and effective justice systems.

A Planet Saved: Environmental Stewardship in Action

Envision a world where our legal systems actively champion the health of our planet. This vision, rooted in the ethical principle of Watan (Homeland), is not an unreachable dream but a feasible reality.

Sustainable Laws: Turning Commitment into Action

Imagine laws that transform environmental responsibility from a choice to a requirement. Picture regulations that compel businesses to prioritize sustainability, akin to the rigorous environmental standards enforced in countries like Denmark. These laws aren't mere idealistic aspirations; they are concrete commitments to preserving our planet for future generations.

The Power of Legal Enforcement

By aligning our legal systems with Watan, we recognize our environment as a sacred trust, not a resource for unchecked exploitation. Legal enforcement becomes a tool to hold accountable those who harm our environment, reflecting actions like the significant fines and restoration mandates seen in the wake of oil spills and industrial accidents.

Climate Justice: Upholding Global Commitments

Imagine international climate agreements that are binding and actionable, similar to the Paris Agreement, but with enhanced enforcement mechanisms. These commitments should ensure equitable and sustainable development for all nations, recognizing our shared responsibility in safeguarding the earth.

Empowering Vulnerable Nations

Legal frameworks must be developed to support vulnerable nations facing the brunt of environmental crises. This support, mirroring initiatives like the Green Climate Fund, should provide necessary resources for adaptation and resilience, embodying global solidarity rather than mere charity.

Seizing the Opportunity for Change

This vision is an opportunity for transformative action. It calls on lawmakers, activists, and citizens to champion legal frameworks that prioritize environmental stewardship. Our legal systems have the potential to be powerful agents of change, safeguarding the future of our planet. It's time for us to demand and implement legal structures that enforce climate justice, protect vulnerable ecosystems, and promote sustainability.

The salvation of our planet is indeed within our grasp. By choosing to protect our homeland through robust legal mechanisms, we commit to a path of sustainability and responsible stewardship. Let's embrace this path, building on current efforts and moving towards a future where our legal systems are guardians of our planet's health.

Global Leadership: The Ethical Vanguard

Envision a world where legal systems transcend national boundaries, wielding their influence to sculpt an ethically governed global community. This vision, rooted in the principles of Maqasid, represents not just an idealistic dream, but a practical roadmap for ethical leadership on a global scale.

Humanitarian Diplomacy: Extending Legal Influence for Human Dignity

Imagine legal frameworks extending beyond national jurisdictions to influence and shape international humanitarian law. Drawing inspiration from the Geneva Conventions, this approach goes beyond traditional diplomacy, committing to international policies that protect human dignity and welfare. It envisions a global legal community that acknowledges a shared responsibility for human rights, transcending geopolitical limits.

Setting a Global Ethical Benchmark

The principles of Maqasid could serve as a universal ethical benchmark, guiding legal systems worldwide. This vision aligns with initiatives like the United Nations' Sustainable Development Goals, aiming not merely for influence but for establishing a global standard of ethical governance. It showcases how a legal system grounded in ethical principles can lead to a more equitable and humane global society.

Inspiring International Change

Legal systems that exemplify ethical leadership can inspire transformative change beyond their own borders. Following the model of the European Court of Human Rights, they can encourage other nations to realign their legal frameworks with universal ethical values. This vision extends beyond national betterment to fostering a global ripple effect of positive change.

Leveraging Influence for Global Good

This concept is more than a utopian ideal; it's a tangible opportunity. Legal systems have the potential to become instruments of global betterment. Legal scholars, diplomats, and policymakers are called to advocate for the integration of ethical principles in international law and relations.

Embracing Ethical Leadership in Challenging Times

In an era marked by complex global challenges, ethical leadership is imperative. The principles of Maqasid provide a robust foundation for ethical governance, guiding us through turbulent times. The moment for ethical leadership is now. Our legal systems, equipped with a vision grounded in ethical values, can be at the vanguard of creating a just, humane, and ethically governed world.

Governance: The Beacon of Hope

Imagine a world where governance transcends bureaucratic norms to become a beacon of hope. In this world, ethical principles are not mere guidelines but the foundation of every government action, turning corruption, injustice, and inequality into rare exceptions rather than prevailing norms.

Ethical Governance: A Force for Societal Transformation

Picture a government so deeply committed to ethical principles that every policy and decision becomes a step toward a fairer society. This vision mirrors initiatives like New Zealand's Wellbeing Budget, which prioritizes citizens' welfare in policy-making. Ethical governance here is not a luxury but an indispensable part of societal progress.

Redefining Corruption as an Aberration

Envision a society where corruption is an anomaly, not a standard practice. Inspired by the transparency models of countries like Denmark, government officials operate not out of self-interest but with a steadfast commitment to the public good. In this society, corruption is a deviation, swiftly addressed and rectified.

Upholding Justice for Every Citizen

Imagine a government system that guarantees justice for every individual, echoing the principles of Maqasid. This system, akin to the rule of law upheld in countries like Canada, ensures that justice is not a slogan but a reality where every citizen, irrespective of their background, receives fair treatment.

Civic Trust as a Democratic Standard

Consider a level of trust between government and citizens that becomes a benchmark for democracies globally. In this society, citizen engagement in governance reflects practices seen in participatory democracies like Switzerland. Here, the government is genuinely representative and accountable to its people.

A Global Model for Ethical Governance

This vision for ethical governance extends beyond national borders, setting a standard for the world. It's a practical goal, achievable through concerted efforts in policy reform, education, and international cooperation. It's a call for governments everywhere to embed ethics at the heart of their actions.

Realizing the Ethical Governance Dream

In a world facing myriad challenges, ethical governance is the beacon of hope we need. This path to a brighter future is not just a theoretical ideal; it's a tangible goal, as demonstrated by nations taking strides in this direction. The time for ethical governance is now. Let's work towards a world where governance is synonymous with justice, ethics guide every decision, and citizens have unwavering trust in their leaders to lead with integrity.

The Time for Groundbreaking Reform is Now: Seizing the Moment for Ethical Governance

In this critical moment, the urgency for transformative reform aligns our legal systems with the ethical principles of Maqasid. This is more than a mere adjustment; it's a leap towards a world steeped in justice and ethical integrity. The moral imperatives are evident, the societal challenges pressing, and a clear blueprint for action is before us. What we need now is the courage to embrace this new era of ethical governance and societal well-being.

A Clear Moral Imperative

In a world beset by challenges like inequality and environmental crises, the ethical alignment based on Maqasid principles is not just necessary; it's imperative. These principles offer us a moral compass, directing us towards a society that values equity and compassion. Ignoring this call means continuing with a status quo that falls short of our ethical potential, much like ignoring climate change despite knowing its impacts.

Addressing Pressing Societal Needs

Our societies face deep-rooted issues – from poverty and inequality to environmental degradation. Ethical alignment in our legal systems provides practical solutions. Take, for example, the implementation of environmental laws in countries like Costa Rica, which has made significant strides in conservation and sustainability. This approach isn't a mere fix; it's a strategy to address societal needs effectively.

A Practical Blueprint for Ethical Governance

The blueprint for this transformation is well-defined. It includes comprehensive legal reforms, such as those seen in Scandinavian countries known for their high standards of social welfare, transparency, and citizen engagement. It calls for constitutional amendments, legislative vigilance, and a commitment to ethical education and accountability. This plan is not a lofty ideal; it's a structured strategy for bringing ethics into the heart of governance.

Striving for an Exceptional Future

We should aspire not just to a satisfactory future but to an exceptional one – where justice and ethics are not merely sought after but are everyday realities. It's about building a society where ethical principles shape every decision and every individual's well-being is a priority, akin to the societal models in nations with high human development indexes.

Resounding Call to Action

This moment calls for action from everyone – policymakers, legal experts, and citizens. It's a call to rise and champion ethical governance, drawing inspiration from global movements advocating for transparency and accountability. It requires boldness to move beyond the current limitations and build a world aligned with our highest ethical ideals.

Seizing the Moment for Ethical Transformation

The time for passive observation has passed. The moment to create a more just, equitable, and compassionate world is now. Let's unite to turn this vision into reality. Let's shape our world into one where ethics reign supreme, justice is tangible, and every individual, irrespective of background, has the opportunity to thrive. This moment is ours to seize –

let's make ethical governance a living reality.

Conclusion: The Transformative Power of Ethical Alignment

The pursuit to align our legal systems with Maqasid principles represents more than a minor adjustment – it's a bold leap towards a world imbued with justice and ethics. This movement is about more than integrating ethical norms; it's a catalyst for sweeping reforms that hold the potential to redefine our societal values, governance structures, and global interactions. We are not just striving for improved laws; we're envisioning a world that is inherently more just, equitable, and compassionate.

Catalyst for Societal Transformation

Integrating Maqasid into our legal systems is not merely a surface-level change. It's a profound shift, akin to the civil rights reforms in the 20th century, which redefined societal norms. It challenges us to look beyond the status quo, imagining a world where ethical decision-making and justice are not aspirations but everyday realities.

Reforming Governance with Ethical Principles

This ethical alignment can revolutionize governance. It compels governments to put citizen welfare at the forefront, to combat corruption actively, and to nurture a trust-based relationship between leaders and citizens. This redefinition of governance moves beyond power dynamics to a model of service and responsibility, similar to the principles seen in Scandinavian countries known for their high levels of trust and social welfare.

Setting a New Global Ethical Standard

On the international stage, embracing Maqasid can establish a new ethical benchmark. This approach echoes the global impact of international treaties like the Universal Declaration of Human Rights, signaling that human dignity and welfare are universal priorities. It proposes a world where each nation commits to ensuring equitable opportunities for all its citizens.

A Vision of a Better World

This alignment is not a distant hope but a tangible goal. It envisions laws that embody ethical principles, a society where justice is foundational, and compassion is a guiding force. It's an invitation to each of us to be part of this ethical transformation, understanding that a better world is not only possible but achievable.

The Urgency of Ethical Transformation

Now is the time to act. We must champion and implement these ethical principles in our legal systems. This journey demands commitment, innovation, and a steadfast belief in the power of ethics to reshape our world. By seizing this opportunity, we can create a society that is not only lawful but just, not merely orderly but equitable, and not simply hopeful but deeply compassionate. The transformative power of ethical alignment is within our reach – let's work together to make it a reality.

11

The Global Impact of Maqasid

Projecting These Sacred Principles Beyond Borders: The Global Mandate of Maqasid

Moral Leadership: A New Frontier of Global Influence

In an era dominated by geopolitics, where the pursuit of power often eclipses ethical considerations, extending Maqasid principles beyond national borders represents a seismic shift. What are these principles? Originating from Islamic jurisprudence, Maqasid refers to the higher objectives of Islamic law, emphasizing values like justice, compassion, and the welfare of the community. This expansion isn't just innovative; it's a radical reimagining of global influence—a pivot from the myopic focus of traditional realpolitik to a world guided by ethical virtues.

The Challenge of Our Times

Today's world, rife with climate change, poverty, conflict, and pandemics, shows the limitations of power politics. These global challenges, not confined by borders, demand solutions that are just as boundless. By applying Maqasid principles, nations can offer a moral compass in these turbulent times.

A Call to Ethical Leadership

Ethical leadership on the world stage means more than military might or economic power. It's defined by the moral values guiding a nation's actions internationally. Consider, for instance, Norway's approach to international relations, often driven by humanitarian concerns and peace mediation, reflecting a commitment to ethical leadership.

An Ethical Imperative

This shift is not about abstract altruism. It's an ethical imperative. Nations upholding Maqasid principles contribute to global welfare. They acknowledge that values like justice and communal welfare are not confined by geography.

The New Frontier

Nations leading with Maqasid principles create a new frontier in global influence. It's not about domination, but about embodying ethical principles. This approach reshapes global discourse, moving from power struggles to ethical responsibilities, setting an example in ethical governance, conflict resolution, and humanitarian action.

A Moral Obligation

In conclusion, embracing these sacred principles globally is more than an option; it's a moral duty to humanity. It's a path towards a collaborative, ethically-driven world, where diplomacy is value-driven, and the well-being of all takes precedence over national interests. This is an opportunity for nations to lead in virtue, shaping a just, equitable, and compassionate global community.

Human Rights Diplomacy: Becoming the Voice for the Voiceless

In the often pragmatic world of international relations, championing human rights with unwavering commitment transforms from a noble aspiration to a moral imperative. Human rights diplomacy, anchored in Maqasid principles—encompassing the sanctity of life (Nafs), justice, and human dignity—stands as a beacon for the voiceless, advocating for humanity's most fundamental values.

Global Advocacy

Proactively advocating for Maqasid-aligned policies in international forums is a responsibility, not a choice. It's about upholding life and dignity as universal values. For instance, when countries like Canada and Sweden raise issues of human rights at the United Nations, they exert moral pressure and challenge global standards. This proactive stance demonstrates how ethical imperatives can influence international debates and policy-making.

Imagine a United Nations where Maqasid principles guide every decision, creating an environment where justice, compassion, and human dignity are not just ideals, but operational mandates. This vision is not mere idealism; it's a tangible path towards a more equitable world.

Ethical Alliances

In pursuing an ethical foreign policy, forming alliances with countries sharing similar values can amplify impact. Such coalitions, driven not by self-interest but by a commitment to human values, can effectively counter human rights violations. Consider the impact of international coalitions in addressing crises like the Rohingya refugee situation, where collective action has been pivotal.

Envision a world where such ethical alliances are commonplace. Here, nations leverage their collective strength to swiftly address human rights issues, transcending traditional geopolitical interests. This vision, grounded in Maqasid principles, prioritizes the welfare and dignity of individuals globally.

In conclusion, human rights diplomacy guided by Maqasid is more than an alternative approach—it's a moral imperative leading to a more just and humane world. It calls for nations to become powerful voices not just in might, but in championing the values that epitomize our shared humanity. This vision of nations collaborating ethically to protect and empower the vulnerable sets a new standard in international relations. Achieving this future is not merely possible; it's within our reach if we boldly embrace these principles.

Economic Diplomacy: Fairness as Foreign Policy

In our globalized world, where economic interests often dominate, adopting economic diplomacy based on Maqasid principles is more than a moral stance; it's a strategic necessity. Economic diplomacy that prioritizes fairness, social welfare (Ummah), and sustainable development (Watan) promises not just goodwill, but also long-term global stability and prosperity.

Sustainable Investments

Leading with sustainable investments goes beyond philanthropy; it's a commitment to ethical foreign policy. For example, when Germany invests in renewable energy projects in developing nations, it sets a powerful precedent for combining economic growth with sustainability. Imagine a world where nations vie not just for economic power but for their contribution to community upliftment and environmental preservation.

Picture a world where economic activities, aligned with Maqasid, bolster community welfare and resource conservation. This approach isn't just ethical; it represents a new model of international cooperation, where prosperity is both shared and sustainable.

Trade Ethics

Incorporating ethical clauses in trade agreements is a powerful tool to redefine international economic relations. Nations advocating for agreements that ensure fair labor practices and equitable wealth distribution (Mal) bring human welfare and social justice to the forefront. Consider how the European Union's trade deals often include human rights clauses, setting a standard for ethical trade.

Imagine a world where such ethical considerations are standard, where economic partnerships are founded on equity and justice. Envision nations working together to create trade agreements that support fair wages, safe working conditions, and balanced wealth distribution. This isn't utopian; it's a practical vision of economic diplomacy that recognizes our global interdependence and prioritizes the well-being of all, from workers to consumers.

In conclusion, Maqasid-based economic diplomacy is not just a moral choice; it's a strategic path towards a more stable, fair, and prosperous world. It's about nations leading by example, demonstrating that economic success can be synonymous with social welfare and environmental sustainability. This vision of international relations, where economic actions are ethically guided and contribute to the greater good, is not just aspirational; it's achievable if we boldly embrace these principles.

Cultural Diplomacy: Bridging Divides Through Shared Values

In a world characterized by rich cultural diversity and, occasionally, divisions, the role of cultural diplomacy, rooted in the principles of Maqasid, is crucial. It's not merely an opportunity but a necessity to use shared ethical values to bridge divides and enhance global unity.

Global Forums

Hosting international events focused on the nexus of culture and Maqasid is a powerful tool. Consider, for example, the World Culture Festival organized by the Art of Living Foundation, which brings together people from various cultures to celebrate unity in diversity. Imagine similar forums where nations unite in exhibitions and conferences, not only to share art and music but also to champion a common moral compass centered on justice, compassion, and well-being.

Visualize a world where cultural diplomacy extends beyond national showcases to highlight a collective commitment to life's sanctity (Nafs), human dignity, and communal harmony (Ummah). These forums can serve as platforms for dialogue, understanding, and cooperation, dismantling cultural barriers and fostering a deeper sense of unity.

Cultural Exchanges

Facilitating educational and cultural exchanges focused on Maqasid principles is an investment in global harmony. For instance, the Fulbright Program, which promotes mutual understanding through educational exchange, could be a model for programs emphasizing ethical and communal values. Imagine students, artists, and scholars engaging in exchanges that not only explore diverse traditions but also immerse participants in the ethical values of Maqasid.

Envision programs where young people from varied backgrounds study, create, and collaborate in environments that prioritize justice, compassion, and community welfare. Such exchanges are more than cultural enrichment; they nurture a generation of global citizens united by an ethical framework, ready to tackle global challenges with empathy and cooperation.

Cultural diplomacy, infused with Maqasid principles, is an effective strategy for building bridges, fostering understanding, and promoting global unity. It envisions international relations where culture is a connector, not a divider; where shared values transcend differences; and where the pursuit of justice and compassion becomes a unifying force. This future is not a distant ideal but a tangible goal, achievable through each cultural exchange and global forum we initiate.

Climate Leadership: The Guardianship of Earth

In an era where the health of our planet is more precarious than ever, applying Maqasid principles to environmental diplomacy is not just a choice but an imperative. As guardians of Earth, our moral duty is to lead by example, advocating for policies that protect our shared homeland (Watan) for both current and future generations.

Environmental Pacts

Leading in the negotiation of international environmental agreements, infused with the ethos of homeland protection (Watan), is a crucial obligation. Consider the Paris Agreement, where nations came together under a common cause, setting tangible targets for reducing greenhouse gas emissions. Envision similar pacts, inspired by the ethical values of Maqasid, that set ambitious yet achievable goals for climate change mitigation, biodiversity protection, and ecosystem preservation.

Imagine a collective commitment to transitioning to renewable energy and sustainable agriculture. These agreements would prioritize long-term ecological well-being over short-term economic interests, embodying justice, equity, and sustainability.

Global Stewardship

Spearheading initiatives for sustainable resource management projects Maqasid principles as solutions to environmental crises. Take, for instance, the collaborative efforts in the Amazon Rainforest to combat deforestation, where nations and organizations work together under a shared ethical commitment to the environment.

These initiatives should prioritize fairness and communal well-being (Ummah), guaranteeing equal access to vital resources such as clean water and fertile land. By advocating for sustainable practices, we recognize the delicate equilibrium of our planet and the interconnectedness of all living beings.

Challenges and Practical Steps

While the vision is clear, achieving it is fraught with challenges such as economic pressures and political resistance. Nations must balance economic growth with environmental preservation, and this often requires innovative policy-making, public-private partnerships, and investment in green technologies. Developing nations, facing different challenges, need support through technology transfer and capacity-building initiatives.

In summary, climate leadership rooted in Maqasid principles is more than an opportunity to address environmental issues; it's a moral duty to safeguard our planet. By advocating for robust environmental pacts and fostering global stewardship, we can lead the way to a world where justice, equity, and ethical guardianship are at the forefront of our actions, ensuring a sustainable future for all generations.

Peacemaking: The Moral High Ground in Conflict Resolution

In a world frequently scarred by violence, a new approach to conflict resolution guided by Maqasid principles isn't just an option; it's a moral imperative. This path represents a commitment to lasting peace, the preservation of life (Nafs), and the promotion of communal harmony (Ummah).

Ethical Mediation

Consider the role of Maqasid in mediating conflicts, as evidenced by the successful peace talks in Northern Ireland. In these negotiations, the emphasis on the sanctity of life (Nafs) and fairness helped overcome longstanding divisions. Ethical mediation, under this perspective, stresses dialogue, empathy, and reconciliation. Nations guided by these principles approach negotiations with a sincere commitment to resolving underlying issues, transcending mere political maneuvers.

Mediators facilitate discussions that consider the well-being of communities (Ummah) and strive for justice and reconciliation. The aim is to create not just a ceasefire but a foundation for lasting peace and cooperative coexistence.

Peacebuilding Initiatives

Imagine international programs for peacebuilding that focus on community welfare (Ummah) and intellectual growth (Aql), similar to the community development projects seen post-conflict in Rwanda. These initiatives transform areas of conflict into communities of reconciliation and growth.

Such programs prioritize the well-being of affected populations, providing support for rebuilding lives and infrastructures. They emphasize education as a tool for understanding, tolerance, and empathy. Nations invest in the future by supporting initiatives that create economic opportunities, healthcare access, and promote cultural exchanges, aiding communities previously torn apart by conflict to heal and rebuild together.

Challenges and Broader Stakeholder Involvement

Implementing this vision in complex geopolitical climates is challenging. It requires overcoming skepticism and resistance, often demanding the involvement of a broad range of stakeholders, including international organizations, NGOs, and local communities. Building trust and ensuring inclusive participation are crucial.

Diverse Perspectives

This approach should be adaptable to various cultural and political contexts, recognizing that the application of Maqasid principles may differ across regions. Respecting local customs and viewpoints is essential in crafting universally acceptable and effective peace solutions.

Peacemaking, infused with Maqasid principles, transcends traditional diplomatic strategies. By embracing ethical mediation and investing in peacebuilding initiatives, we can transform conflict zones into communities of hope and cooperation. This approach is not just about resolving disputes; it's about fostering a world where conflicts are ethically addressed, lives are preserved, and communities thrive in harmony. Embracing this vision is essential for the well-being of all, paving the way for a more peaceful global society.

The Ethical Vanguard of a New Global Order

As the world stands at a pivotal crossroads, the path we choose now will indelibly shape our collective future. Embracing the sacred principles of Maqasid in our global interactions is more than a choice; it's a profound commitment to forge a new era of ethical global engagement.

In this envisioned global order, ethics are not just an addendum but the cornerstone of international relations. This approach is not solely about doing what's right; it's about pursuing justice, equity, and sustainability. Leading with moral integrity demonstrates that ethical considerations, far from being weaknesses, are the most formidable assets in global diplomacy.

However, this ideal faces real challenges. In the current landscape of realpolitik, where power and self-interest often prevail, shifting to an ethics-centered approach requires gradual, strategic steps. Nations must navigate complex geopolitical realities and sometimes conflicting interests. Building consensus, particularly with nations or entities that may not initially share this vision, is a critical and ongoing process.

To operationalize this ethical paradigm, nations can start by embedding Maqasid principles into bilateral and multilateral agreements. International forums and organizations can serve as platforms for advocating these values, influencing policies and decisions across various levels. Current trends, such as the increasing focus on sustainable development and human rights in global forums, indicate the beginnings of this shift.

This new order redefines global diplomacy, advocating collaboration not just for national interests but for the collective welfare of humanity. It's a call to elevate our discourse, to move beyond short-term gains, and to embrace a holistic vision of progress.

By championing these principles, nations become beacons of ethical leadership, inspiring others and forming alliances based on shared values. This transformed international stage becomes a platform for ethical collaboration, where every nation, irrespective of its size or influence, is valued for its commitment to justice, compassion, and sustainability.

In this ethical vanguard, human rights, economic fairness, cultural exchange, environmental stewardship, and peacemaking are not isolated endeavors but interconnected facets of a global movement. This movement, embodying the ideals of Maqasid, becomes a powerful force for change, proving that a better world is not just possible but imperative.

In conclusion, projecting Maqasid principles beyond our borders is more than a diplomatic strategy; it is a declaration of our dedication to a more ethical, just, and equitable world. It underscores the belief that nations can and should lead with values, proving that ethical considerations are essential in shaping a better future. The path is clear, and the choice, while challenging, is one worth making for the well-being of our global community and for generations to come.

The Ethical Vanguard: Shaping a Global Community

Projecting Maqasid principles onto the global stage represents more than policy shifts; it's a profound declaration of our global intentions. It signifies a commitment to being part of an international community that is guided by a moral compass, one that values justice, compassion, and the common good. This endeavor isn't about remolding the world in our own image, but in the image of our collective best selves.

In a world often dominated by geopolitical interests and national self-prioritization, advocating these sacred principles globally marks a significant departure from conventional norms. It's a declaration that we refuse to remain passive in a world facing diverse challenges. Instead, we choose to be active creators of a global community that mirrors the highest aspirations of our shared humanity.

For example, the application of these principles can be seen in initiatives like the United Nations Sustainable Development Goals (SDGs), which unite nations in a global effort to address major challenges such as poverty, inequality, and climate change. This commitment transcends national borders and cultural or religious divides, embodying a universal call to respect individual dignity, uphold life's sanctity, and promote communal welfare.

By projecting Maqasid principles in our global interactions, we aim to create a world where diplomacy is ethically driven, where nations collaborate not only for their own benefit but for the collective good. This vision reshapes international relations dynamics, moving away from zero-sum perspectives to a mindset of shared ethical prosperity.

However, this vision is not without its challenges. In the complex landscape of international politics, aligning diverse nations with varying interests and values to a common ethical framework requires diplomacy, patience, and often, compromise. It's a gradual process that involves balancing idealism with the practical realities of the world.

This endeavor also reflects our belief in the potential for positive change. It's a rejection of the notion that the world must remain entrenched in conflict, inequality, and environmental degradation. Instead, it asserts that we can and must strive for a world where peace supersedes conflict, fairness outweighs injustice, and environmental stewardship is a priority.

In conclusion, embracing Maqasid principles on a global scale is a bold move towards redefining our international community. It's a commitment to a world where ethics, justice, and compassion are not mere aspirations but central guiding principles. It's a declaration of our choice to be architects of a better, more ethically aligned world, reflecting our shared values and highest ideals.

Conclusion: Your Call to Action - Making a Better World Inevitable

Today, you stand at a crossroads, equipped not with weapons, but with transformative ideas and principles. This is your call to action, a call that transcends rhetoric and demands tangible change. It urges you to move these ideas from academic theory and bureaucratic planning into the realm of practical implementation. Your mission is to advocate, implement, and embody these principles, turning a better world from a possibility into an inevitability.

In the grand tapestry of history, moments like this are rare. They are times when visionaries and leaders converge to redefine humanity's narrative. Now is such a moment—a chance to embed the aspirations of justice, compassion, and ethical governance into our societal fabric. However, this window of opportunity is brief, and the challenges are significant.

You have the blueprint for a world where ethical governance is standard.

This involves practical steps like advocating for transparent decision-making processes, supporting policies that prioritize sustainable development, and fostering international relations driven by empathy and mutual respect. It's about promoting diplomacy that acknowledges the common welfare of all humanity, not just geopolitical interests.

But remember, with every opportunity come challenges. The path to transformative change is fraught with obstacles. Resistance, inertia, and setbacks are inevitable. Yet, it is in adversity that true leaders are forged—those unwavering in their quest for justice and compassion.

To realize this vision, advocate relentlessly for ethical governance and human rights, both locally and globally. Challenge leaders, disrupt the status quo, and be the catalysts of change. Implement policies that reflect Maqasid principles, and be the voices that resonate with power, urging decision-makers towards ethical leadership.

Beyond advocacy, live these principles. As individuals and communities, embody the values you champion. Let your actions reflect your commitment to justice and compassion, serving as a beacon for others.

In conclusion, history is shaped by those who seize the moment, who rise to the challenge, and who turn vision into reality. This is your call to action. The better world you envision is not only possible; it is within reach if you approach it with courage, determination, and a clear plan. Your actions and commitment can ensure that this vision becomes an inevitable part of our collective future.

The Opportunities for Global Peace and Collaboration: The Maqasid Imperative

A New Blueprint for Global Harmony: Unleashing the Untapped Potential

As we navigate a world often characterized by conflict, inequality, and environmental challenges, the application of Maqasid principles on the international stage offers a unique opportunity to reshape global dynamics. This is more than a lofty ideal; it's a practical, ethical vision with the potential to fundamentally alter the nature of international relations.

Envision a world where nations collaborate as partners in the pursuit of the common good. This global landscape would not only champion peace as a diplomatic objective but embed it in the very core of international policy, driven by the sanctity of life (Nafs), the welfare of communities (Ummah), environmental protection (Watan), equitable wealth distribution (Mal), and intellectual and cultural development (Aql). This vision, far from being a pipe dream, is an achievable reality.

Implementing Maqasid principles, however, does not come without challenges. The path to global harmony requires navigating complex political landscapes and overcoming barriers of mistrust and competing interests. For example, the Paris Agreement on climate change exemplifies how nations can come together for a common environmental cause, yet it also shows the difficulties in achieving unified action.

Central to Maqasid is the preservation of human life (Nafs). We can draw inspiration from international initiatives like the Geneva Conventions, which set standards in international law for humanitarian treatment in war. A world where diplomatic efforts prioritize peace and conflict resolution as non-negotiable goals is within our reach, but it requires persistent dialogue and a steadfast commitment to humanitarian principles.

The well-being of communities (Ummah) is vital. A practical step towards this goal is enhancing international aid effectiveness, ensuring it is not merely symbolic but genuinely addresses the needs of recipient communities, enabling them to become self-sustaining.

Environmental stewardship (Watan) calls for global cooperation beyond mere political agreements. Successful models like the international collaboration in the ozone layer's preservation through the Montreal Protocol illustrate how collective action can yield significant environmental benefits. This principle can guide us toward international agreements that genuinely address critical issues like climate change, deforestation, and resource depletion.

Equitable wealth distribution (Mal) challenges existing economic disparities. An effective approach could involve rethinking international trade policies to support fair trade, ensuring that wealth generated benefits all parties equitably, especially those in less developed nations. Models like the microfinance initiatives in developing countries, which empower local economies, can serve as examples of how to bridge the wealth gap on a global scale.

The nurturing of intellect and culture (Aql) emphasizes the role of education and cultural exchange. International education programs, like student exchange initiatives, can foster a global understanding and respect, breaking down barriers of ignorance and prejudice.

This vision for a global community guided by Maqasid principles is grounded in pragmatic approaches that resonate across diverse cultures and political systems. It's a call to action for all nations to move beyond outdated paradigms and embrace a future where peace, justice, and sustainability are not just ideals, but realities.

In conclusion, the Maqasid framework offers a transformative blueprint for global relations. While challenges exist, the successful implementation of these principles in various contexts demonstrates their viability. This isn't just a theoretical concept; it's a practical imperative for our time, demanding collective action to forge a better world for all.

Conflict Resolution: The Ethical Route to Peace

Envision a world where conflicts are not resolved through force or power struggles but through the application of shared human values and dialogue. This vision, grounded in the ethical principles of Maqasid, offers a practical and ethical route to lasting peace. It's a vision where global disputes are approached not with weapons, but with a commitment to understanding, compassion, and reconciliation.

At the core of Maqasid lies the recognition of universal human values that transcend national, cultural, and religious differences. These values could become the common ground for conflict mediation, offering a means to bridge divides and foster meaningful discussions. In this ideal scenario, diplomacy shifts from a competitive exercise to a collaborative process that respects life (Nafs) and promotes communal harmony (Ummah).

However, translating this vision into reality presents significant challenges. Conflicts often stem from deep-rooted historical grievances, economic disparities, and cultural misunderstandings. Effective mediation requires not just goodwill but also a nuanced understanding of these complex factors. Real-world examples like the peace negotiations in South Africa post-apartheid or the Northern Ireland peace process illustrate how applying shared values, along with a deep understanding of the underlying issues, can lead to successful conflict resolution.

Preventive diplomacy, a proactive approach to addressing emerging conflicts, is vital in this framework. By actively engaging in dialogue and understanding potential conflict drivers, nations can work to defuse tensions before they escalate. This approach demands a shift from reactive to proactive diplomacy, where the sanctity of life (Nafs) and communal well-being (Ummah) are prioritized to prevent conflicts from arising.

In this envisioned world, ethical responsibility extends beyond national interests. Nations recognize the interconnectedness of the global community and understand that their actions have far-reaching consequences. The pursuit of peace becomes not just a strategic choice but a moral imperative, where leaders are not only accountable to their citizens but also to the broader international community.

The inclusion of various actors – international organizations, NGOs, civil society groups, and even individuals – is crucial in this process. Each plays a distinct role in conflict resolution, from providing humanitarian aid and facilitating dialogue to monitoring ceasefires and rebuilding post-conflict societies.

This vision for global peace and collaboration is not a distant dream, but a path that requires concerted effort and dedication. It challenges us to prioritize the sanctity of life, the welfare of communities, and the prevention of conflict-related suffering. By embracing the Maqasid principles as a guide, we can move from being passive observers to active participants in creating a more just, peaceful, and harmonious world. The ethical route to peace is before us, and it is our collective responsibility to pursue it with commitment and action.

Global Alliances: Beyond Political Expediency

Imagine a world where alliances among nations are grounded not in fleeting political expediency but in a steadfast commitment to ethical principles. Envision international coalitions that serve as powerful drivers of collective well-being, transcending traditional security concerns. This vision, rooted in the ethical bedrock of Maqasid, offers a transformative approach to global alliances, reshaping international relations with a focus on shared human values.

In this world, nations unite to form ethical coalitions guided by Maqasid principles, transcending narrow political interests. These alliances emerge as beacons of shared values, championing the welfare of humanity (Ummah) and the common good. They represent a shift from a paradigm where security is synonymous with military might, to one where addressing the root causes of conflict, poverty, and inequality is paramount.

However, transitioning to this new form of global alliance poses significant challenges. The current geopolitical landscape is often driven by power dynamics and national interests. Overcoming these entrenched systems requires a gradual approach, starting with small-scale collaborations focused on specific issues like climate change or public health. Successful models like the European Union's humanitarian aid initiatives, which often transcend political interests for the greater good, provide a blueprint for how ethical considerations can be integrated into international cooperation.

These ethical coalitions, promoting the sanctity of life (Nafs), communal well-being (Ummah), and principles of justice and equity, could reshape global policy-making. They would work towards tackling issues like climate change and poverty with a collective dedication to ethical values, transcending mere rhetoric.

A reimagined global governance system could also emerge from these ethical coalitions. Proposals to restructure international organizations, like the United Nations, to incorporate Maqasid principles into decision-making processes reflect this change. It's a shift from power politics to a system centered on ethics, justice, and global well-being.

The impact of such coalitions and a renewed governance framework could be profound. The pursuit of peace, justice, and prosperity would become a collective goal, transcending the interests of a few powerful nations. This approach would protect the vulnerable, address inequalities, and uphold human dignity.

This vision is not mere idealism; it's a necessary response to today's global challenges. Climate change, health crises, and the plight of refugees all demand collaborative solutions rooted in ethical frameworks. Moving beyond narrow national interests to embrace the greater good is imperative.

Creating alliances based on shared ethical values is not just a call to action; it's a necessity to shape a better world. This future, guided by Maqasid principles and collective well-being, is within reach, awaiting our commitment and collective action to realize it.

Economic Partnerships: Prosperity Through Ethics

Imagine a world where economic partnerships extend beyond profit and loss, anchored in ethical principles that champion sustainable development and equitable wealth distribution. This vision, guided by the principles of Maqasid, transforms economic partnerships into ethical partnerships – not just a possibility, but an imperative for our times.

In this envisioned world, nations lead by example, engaging in global development projects that align with Maqasid principles. These initiatives prioritize sustainable development (Watan) and equitable wealth distribution (Mal). Economic prosperity is pursued not at the expense of the environment or communities but in harmony with the greater good.

Real-world examples, such as the microfinance programs in Bangladesh or sustainable trade initiatives like Fair Trade, demonstrate how ethical considerations can be integrated into economic models. These programs have shown that financial success can coincide with social and environmental responsibility.

However, transitioning to this model is not without challenges. Overcoming entrenched economic systems driven by profit requires innovative approaches, policy reform, and often, a shift in consumer behavior. Corporate interests and political resistance can pose significant obstacles, but these can be mitigated through regulations, incentives, and public awareness campaigns.

Ethical economic partnerships are based on the concept that wealth extends beyond mere monetary value to include the welfare of both people and the planet. In this model, economic decisions prioritize fairness and equality, questioning conventional practices and reforming economic policies.

Moreover, these partnerships aim to reform trade relations, promoting systems where benefits are shared equitably among all parties. It's about building a global economic ecosystem where prosperity is shared, and disparities are actively addressed.

The impact of such partnerships would be profound. Economic growth would become synonymous with environmental sustainability. Impoverished nations would receive fair opportunities for growth, not burdened by debt but empowered by equitable economic relationships. Wealth would not be hoarded by a few but distributed fairly, upholding the dignity of every individual.

This vision is an ethical imperative in response to the environmental crises, wealth disparities, and social injustices exacerbated by our current economic models. It calls for a shift to an economic framework where ethics are integral, not an afterthought.

Ethical economic partnerships are about more than prosperity; they are about justice, sustainability, and the collective well-being. This future, where economic decisions are made conscientiously, and wealth is pursued ethically, is within reach. It calls for the collective action of governments, businesses, international organizations, and consumers. This isn't just a call to action; it's a call to reshape the world's economic landscape, one ethical partnership at a time. This future is not just a dream but a feasible reality, waiting for us to embrace it.

Environmental Stewardship: Collective Care of the Planet

Imagine a world where nations transcend rhetoric and actively unite to protect our planet. Envision a future where caring for the Earth (Watan) is a shared global responsibility, integral to international relations. This world sees environmental stewardship not just as a local concern but as a cornerstone of global cooperation.

In this envisioned world, nations prioritize the planet's well-being over narrow self-interest. They lead or support global sustainability initiatives that align with the sacred principle of homeland protection (Watan). These initiatives are impactful, driving responsible stewardship on a global scale. Environmental preservation becomes an ethical obligation, not a mere choice.

For instance, the global response to the ozone layer depletion, culminating in the Montreal Protocol, demonstrates how collaborative action can effectively address environmental crises. Imagine expanding this cooperative spirit to other areas such as reforestation, wildlife preservation, and combating climate change. Nations work together on transnational conservation efforts, recognizing our planet's health as interconnected with all life.

Ethical environmental stewardship presents an opportunity for unity. It's a chance for nations to pool resources, knowledge, and technologies to combat environmental challenges. It fosters diplomatic ties, builds trust, and establishes collective responsibility. This cooperation isn't a burden but a chance to build a more harmonious global community.

Moreover, this stewardship is an investment in our future. Recognizing that today's actions impact future generations, it's a commitment to safeguard the planet for our children and beyond. It's an understanding that the Earth, a finite resource, requires careful and respectful management.

In this vision, nations become leaders in responsible resource management. Economic growth aligns with sustainable practices, ensuring the well-being of current and future generations. Natural resource policies are guided by ethical considerations, shifting from exploitation to sustainable utilization.

This vision is an ethical imperative, not a distant dream. The environmental challenges we face, from climate change to biodiversity loss, demand collective, actionable solutions. It's time for nations to move from promises to concrete measures, embracing their stewardship role.

Collective care for our planet isn't solely about preserving nature; it's about safeguarding our shared future. This vision is a call to all nations to embrace their moral duty to protect the Earth. It's a call for unified action and sustainable harmony—a future that we must actively work towards for the sake of our planet and all its inhabitants.

Social Justice: A Global Movement

Imagine a world where nations champion social justice not as a secondary agenda but as a primary global commitment. This future, rooted in the ethical framework of Maqasid, envisages a concerted effort to eradicate poverty, expand educational access, and ensure universal healthcare. This vision goes beyond borders, transforming social justice into a movement that resonates globally.

In this envisioned world, international platforms become arenas not just for advancing national interests but for vigorously advocating social issues aligned with Maqasid principles. Nations become vocal in their fight against poverty, not out of charity, but driven by a moral imperative. They champion education as a fundamental right, understanding that knowledge (Aql) is essential for human potential and societal growth.

Moreover, these nations advocate for universal healthcare, upholding the preservation of life (Nafs) as paramount. They recognize that social justice entails more than wealth redistribution; it's about ensuring equitable opportunities for dignity and well-being for all.

For example, initiatives like the United Nations Sustainable Development Goals (SDGs) provide a blueprint for how nations can collaborate on these fronts. However, the challenge lies in moving from policy to action. Overcoming political inertia, cultural differences, and economic barriers requires a concerted effort, innovative policies, and robust international cooperation.

In this world, humanitarian leadership overshadows military and economic dominance. Nations initiate or support humanitarian missions reflecting Maqasid principles, prioritizing life preservation (Nafs) and community welfare (Ummah). This approach sets a precedent for ethical global action, where compassion transcends borders.

This vision of social justice is not about empty promises but about tangible actions and measurable impacts. Nations collaborate to tackle root causes of social injustices, creating sustainable and long-term solutions. Social justice becomes a unifying goal, transcending political and cultural differences, reminding us of our shared humanity and interconnected destinies.

Acknowledging the diversity of global contexts, this vision for social justice adapts the Maqasid principles to fit various cultural and political frameworks, ensuring inclusivity and relevance. It's a call for global solidarity, where each nation contributes according to its capabilities and context.

This is not a utopian dream but an ethical imperative. The pressing challenges of poverty, educational disparity, and healthcare inadequacy demand a global response. It's time for nations to rise above self-interest and embrace their role as champions of social justice.

Nations must not only pursue their well-being but contribute actively to humanity's collective welfare. A world where social justice thrives is a world of greater stability, prosperity, and harmony. It's a future where every individual has the chance to achieve their potential, enriching the global human experience.

The call for social justice is both a moral imperative and a practical call to action. It invites nations to collaborate, innovate, and make a substantial difference in billions of lives. This future, where social justice is a global reality, is not just achievable; it's essential and within our collective reach.

Maqasid: Paving the Way for Ethical Global Unity

In a world frequently marred by conflict, inequality, and environmental degradation, the prospect of global peace and collaboration can seem distant. Yet, the application of Maqasid principles offers a pragmatic blueprint for overhauling international relations. This approach is not a utopian fantasy but a tangible strategy rooted in the interconnected realities of our world.

Maqasid provides a comprehensive framework addressing key global challenges, emphasizing life preservation, community welfare, sustainable development, equitable wealth distribution, intellectual growth, and environmental protection. These are tangible goals, exemplified by initiatives like the United Nations Sustainable Development Goals (SDGs), which echo the spirit of Maqasid in their global outreach and ambition.

Nations can choose a different path in conflict resolution by prioritizing the sanctity of life (Nafs) and communal harmony (Ummah). Ethical mediation, as seen in the diplomatic efforts that led to the Paris Agreement on climate change, demonstrates how common ground can be found without resorting to violence. This approach is not idealistic but a conscious choice accessible to nations today.

Consider an economic landscape where trade agreements prioritize fairness and ethical labor practices (Mal). Nations can set an example by investing in projects that focus on social welfare (Ummah) and sustainable development (Watan). Such transformation is already taking shape in initiatives like the European Union's trade policies, which increasingly incorporate social and environmental standards.

Moreover, envision humanitarian aid prioritizing sustainable development over short-term fixes, guided by the principles of life preservation (Nafs) and community welfare (Ummah). Collaborative efforts, like the global response to the COVID-19 pandemic, show how nations can unite to address immediate needs while keeping long-term sustainability in focus.

Global alliances can evolve beyond political convenience, forming around shared values and a commitment to Maqasid principles. Such alliances could advocate for ethical governance and influence international bodies like the United Nations, shifting from power-centric to ethics-centric global governance.

Environmental diplomacy, underpinned by Maqasid, can lead to meaningful climate agreements. Nations collaborating on ambitious environmental targets show that protecting our shared planet (Watan) is not wishful thinking but a collective goal within reach.

This vision is not just aspirational; it's a practical call to action. The challenges we face demand a collective response grounded in ethical principles. It's a call for leaders, policymakers, and citizens to adopt a transformative vision and collaborate toward a more just, equitable, and sustainable global order.

Let's start this journey now. By replacing conflict with collaboration and division with unity, we can reshape the narrative of international relations. This is our chance to not just make history but to redefine it according to our highest ethical ideals. Let's seize this moment to create a cherished legacy for future generations. The path to a better world starts with us and it starts today.

Redefining the Future: A Call for Ethical Unity in Global Relations

Throughout history, there have been pivotal moments when civilizations have risen to meet formidable challenges, driven by visionaries and leaders who dared to imagine a better world. Today, we stand at the cusp of a similar transformative opportunity. The long-standing narrative of international relations, characterized by power struggles and divisions, is ripe for change. We possess the collective power to redefine this narrative, steering it towards collaboration, unity, and ethical governance.

Imagine a world where nations shift their perspectives from adversarial to cooperative, uniting in the face of global challenges such as poverty, climate change, and health crises. Picture a global community where dialogue triumphs over conflict, and mutual well-being eclipses narrow national interests. This vision is not mere fantasy; it's a realistic goal that begins with a fundamental shift in how we approach global relations.

Achieving this vision, however, requires us to navigate real challenges. Political inertia, economic disparities, and cultural differences are significant obstacles. To overcome them, nations can start by engaging in small-scale collaborative efforts, building trust and mutual understanding. These initial steps can lay the groundwork for more extensive cooperation.

The principles of Maqasid – prioritizing the well-being of all, preserving life, and pursuing justice – offer a moral compass in this journey. Instead of letting divisions dictate our interactions, we can align our policies and actions with these ethical principles. This approach, however, must be adaptable to the diverse political and cultural landscapes of our world, ensuring that these principles resonate universally.

Now is the time for action, not complacency. We are tasked with steering history towards a world marked by justice, equity, and ethical governance. This is not a responsibility to be deferred to future generations but an immediate calling for today's leaders and citizens.

As we embark on this path, we must commit to unity over division, collaboration over conflict. Each decision, alliance, and policy must reflect our commitment to ethical ideals. The journey towards a better world begins with our choices today.

This new chapter in human history is not just about redefining how nations interact; it's about creating a legacy that future generations will cherish – a world where justice, unity, and collaboration are not just ideals but realities. The path forward starts with us, and it starts now. Let's seize this moment with determination and hope, embracing our role in shaping a world defined by our highest ethical aspirations.

Conclusion: The Dawning of a New Era in Global Relations

Envision a world where traditional paradigms of power politics give way to a new era in global relations, anchored in the profound principles of Maqasid. This transformative vision redefines our engagement with the world, advocating for a harmonious and ethical global community.

In this future, the international stage transforms from a battleground of supremacy into a forum for collaboration and shared progress. Nations unite not merely for coexistence but for active cooperation, addressing humanity's pressing challenges from poverty and conflict to climate change and social injustice.

The bedrock of this new era is ethical governance. Nations commit to Maqasid principles in their international dealings, pledging to uphold life preservation (Nafs), community welfare (Ummah), sustainable development (Watan), equitable wealth (Mal), intellectual growth (Aql), and protection of our planet (Watan).

Imagine a United Nations where Maqasid principles guide every decision, fostering a world that seeks the greater good beyond narrow national interests. Diplomacy evolves into moral engagement, with conflicts resolved through ethical mediation, emphasizing life sanctity (Nafs) and communal harmony (Ummah).

However, realizing this vision faces significant challenges. The shift from entrenched power dynamics to a Maqasid-based approach requires navigating complex geopolitical landscapes, overcoming economic interests, and bridging cultural differences.

To transition to this new era, nations can start with small-scale collaborations focused on shared global issues, gradually building trust and understanding. Incorporating Maqasid principles into international treaties and agreements, and fostering global economic policies that prioritize equitable wealth distribution and environmental sustainability, are practical steps towards this vision.

In this transformed world, global alliances form not for political gain but for shared ethical values. Nations advocate for integrating Maqasid principles into international governance, moving from a power-centric to an ethics-centric model. Environmental diplomacy, underpinned by a commitment to sustainability and equitable resource policies, becomes a key aspect of international relations.

This new era is not a utopian dream but a feasible reality, rooted in our shared humanity and capacity for moral growth. The challenges our planet faces demand a collective and ethical response. It's a call to action for nations, leaders, and citizens to rise above self-interest and embrace a global community guided by moral values.

Let us work to create this world, becoming architects of a new era in global relations. This future, where nations cooperate out of shared values and a common destiny, is not just a possibility; it's an imperative. It's a future where global peace, justice, and collaboration are not aspirational goals but achievable objectives, waiting for us to seize them.

IV

Future Prospects

Maqasid redefines governance with a focus on justice and societal welfare, urging us from mere concepts to ethical action. This isn't an end but a start towards continuous improvement in an evolving world. Facing the choice between short-term pragmatism and a principled future, Maqasid prompts a revolutionary leap towards equitable, sustainable governance. Challenges exist, they highlight our mission's urgency. Let's embrace Maqasid, shaping a just, equitable future. The time for action is now.

12

The Challenges and Pitfalls

Recognizing and Mitigating the Potential Downsides: A Proactive Strategy for Ethical Governance

The Crucible of Transformation: Confronting Complexity with Courage

As we embark on integrating Maqasid into governance, it's vital to proactively address its challenges, not as a sign of doubt, but as a testament to our commitment to responsible governance. Here, we succinctly explore these challenges and propose strategic solutions:

1. **Resistance to Change:** Change often breeds resistance. To ease this, focused public awareness campaigns and educational initiatives are key. By clearly articulating Maqasid's ethical benefits and practical improvements, we can transform skepticism into support.
2. **Interpretation Disputes:** The flexibility of Maqasid's principles can lead to disagreements. Establishing councils of experts for guidance and maintaining transparent decision-making processes will be crucial in navigating these disputes.

3. **Economic Adjustments:** Shifting to an ethically-focused governance model might disrupt certain economic sectors. A gradual transition, coupled with support for affected industries, can ease this shift. Highlighting the long-term benefits, such as sustainable growth and fair wealth distribution, can also rally support.

4. **Global Relations:** Our ethical stance might not align with all international practices, posing diplomatic challenges. Engaging in open dialogue and seeking common ethical ground, while leveraging our commitment to justice and sustainability, can strengthen international relations.

5. **Bureaucratic Adaptation:** Bureaucracies may resist changes to their established systems. Targeted training programs and clear communication on the advantages of ethical governance can foster internal support.

6. **Political Exploitation:** There's a risk of Maqasid's principles being co-opted for political gain. Establishing robust monitoring and accountability mechanisms, with civil society and media involvement, can ensure genuine adherence to these principles.

7. **International Relations:** Balancing our ethical approach with international interests requires a principled yet pragmatic stance. Diplomacy and mediation become key tools in maintaining our values while resolving global disputes.

Consider the example of a country that successfully navigated similar challenges while transitioning to a more ethical governance model. Their approach, involving inclusive dialogue and phased policy implementation, proved effective in overcoming resistance and building consensus.

In conclusion, recognizing and addressing these challenges is integral to our journey towards ethical governance. By employing wisdom and courage, we can navigate these complexities, ever mindful of our ultimate goal: a just, equitable, and compassionate society for all.

Intellectual Rigor: Safeguarding Against Misinterpretation

In the pursuit of a just and ethical society, ensuring the precise interpretation and application of Maqasid principles in governance is indispensable. To prevent potential misinterpretations and foster intellectual depth, we propose a dual strategy:

Scholarly Oversight: Establish Diverse Boards of Scholars

The cornerstone of preventing misinterpretation lies in forming boards of scholars deeply versed in Islamic jurisprudence and ethics. These scholars will provide essential insights into the practical application of Maqasid in policymaking. Importantly, these boards must represent a spectrum of viewpoints within Islamic thought, ensuring a balanced and holistic approach. Their diverse perspectives will prevent any single interpretation from prevailing and will guide policymakers and legislators in making decisions that truly embody Maqasid's ethical objectives.

Consider, for example, the successful implementation of a similar advisory board in Norway, which played a pivotal role in harmonizing traditional ethical principles with contemporary governance challenges.

Public Education: Implement Comprehensive Awareness Campaigns

A common root of misinterpretation is a fundamental lack of public understanding. Addressing this requires comprehensive awareness campaigns that explain Maqasid's ethical underpinnings and its goals of justice, equality, and human welfare. Utilizing various media channels and community engagement programs, these campaigns should not only educate but also showcase real-life impacts of Maqasid principles, thereby bridging the gap between abstract concepts and tangible outcomes.

Moreover, these educational efforts should foster critical thinking and open dialogue among citizens, empowering them to actively engage with and question the application of Maqasid in governance. This approach not only deepens societal understanding but also cultivates an informed and proactive community.

However, implementing these strategies is not without challenges. For instance, securing funding for extensive educational campaigns and ensuring genuine representation on scholarly boards are significant hurdles. These challenges call for collaborative solutions and a commitment from both governmental and non-governmental organizations.

In conclusion, by establishing diverse scholarly boards and launching far-reaching educational campaigns, we can protect against misinterpretation of Maqasid, steering towards a more ethically grounded and just society. These measures, while demanding, are critical steps in our journey towards responsible governance.

Transparency and Accountability: Preventing Political Exploitation

To ensure genuine integration of Maqasid principles into governance and prevent their political exploitation, robust transparency and accountability mechanisms are essential. Here are two key strategies to achieve this:

Regular Audits: Conduct Independent Audits

Regular, independent audits are vital in verifying that Maqasid principles are truly ingrained in governance practices, not merely as symbolic gestures. These audits, conducted by impartial bodies proficient in Islamic jurisprudence and ethics, should critically evaluate a range of policies from economic initiatives to foreign affairs. They must assess both the intended goals and the real societal impact: Are they fostering justice, equality, and overall well-being?

For instance, the implementation of similar audit systems in Canada has shown significant success in aligning governance with ethical principles. These systems critically analyze both policy intentions and outcomes, ensuring alignment with ethical standards.

These audits should also incorporate insights from Maqasid scholars and experts, enhancing the depth of evaluation. The findings must be transparently shared with the public, fostering trust and accountability in the government.

Public Reporting: Enhance Transparency in Governance

The results of these audits should be publicly accessible, underlining the commitment to transparency in governance. This public reporting serves multiple purposes: it informs citizens about the government's adherence to Maqasid, enables monitoring by civil society organizations, and encourages a culture of openness within government circles.

Utilizing modern technology, such as digital platforms, can make these reports more accessible and engage a wider audience. This approach not only ensures transparency but also facilitates an easier way for the public to engage with and understand the findings.

Additionally, the government should actively engage in dialogues with civil society groups, religious leaders, and citizens, inviting feedback and participation. This not only upholds Maqasid principles but also adapts them to evolving societal needs.

However, challenges such as ensuring the independence of auditors and effectively disseminating information to a diverse population must be addressed. Strategies like appointing auditors from varied backgrounds and leveraging multiple communication channels can help overcome these obstacles.

In conclusion, through regular independent audits and transparent public reporting, we can cultivate a culture of ethical governance. These strategies ensure that Maqasid principles are authentically integrated into governance, empowering citizens, building trust, and maintaining the highest ethical standards.

Social Engagement: Overcoming Social Resistance

Effective implementation of Maqasid principles in governance, especially in overcoming social resistance, necessitates open dialogue and collaboration with communities and stakeholders. Here are two key strategies streamlined for better understanding and broader accessibility:

Community Dialogues: Facilitate Inclusive Discussions

Organizing community dialogues and town hall meetings is crucial for understanding and addressing concerns and cultural nuances related to Maqasid. These discussions should provide a welcoming platform for everyone to voice their opinions and questions. The benefits of such engagement include:

- **Building Trust:** Transparent and open dialogues demonstrate the government's willingness to listen, fostering trust and social acceptance.
- **Clarifying Misconceptions:** Direct interactions allow for the clarification of any misunderstandings about Maqasid, ensuring accurate community understanding.
- **Identifying Cultural Nuances:** Dialogues help uncover unique cultural interpretations of Maqasid, essential for tailoring governance approaches.
- **Resolving Conflicts:** These discussions offer a peaceful platform to address disagreements and align solutions with Maqasid principles.

For instance, a successful case in New Zealand demonstrated how community dialogues significantly eased the integration of new governance principles, aligning them more closely with public expectations and cultural values.

Multi-Stakeholder Involvement: Enhance Collaborative Decision-Making

Inclusivity is vital in the application of Maqasid. Engaging religious leaders, scholars, activists, and civil society organizations in the decision-making process ensures a well-rounded and ethically sound approach. This collaborative effort offers:

- **Diverse Perspectives:** Each group contributes unique insights, creating a more comprehensive understanding of societal needs.
- **Checks and Balances:** This diversity prevents power concentration and promotes broader ethical consensus.
- **Enhanced Legitimacy:** Inclusive decision-making processes are perceived as more legitimate and representative.
- **Conflict Resolution:** Multi-stakeholder forums are instrumental in finding common ground and reducing resistance.

However, organizing effective community dialogues and stakeholder meetings can face challenges such as logistical constraints and varying political agendas. These can be mitigated by leveraging digital platforms for wider participation and establishing clear, structured dialogue processes.

In conclusion, overcoming social resistance to Maqasid principles requires a dual approach of facilitating community dialogues and encouraging multi-stakeholder involvement. This strategy not only promotes transparency and inclusivity but also respects cultural diversity, leading to broader acceptance and successful integration of Maqasid principles in governance.

Systemic Transformation: Navigating Institutional Barriers

The integration of Maqasid principles into governance represents a significant systemic shift, often hindered by institutional barriers. However, these challenges can be managed with strategic and proactive measures.

Here are two key strategies refined for effectiveness:

Pilot Programs: Phased Testing and Scaling

Embarking on systemic transformation can be made less daunting through carefully designed pilot programs. These allow governments to:

- **Test Feasibility:** Pilot programs act as practical trials, testing how well policies aligned with Maqasid principles can be integrated into existing systems.
- **Collect Valuable Data:** They provide an opportunity to gather data and feedback, which is crucial for policy refinement and improvement.
- **Showcase Successes:** When successful, these pilots serve as persuasive evidence of the benefits of Maqasid, building public and political support.
- **Identify and Address Challenges Early:** Early detection of potential issues enables timely adjustments.

For example, a pilot program in Indonesia successfully introduced Maqasid-based policies in a specific sector, demonstrating improved social outcomes and gaining wider acceptance for a subsequent nationwide rollout.

Once proven effective, these programs can be expanded gradually, easing the transition and reducing the risks associated with systemic change.

Resource Pooling: Collaborative Approach to Resource Allocation

The transition to Maqasid governance can be resource-intensive. Governments, especially those with constrained budgets, can overcome this through resource pooling, partnering with private sectors, NGOs, and international bodies. This approach offers:

- **Financial Support:** External partners can fund various transition aspects, from research to capacity building.

- **Shared Expertise:** Collaborating with NGOs and international organizations can bring in specialized knowledge, particularly in areas like social justice and environmental sustainability.
- **Efficient Use of Resources:** Pooling resources can streamline efforts, avoiding duplication and promoting logistical efficiency.
- **Global Best Practices:** Working with international bodies allows governments to learn from global experiences in ethical governance.

Integrating technology in these processes, such as using data analysis tools for pilot program assessment or digital platforms for collaboration, can further enhance efficiency and impact.

However, challenges such as bureaucratic resistance to pilot programs or complexities in managing public-private partnerships must be navigated carefully. Clear communication, defined roles, and transparent processes are key to addressing these challenges.

In conclusion, by implementing phased pilot programs and fostering collaborative resource pooling, governments can effectively navigate the institutional barriers to Maqasid governance. This approach not only ensures a smoother transition but also leverages shared resources and expertise, setting a strong foundation for long-term ethical governance success.

Diplomatic Finesse: Resolving Global Dilemmas

In the complex realm of international relations, integrating Maqasid principles into diplomatic practices is crucial for fostering ethical governance on a global scale. Here's how governments can effectively navigate and resolve international challenges:

Ethical Diplomacy

- **Nuanced Approach:** Diplomacy on the global stage requires balancing diverse interests and cultures. An ethical approach, guided by Maqasid, involves finding shared values with other nations while respecting their sovereignty and cultural contexts. For example, Malaysia's recent diplomatic efforts in the South China Sea negotiations showcased how mutual respect and understanding, grounded in Maqasid principles, led to a breakthrough in negotiations.
- **Conflict Resolution:** Ethical diplomacy should be employed to peacefully resolve conflicts. Encouraging dialogue and negotiations based on shared human values can de-escalate tensions and promote lasting peace. The principles of Maqasid, such as the preservation of life ('Nafs') and community welfare ('Ummah'), offer a common ground that transcends national boundaries.
- **Soft Power:** Utilize soft power by showcasing the benefits of governance aligned with Maqasid, such as social justice and environmental stewardship. This approach can positively influence global perceptions and support ethical governance.

Global Partnerships

- **Ethical Coalitions:** Form or join international coalitions committed to ethical governance based on Maqasid. These coalitions can address global challenges while promoting collective well-being. An example is the Alliance for Multilateralism, which has brought together nations to tackle issues like poverty and climate change through shared ethical principles.
- **Global Governance Reform:** Advocate for incorporating Maqasid principles in the decision-making processes of international organizations like the United Nations. This reform can lead to more inclusive and ethical global governance.
- **Humanitarian Leadership:** Lead in international humanitarian

efforts that reflect Maqasid principles. Active participation in global humanitarian missions demonstrates a commitment to ethical action and inspires other nations.

However, integrating Maqasid in global diplomacy is not without challenges. Balancing national interests with ethical principles, navigating diverse political landscapes, and addressing criticisms from different cultural and ethical perspectives are significant considerations.

In conclusion, practicing ethical diplomacy and engaging in global partnerships are key to resolving international dilemmas and promoting ethical governance worldwide. By adopting these strategies, governments can contribute to a more just, equitable, and harmonious global community, while navigating the intricacies of international relations with Maqasid principles as a guiding light.

Turning Challenges into Catalysts for Progress

As governments endeavor to integrate Maqasid into their governance frameworks, it's imperative to view arising challenges not as roadblocks but as opportunities for development and refinement. This mindset shift is key for several reasons:

Intellectual Rigor and Scholarly Oversight

- **Strengthening Governance:** Robust scholarly oversight ensures Maqasid principles are upheld with integrity. This approach, far from impeding progress, actually enriches governance and decision-making. For instance, the implementation of Maqasid in Morocco's policy reform demonstrated how academic rigor significantly improved policy outcomes.
- **Educated Citizenry:** Effective public education initiatives cultivate a knowledgeable and engaged citizenry. This leads to a society that actively participates in ethical governance, reinforcing the social

contract between the government and the people.

Transparency and Accountability

- **Trust in Governance:** Regular audits and transparent reporting not only deter political exploitation but also foster public trust. This approach has been successful in Denmark, where increased transparency led to higher public confidence in government actions.
- **Government Credibility:** Internationally, such transparency elevates a nation's credibility, positioning it as an ethical leader and fostering global collaborations.

Social Engagement and Multi-Stakeholder Involvement

- **Inclusive Governance:** Engaging communities in dialogues creates inclusive policies that reflect diverse societal needs. This strategy has been effective in resolving conflicts and enhancing social harmony, as seen in the peace-building process in Northern Ireland.
- **Conflict Resolution:** Utilizing these platforms for conflict resolution contributes to societal stability.

Systemic Transformation and Resource Pooling

- **Progressive Transition:** Pilot programs enable a gradual, adaptable transition to ethical governance. Learning from these smaller initiatives allows for scaling successful strategies, as exemplified by the Smart Cities Mission in India.
- **Financial Viability:** Collaborative financial strategies with private sector organizations, NGOs, and international bodies ensure sustainable transformation. This approach was instrumental in the successful governance reforms in Rwanda.

By embracing challenges as catalysts for progress, governments can not only navigate potential difficulties but also enhance the essence of governance. The journey of integrating Maqasid principles becomes one of continuous improvement and learning, where each challenge surmounted fortifies the commitment to ethical governance. It's a path that leads to a more ethical, prosperous, and harmonious society—a path that, while demanding, is immensely rewarding and crucial for future generations.

Conclusion: Embrace Complexity - Transforming Challenges into Opportunities

In our endeavor to weave Maqasid principles into the fabric of governance, let's wholeheartedly embrace the inherent complexities of this transformative journey. These intricacies should not be viewed as barriers but as vital catalysts in refining and perfecting our governance systems. Here's how embracing complexity becomes a conduit for success:

Testing Ground for Innovation

- **Continuous Improvement:** The complexities of integrating Maqasid challenge us to innovate, fostering a dynamic and adaptable governance system. For instance, the introduction of Maqasid-based environmental policies in Costa Rica led to breakthroughs in sustainable development, showcasing how complexity can drive creative solutions.
- **Inclusive Decision-Making:** Complex issues necessitate a multi-faceted decision-making process. By engaging a diverse range of voices, from grassroots activists to policy experts, governance becomes more democratic and equitable.

Resilience and Determination

- **Character Building:** Tackling these challenges head-on builds resilience and fortifies our collective determination. It instills the courage needed to pursue ethical governance, even in the face of adversity.
- **Societal Cohesion:** Overcoming complex challenges together can significantly strengthen societal bonds. This shared journey towards ethical governance fosters unity and a sense of common purpose.

Collective Action and Progress

- **Collaborative Solutions:** The multifaceted nature of Maqasid principles often requires collaborative efforts. This has been evident in global partnerships, like the United Nations Sustainable Development Goals, where countries work together to address complex global issues, reinforcing the importance of cooperation for collective well-being.
- **Measuring Success:** By embracing complexity, we develop more holistic success metrics, evaluating governance not just quantitatively but also qualitatively, in terms of adherence to ethical principles and societal impact.

Seizing the Moment

- **Timely Action:** The urgent need to address these complexities propels us to take decisive action. The time to transform governance in line with Maqasid principles is now, not in some distant future.
- **Achieving the Possible:** By embracing complexity, we turn aspirations into tangible realities. It's a reminder that the ethical and just society we envision is within reach.

So, as we roll up our sleeves, let's unite in our resolve to transform these complexities into stepping stones. Integrating Maqasid into governance

332

goes beyond theory; it's a practical pathway to a future where ethical governance and Maqasid principles are at the heart of a just, equitable, and prosperous society. The time for collaborative action and bold strides forward is now.

Strategies for Overcoming Political Resistance and Social Challenges: A Tactical Approach for Ethical Governance

The Roadblock as the Road: Turning Opposition into Opportunity

In integrating Maqasid principles into governance, a path fraught with political resistance and social challenges, it's crucial to transform these hurdles into catalysts for positive change. Let's explore how to navigate these challenges effectively:

Inclusive Dialogue

- **Political Engagement:** Proactively engage with political actors and stakeholders. Understanding their concerns and incorporating their views can create a more robust and inclusive system. For instance, in South Africa, engaging opposition parties in dialogue helped refine and gain broader support for new policies.
- **Public Discourse:** Encourage public debates and discussions about Maqasid integration. This transparency ensures that governance reflects the values and aspirations of the people, enhancing democratic participation.

Education and Awareness

- **Social Awareness Campaigns:** Launch campaigns to educate society about Maqasid's principles and objectives. Address misconceptions to build understanding and acceptance.
- **Leadership Role:** Empower religious and community leaders to educate and guide public perception towards ethical governance. Their influential voices can significantly shift public opinion.

Pragmatic Implementation

- **Gradual Transition:** Recognize that governance change takes time. Start with broadly supported policies, demonstrating Maqasid's benefits to win over skeptics.
- **Pilot Programs:** Implement pilot programs in specific areas to test Maqasid principles. Positive outcomes from these pilots, like those seen in the Green City Initiative in Curitiba, Brazil, can build credibility and support.

Collaboration and Coalition Building

- **International Alliances:** Forge alliances with countries advocating similar governance goals. Collective efforts, such as the Paris Agreement on Climate Change, bolster support and add legitimacy.
- **Multi-Stakeholder Partnerships:** Work with civil society, academia, and the private sector to shape and oversee governance, ensuring collective ownership and diverse perspectives.

Accountability and Transparency

- **Independent Oversight:** Establish commissions for monitoring Maqasid application, ensuring adherence and preventing superficial implementation.

- **Public Reporting:** Share oversight findings publicly, utilizing digital platforms for broader accessibility and engagement, reinforcing government accountability.

Adaptation and Flexibility

- **Contextual Application:** Tailor Maqasid application to cultural, social, and economic contexts, while upholding universal values of justice and equity.
- **Learning from Challenges:** View setbacks as learning opportunities. A flexible governance model evolves from both successes and failures, adapting to changing circumstances.

In conclusion, rather than being deterred by opposition and resistance, we should view these as impetuses for pursuing more ethical governance. Through inclusive dialogue, education, pragmatic implementation, collaboration, accountability, and adaptation, political and social challenges can be turned into stepping stones towards progress. The path towards ethical governance, underpinned by Maqasid principles, may be challenging but is ultimately rewarding, leading to a society founded on justice, compassion, and human dignity. Embracing these strategies, we can transform opposition into an opportunity for a brighter future.

The Political Landscape: Overcoming Resistance in Governance

Navigating the political intricacies when introducing transformative concepts like Maqasid into governance requires a blend of strategic planning and persuasive advocacy. Here are refined strategies for securing political support:

Building Alliances

- **Coalition Building:** Form alliances with political figures and organizations advocating for ethical governance. This unified front amplifies influence, as seen in Spain where a coalition of diverse parties successfully advocated for governance reform.
- **Interfaith Engagement:** Collaborate with leaders across faith communities, emphasizing Maqasid's shared ethical values. Such partnerships were instrumental in the Interfaith Rainforest Initiative, bridging cultural divides.

Public-Private Partnerships

- **Economic Rationale:** Highlight Maqasid's long-term economic benefits, like a healthier, better-educated workforce. Businesses tend to support initiatives that align with their interests, as demonstrated in the partnership between multinational corporations and the Global Education Initiative.
- **Corporate Responsibility:** Encourage businesses to adopt CSR initiatives that resonate with Maqasid principles. This approach can enhance their reputation and customer loyalty.

Transparency and Accountability

- **Clear Metrics:** Develop measurable metrics for policies based on Maqasid, such as improved healthcare coverage or education quality. Transparent reporting, as practiced in Finland's Education System Reform, enables objective assessment.
- **Public Accessibility:** Make policy-related data publicly available. This transparency builds trust and validates the positive impacts of ethical governance.

Policy Pilot Programs

- **Demonstrable Impact:** Initiate pilot programs to illustrate Maqasid's effectiveness. For instance, a pilot project in Kuala Lumpur focusing on affordable housing showed remarkable improvements in community welfare, building a case for broader implementation.
- **Stakeholder Engagement:** Include citizens, experts, and community leaders in designing and evaluating pilot programs. Their involvement ensures a more comprehensive approach and grassroots support.

Public Engagement and Education

- **Community Dialogues:** Host forums for open discussion about Maqasid. Addressing concerns directly, as done in the "Voices of Youth" town hall meetings in Amman, Jordan, can clarify misconceptions and demonstrate societal benefits.
- **Educational Campaigns:** Launch campaigns to educate the public, using varied media to reach different audiences. Tailor messages to resonate with specific groups, from policymakers to the general populace.

While these strategies are robust, they come with challenges, such as potential political opposition or complexities in forming effective public-private partnerships. These obstacles require careful navigation and adaptability.

In conclusion, transforming political and social resistance into support for ethical governance is a complex yet achievable goal. Through inclusive dialogue, pragmatic implementation, collaborative efforts, and transparent practices, we can pave the way for a more just, equitable, and compassionate society. It's a journey that, despite its challenges, offers significant rewards in bettering the nation and its people.

The Social Sphere: Navigating Societal Challenges

Securing societal support is crucial in the pursuit of ethical governance guided by Maqasid principles. This endeavor, while challenging, can be successful with a well-crafted approach that builds understanding, inclusivity, and active public participation. Here are enhanced strategies to achieve this:

Public Awareness Campaigns

- **Media Campaigns:** Implement comprehensive media campaigns across television, radio, social media, and other platforms to educate the public on Maqasid's universal values. For example, a campaign in Malaysia effectively increased public awareness and acceptance of governance reforms.
- **Myth Disarmament:** Actively address and debunk common myths about Maqasid, providing clear and accurate information to alleviate fears and misconceptions.

Community Engagement

- **Inclusive Forums:** Host community forums, town hall meetings, and discussions to give citizens a platform to express their views. These forums should be designed to make everyone feel heard and valued, similar to successful community engagement initiatives seen in the Participatory Budgeting Project in Porto Alegre, Brazil.
- **Local Input:** Ensure local insights are integrated into decision-making, allowing communities to influence how Maqasid principles address their specific needs.

Education and Training

- **Curricular Integration:** Advocate for the inclusion of Maqasid principles in school curricula, fostering early understanding. This approach was successfully implemented in the International Islamic University Malaysia's educational programs.
- **Adult Education:** Offer accessible adult education courses on Maqasid, focusing on its practical applications in daily life, ensuring broad community engagement.

Celebrate Success Stories

- **Showcase Impact:** Publicize success stories where Maqasid's application has led to tangible community improvements, like in the development of affordable housing projects in Indonesia, where it contributed to notable social advancements.
- **Recognition and Awards:** Establish programs to celebrate individuals and organizations that effectively implement Maqasid principles, fostering a culture of recognition and inspiration.

While these strategies are robust, they come with challenges such as overcoming public skepticism or logistical difficulties in organizing large-scale events. These can be mitigated through targeted communication strategies tailored to different community segments and by establishing efficient feedback mechanisms to continuously adapt and improve initiatives.

In conclusion, engaging the public in ethical governance requires active effort in building awareness, facilitating dialogue, and recognizing achievements. By implementing these strategies with a focus on inclusivity and responsiveness, the transition to a Maqasid-based governance system can be smoother and more widely accepted. It's a journey towards a society that not only upholds universal values but also cherishes the well-being of every citizen.

Crafting a Masterplan for Societal Transformation: The Power of Strategy

In the grand narrative of societal change, significant transformations, like the integration of Maqasid principles into governance, often face resistance. This journey isn't merely about confronting opposition; it's about mastering the art of strategic transformation. A well-crafted masterplan is crucial, combining finesse in political maneuvering with deep connections in the communities we serve.

Understanding the Power of Strategy: A robust strategy transforms challenges into opportunities. It's a guiding blueprint, turning resistance into resilience and obstacles into stepping stones. This approach has been exemplified in movements like the Civil Rights Movement in the United States, where strategic planning and community mobilization led to profound societal change.

Components of a Masterplan

1. **Coalitions and Alliances:** Take the Amazon Alliance, where various environmental organizations, Indigenous groups, and concerned citizens collaborate to protect the Amazon rainforest from deforestation and industrial exploitation.
2. **Economic Leverage:** Engaging the business sector by highlighting the long-term economic benefits of Maqasid, such as sustainable growth, can be pivotal. This strategy mirrors successful initiatives like the Business Roundtable's commitment to stakeholder capitalism in the United States.
3. **Transparency and Accountability:** Clear metrics for evaluating Maqasid policies, coupled with public accessibility to this data, build credibility and trust, much like the approach taken in Sweden's Open Government Initiative.
4. **Pilot Programs:** Implementing pilot programs to demonstrate Maqasid's impact is vital. These small-scale initiatives, such as the

Green Belt Movement in Kenya, serve as tangible evidence of the benefits of ethical governance.

The Masterplan in Action

This masterplan is not static but adapts to new challenges and opportunities. It's a roadmap through political and social resistance, with each step designed to convert opposition into support. For example, in engaging with resistant stakeholders, tailored communication strategies and inclusive dialogues, as seen in the Truth and Reconciliation Commission in South Africa, can be effective.

The Commitment to Transformation

Central to this plan is an unwavering commitment to Maqasid's transformative power. This commitment, echoing the dedication seen in Nelson Mandela, should be evident in every action, inspiring others to join the cause.

Measuring Success

Success will be measured not only in policy outcomes but in the more nuanced indicators of societal change, like public engagement levels and shifts in societal attitudes towards governance.

In conclusion, crafting a masterplan for societal transformation is a dynamic and complex task. By strategically building alliances, leveraging economic arguments, ensuring transparency, and demonstrating success through pilot programs, we can turn the tide of resistance. It's a journey that calls for patience, commitment, and strategic savvy, but one that leads to a society rooted in the principles of Maqasid. Let us embark on this journey with the resolve to see it through, step by strategic step.

Embracing Challenges as Catalysts for Transformation: The Power to Shape a New Reality

In our quest to establish a society guided by Maqasid principles, we must view challenges not with trepidation but as opportunities for growth and transformation. Resistance should be seen not as a sign of failure but as a testament to the profound impact of our endeavor. The journey towards a Maqasid-based society, though strewn with obstacles, is one filled with purpose and promise.

The Catalyst of Challenges

Challenges in this journey are not barriers but catalysts for change. They test and strengthen our commitment to ethical governance. For instance, when the Women's Suffrage Movement faced resistance, they used it as an opportunity to refine their strategies and strengthen their resolve, ultimately leading to significant societal progress.

Harnessing the Transformative Power

The resistance we encounter underlines the potential of Maqasid to reshape societal norms. It's not merely an idealistic vision; it's a practical, transformative force, as demonstrated in the implementation of the Nordic Model in Scandinavian countries, where alignment with ethical principles led to profound changes in governance and social welfare.

The Road Less Traveled

Embarking on this path is challenging. It's a road less traveled, filled with complexities and uncertainties. Yet, these challenges enrich our journey, underscoring our dedication to higher ethical standards and a more equitable world.

The Call to Action

We must be active agents of change, not passive observers. This involves engaging in strategic planning and decisive action. For example, through community engagement initiatives like the Participatory Budgeting Project in New York City, we can involve diverse stakeholders in meaningful dialogue and collaborative action.

Our Power to Shape the Future

The society we aspire to is within reach. It requires our collective will and dedication to the principles of Maqasid. We hold the power to realize this vision, as seen in the transformative efforts of Mahatma Gandhi and the Indian Independence Movement, who, against all odds, shaped a more just and ethical society.

Navigating the Challenges

As we confront these challenges, we should anticipate specific obstacles such as political opposition or cultural resistance. Addressing them requires tailored strategies, clear communication, and a commitment to continuous learning and adaptation.

In conclusion, let us embrace the challenges ahead as opportunities for growth and societal advancement. Our journey towards ethical governance, guided by Maqasid, is not merely a dream but a tangible reality in the making. By rising to the occasion and overcoming obstacles, we can usher in an era of ethical governance. The time for action is now, and the future we envision is in our hands.

Conclusion: The Art of Tactical Transformation

Embracing the journey towards ethical governance underpinned by Maqasid principles is more than a test of resolve; it's an art form that requires tactical intelligence, strategic patience, and an unwavering belief in the transformative potential of these principles.

Tactical Intelligence

Navigating the political terrain calls for astute coalition-building with politicians, parties, and organizations committed to ethical governance. Such alliances, exemplified by the successful coalition in Germany, enhance collective influence and support policy advancement. Equally strategic is engaging the business sector, highlighting the long-term economic benefits of ethical governance, such as a skilled workforce and sustainable growth, much like the UN Global Compact that aligned corporate goals with ethical standards.

Strategic Patience

Patience is indispensable when facing resistance and fostering societal change. Adopting transparency and accountability, as seen in New Zealand's Public Service Act 2020, helps win skeptics over. Establish clear metrics to gauge policy success, and ensure this data is publicly accessible to build credibility and trust. Implementing pilot programs, similar to the Maqasid-based community development projects in Jordan, provides concrete proof of Maqasid's positive societal impact, paving the way for broader implementation.

Unwavering Commitment

The core driving force is a deep commitment to Maqasid's universal values and their capacity to create a fairer, more prosperous society. Let this commitment be evident in every action and communication, serving as an inspiration to others.

Acknowledging Challenges

It's crucial to recognize and address challenges such as political opposition or cultural barriers. Approaching these with adaptive strategies, including digital engagement and international cooperation, ensures a more robust and inclusive process.

Measuring and Celebrating Impact

Beyond metrics, it's important to communicate and celebrate the successes of Maqasid integration, fostering wider support. Publicizing improvements in community well-being or governance efficiency can galvanize public and political backing.

In conclusion, the art of tactical transformation in integrating Maqasid principles into governance is a multifaceted endeavor. It involves forming alliances, demonstrating economic benefits, maintaining transparency, and committing to the ethical transformation journey. Through this approach, challenges can be converted into support, making the vision of a better future a tangible reality. As we navigate this complex yet rewarding path, staying focused, patient, and committed to ethical governance is paramount. Together, we can unlock the full potential of Maqasid and foster a society that thrives on its principles.

13

Maqasid for a New Age

Adapting These Timeless Principles for the 21st Century: The Blueprint for Modern Ethical Governance

The Power of Timelessness: Meeting Modernity with Ancient Wisdom

Introducing Maqasid: Foundations of Ethical Governance

In our rapidly changing world, where technology and societal norms evolve constantly, the ancient principles of Maqasid stand out as pillars of enduring wisdom. Originating from classical Islamic thought, Maqasid encompasses core objectives such as the preservation of life, intellect, faith, lineage, and property, forming a holistic approach to ethical governance and societal well-being.

Adaptation, Not Stagnation: Reimagining Ancient Wisdom

The beauty of Maqasid lies not in rigid adherence to past interpretations but in its dynamic adaptability. It challenges us to breathe new life into these timeless principles, ensuring their relevance in addressing contemporary challenges. Consider the evolving notion of justice, central to Maqasid. In a world grappling with issues like digital privacy, economic disparity, and climate change, this age-old concept guides us toward equitable solutions rooted in fairness and human dignity.

A Modern Context: Specific Challenges and Maqasid

For instance, when tackling climate change, Maqasid's emphasis on the preservation of life and property becomes crucial in formulating policies that protect the environment while ensuring sustainable development. In the realm of digital privacy, the principle of protecting intellect guides us in balancing technological innovation with the safeguarding of personal information.

Personal Narratives: Maqasid in Action

Imagine a city council using Maqasid to frame its urban development plan, prioritizing green spaces and public amenities that enhance community life and well-being, a practical demonstration of these principles at work in modern governance.

The Call to Action: Embracing Timeless Wisdom Today

As we confront the challenges of our era, the call for ethical governance grounded in Maqasid's timeless wisdom grows louder. This is a call to action for policymakers, community leaders, and individuals. We must integrate these principles into our societies' fabric, not as historical relics but as guiding lights leading us towards a more equitable, sustainable, and harmonious future.

A Practical Step Forward

This journey begins with education and awareness. Workshops and policy discussions incorporating Maqasid can enlighten leaders and citizens alike, fostering a collective commitment to these principles. From there, the incorporation of Maqasid into legislative processes and community initiatives can mark the start of a profound transformation in how we govern and live.

21st Century Governance: Forging a Path of Clarity Amidst Complexity

In an era marked by rapid technological advancement and environmental crises, clarity in governance is paramount. Maqasid, an ancient set of principles rooted in Islamic jurisprudence, offers this much-needed clarity. These principles, which prioritize human dignity, justice, and the preservation of the natural world, can be our compass in navigating the complexities of the 21st century.

Technological Ethics: Guiding Innovation with Wisdom

The digital age presents extraordinary opportunities alongside significant ethical dilemmas. The Maqasid principle of intellect (Aql) urges us to use our advancements wisely. For instance, consider the development of AI. Instead of solely focusing on efficiency, incorporating Aql means building AI systems that respect privacy (Nafs) and intellectual property (Mal), mirroring our shared ethical values.

In practice, this approach has seen tech companies in places like Singapore collaborate with ethicists to design AI that respects user privacy while enhancing service quality. Such initiatives demonstrate how Maqasid can direct technological innovation towards societal benefit.

Environmental Sustainability: A Moral Imperative

The principle of protecting the homeland (Watan) within Maqasid aligns perfectly with the urgent need for environmental sustainability. This principle has inspired initiatives like Indonesia's 'Green Fatwa,' a religious decree encouraging Muslims to combat climate change. It illustrates how religious principles can motivate environmental stewardship on a large scale.

A world where nations embrace clean energy, equitable resource distribution, and environmental justice is achievable. By applying the collective principle of Ummah from Maqasid, countries can unite in their efforts against climate change, setting an example of global cooperation and mutual responsibility.

The Call to Embrace Clarity

As we confront the complexities of our times, from AI ethics to environmental degradation, the clarity offered by Maqasid is indispensable. It's a call for leaders and policymakers to adopt these timeless principles, creating governance models that respect both technological progress and our planet's health.

Embracing Maqasid in Policy and Practice

To make this vision a reality, we must begin by incorporating Maqasid into educational curricula, public policy discussions, and corporate governance. Practical workshops and policy frameworks can facilitate this integration, ensuring that the next generation of leaders is equipped with both the knowledge and the ethical compass to navigate the challenges of our time.

In this age of uncertainty and rapid change, let Maqasid guide us, offering a path of clarity and wisdom that leads to a more just, sustainable, and prosperous world for all.

Social Equity: Paving the Way to a Fairer Future

As we navigate an era defined by both remarkable progress and deep-rooted disparities, the quest for social equity transcends aspiration to become an imperative. The ancient principles of Maqasid, originating from Islamic jurisprudence and emphasizing human dignity and justice, provide a timeless framework that can guide us in shaping a more equitable society in our contemporary world.

Universal Healthcare: A Right, Not a Privilege

At the heart of Maqasid lies the principle of life (Nafs), valuing each human existence. This principle, when applied to our modern context, becomes a compelling argument for universal healthcare. It advocates for a system where healthcare is a fundamental right, accessible to all regardless of economic status.

Consider the example of countries like Canada and Scandinavian nations, where universal healthcare systems have been successfully implemented. These models demonstrate how the commitment to the sanctity of life, a core Maqasid principle, can be realized in policy, ensuring that all citizens have the healthcare they need to live fulfilling lives.

Bridging the Wealth Gap: Towards Economic Justice

The Maqasid principle of wealth (Mal) stresses the equitable distribution of resources. In today's world, this translates into addressing income inequality through measures like progressive taxation and social safety nets. These policies aim to reduce the gap between the wealthy and the poor, creating opportunities for all.

Take, for instance, the progressive tax systems in countries like Germany and New Zealand. These systems exemplify how Maqasid's guidance on wealth distribution can be manifested in policy to nurture shared prosperity and social cohesion.

The Path to Social Equity: Overcoming Challenges

Achieving social equity is complex, involving not just policy change but also shifts in societal attitudes and practices. Challenges such as political resistance, budgetary constraints, and differing societal values must be navigated carefully.

A Collective Call to Action

The journey towards social equity, guided by Maqasid, requires concerted efforts from policymakers, community leaders, and citizens. It involves not only formulating equitable policies but also fostering a culture of inclusivity and empathy. Workshops, community dialogues, and educational campaigns can play a pivotal role in this process, spreading awareness and garnering support for equitable practices.

In our quest for a fairer future, let the principles of Maqasid be our guide, steering us towards a world where fairness and justice are not just ideals but realities. By aligning our collective efforts with these age-old principles, we can build a society where every individual has the opportunity to thrive, contributing to a stable, prosperous, and equitable world.

Modern Education: Forging Ethical Leaders of Tomorrow

In this rapidly evolving 21st-century landscape, education extends beyond a mere pathway to knowledge – it becomes a crucible for shaping the future. By integrating the principles of Maqasid into our educational frameworks, we can equip our youth with the values, skills, and ethics vital for the challenges of our times.

Digital Literacy: Embracing Intellectual Responsibility

The Maqasid principle of intellect (Aql) underscores the importance of knowledge and critical thinking. In our digital era, this translates into an educational imperative to offer comprehensive digital literacy programs. For example, initiatives like Finland's national curriculum, which integrates digital literacy and critical thinking from an early age, serve as a model for how we can incorporate Aql into education.

Students today need to be more than just tech-savvy; they must also be discerning digital citizens, capable of navigating the complexities of the online world with wisdom and ethical consideration. By aligning educational practices with Aql, we can prepare students to use technology in ways that enhance our shared humanity.

Ethical Citizenship: Cultivating Compassionate Global Leaders

The principles of community (Ummah) and religion (Din) in Maqasid speak to the heart of social responsibility and ethical conduct. It's essential for modern education to not only cover academic subjects but also to foster ethical citizenship. This can be seen in programs like the International Baccalaureate (IB), which emphasizes global-mindedness and ethical understanding.

Envision a generation of students who are not only academically proficient but also deeply attuned to the needs of their communities and the wider world. By weaving the principles of Ummah and Din into our educational systems, we can nurture leaders who are committed to collective well-being and capable of bridging cultural and societal divides.

Addressing Real-World Challenges

Implementing these ideals is not without its challenges. Schools in resource-limited settings might struggle with integrating digital literacy or global ethics into their curricula. Collaborations between governments, NGOs, and private sectors can play a crucial role in providing the necessary resources and training to bridge these gaps.

MAQASID FOR A NEW AGE

A Concrete Path Forward

To make this vision a reality, educators and policymakers must collaborate to develop curricula that reflect these values. Professional development for teachers, investment in technology infrastructure, and community engagement are key steps in this direction.

The Future of Education: Knowledge Meets Values

Modern education, guided by the timeless wisdom of Maqasid, can become a powerful force for good. It's about more than imparting information; it's about molding ethical, responsible, and compassionate leaders for an interconnected world. By embracing these principles, we pave the way for a generation that not only excels academically but also carries forward the torch of ethical values, lighting the path to a brighter, more equitable future for all.

Global Diplomacy: Shaping a New Paradigm for Global Ethics

In the interconnected world of the 21st century, diplomacy transcends traditional negotiations between nations. It becomes a platform for advocating ethical principles that cross borders. By infusing global diplomacy with the values of Maqasid, we can promote human rights and work towards sustainable development, forging a more just and harmonious world.

Human Rights Advocacy: Beyond Diplomatic Strategy

The Maqasid principle of preserving life (Nafs) emphasizes the sanctity of human life. This ethic, when carried into the international arena, transforms human rights advocacy from a diplomatic strategy into a moral imperative. For instance, the international response to the refugee crisis in recent years, where some nations have taken significant steps to provide asylum and support, reflects the integration of Nafs into diplomatic actions.

Envision a world where nations unite not just in self-interest but in defense of universal human rights. By rooting our diplomatic efforts in Nafs, we strive for a global community where each person's right to life, liberty, and security is respected and protected, free from discrimination and violence.

Championing Sustainable Development Goals: A Unified Ethical Mission

The principles of community welfare (Ummah) and homeland protection (Watan) align closely with the Sustainable Development Goals (SDGs). These goals, encompassing justice, equity, and sustainability, provide a blueprint for a better future. An example of this alignment is seen in global climate agreements, where nations come together to tackle environmental challenges, reflecting both Ummah and Watan principles.

Imagine international collaborations driven not just by strategic interests but by a commitment to the SDGs. Through diplomatic efforts grounded in these Maqasid principles, we can address global challenges like poverty, inequality, and climate change more ethically and effectively.

Navigating Complexities in Diplomatic Ethics

Implementing these principles in the complex world of international relations is not without its challenges. Differences in cultural, political, and economic backgrounds can pose significant barriers. Diplomats must navigate these realities while striving to uphold ethical standards.

Towards an Ethical Diplomatic Framework

To reshape global diplomacy, we must encourage training programs for diplomats that emphasize these ethical principles. International forums and think tanks can play a crucial role in fostering discussions and strategies that align with Maqasid values.

The Future of Diplomacy: Anchored in Ethics

Global diplomacy, guided by Maqasid, can transcend national interests to uphold values benefiting humanity at large. With a moral compass rooted in justice, compassion, and the common good, diplomatic efforts can transform from mere statecraft into a force for positive global change. As we embrace these principles, we contribute to building a world where diplomacy champions the well-being of all people and the planet we share.

Embracing Timeless Wisdom for a Better Tomorrow

In our rapidly evolving world, filled with complex challenges and changes, the principles of Maqasid stand as a beacon of enduring wisdom. Our mission goes beyond merely preserving this ancient knowledge; it's about revitalizing it to resonate with our current global issues. This endeavor isn't just about honoring the past but about forging a better future – and the urgency to do so is now.

Revitalizing Ancient Wisdom for Contemporary Relevance

Maqasid is not a static relic but a dynamic philosophy, vibrant and applicable to our modern context. By adapting its tenets to address 21st-century issues, we reinvigorate its essence. This is not a rejection of our heritage but a celebration of its ongoing relevance. For instance, the principles of Maqasid are being applied in modern urban planning in cities like Kuala Lumpur, where sustainable development and community welfare are prioritized, demonstrating how ancient wisdom can address contemporary urban challenges.

A Blueprint for Ethical Governance in a Complex World

As we confront issues like climate change, technological disruption, and social inequality, Maqasid offers a framework for ethical governance. It's a navigational tool guiding us toward solutions that uphold justice, human dignity, and communal well-being. Ethical governance, as outlined by Maqasid, becomes a tangible goal, not just an idealistic vision.

The Urgency of Now: Taking Action

The challenges of our time are immediate, and the need for ethical guidance is critical. Embracing Maqasid's wisdom propels us not just to reflect on the past but to actively shape the future. This is about creating a world where decisions and actions are influenced by justice, compassion, and ethical considerations. For example, incorporating Maqasid principles in educational reforms or corporate social responsibility initiatives can lead to tangible positive changes in society.

Building a Future Rooted in Ethical Principles

Adapting Maqasid for our era makes us architects of a hopeful future. We lay the groundwork for a world where ethical governance, social justice, and environmental sustainability are not aspirational concepts but lived experiences. This transformation of ancient wisdom into a guiding light for today paves the way for a brighter, more equitable world.

A Call to Universal Action

The future is shaped by our present actions. The universal applicability of Maqasid principles across different cultures and political systems underscores their potential as a force for global positive change. Let's embrace the timelessness of these principles and actively apply them in various spheres of our lives. The time for action is now, and the potential for a better future is in our hands.

Unlocking the Transformative Potential: A Vision for the Future

We stand at a pivotal moment where we can harness transformative potential to shape a better world. Envision a future where governance embodies deep ethical values, where technology enhances the human experience, and where a global community not only dialogues but actively listens and learns. This future is not a distant dream but an urgent necessity, especially in a 21st century that doesn't just welcome but demands the adaptation of Maqasid principles.

Ethical Governance for a Better Society

Ethical governance can move from concept to reality, profoundly impacting lives. Integrating Maqasid into governance has shown promising results in places like Norway, where policies prioritize social welfare and justice, embodying fairness and compassion. By following this model, ethical governance becomes a pragmatic route to improving societal wellbeing.

Technology as a Force for Good

In the realm of technology, innovation must be paired with humanity. Consider how ethical AI initiatives, like those undertaken in Japan, focus on aligning technological advancements with human dignity and ethical considerations. This approach ensures that technological progress benefits society holistically, making it not just an ambition but a necessity in our tech-driven age.

A Global Community that Listens

Amidst global division, the importance of a community that listens – to diverse voices, ancient wisdom, and shared human values – is paramount. The principles of Maqasid can guide international forums, such as the United Nations, fostering genuine dialogue and understanding. This approach is crucial for building a world more unified and empathetic.

An Urgent Call to Adapt and Thrive

As we navigate the complexities of the 21st century, adapting our values to contemporary challenges becomes essential. Maqasid offers a pathway not just to preserve the past but to enrich the present and secure a sustainable future. For instance, incorporating these principles into education can empower future generations with values of ethics, innovation, and unity.

The potential for creating a world where ethics, technological advancement, and global unity thrive together is immense. This isn't just a theoretical model; practical examples around the world show it's achievable. Let's seize this opportunity to transform our global society, embracing Maqasid principles as a cornerstone for positive change. The time for action is now; the future we shape today is the legacy we leave for tomorrow.

Conclusion: From History's Pages to Modern Governance - Timeless Principles for a Timely Future

As we embark on a journey from the annals of history to the forefront of modern governance, we find that the principles of Maqasid are not mere relics of the past but foundational stones for a future filled with promise. These principles, rooted in the preservation of faith, life, intellect, lineage, and property, offer a blueprint for ethical governance and human flourishing.

Making Timeless Principles Timely

In an era marked by unprecedented challenges, from climate change to technological upheaval, applying the timeless principles of Maqasid is not just an option but a moral imperative. These principles serve as a moral compass, guiding us through the complexities of our times with a focus on justice, equity, and compassion.

Shaping the 21st Century with Ethical Foundations

We are not mere spectators of the 21st century; we are its shapers. By integrating Maqasid into our governance models, we can build societies where justice and compassion are not aspirational but actualized. For instance, the incorporation of these principles in policies like New Zealand's wellbeing budget demonstrates how ancient wisdom can inform modern policy-making for societal benefit.

Defining the Future with Conscious Actions

Our actions today paint the canvas of tomorrow. As we face the future, let us define it with principles that uphold our shared humanity. This means transcending divisions and uniting in our common pursuit of a better world. Maqasid's emphasis on communal welfare and human dignity provides a framework for this unification.

The Time to Act is Now

The future is a tapestry woven from our present choices and actions. It beckons us to weave it with threads of ethics, compassion, and wisdom. The time for action is not in a distant future; it is now. We must seize this moment to apply the wisdom of Maqasid, crafting policies and societal structures that reflect these values. For instance, integrating these principles into educational curricula can prepare future generations to continue this ethical legacy.

Let us harness the timeless wisdom of Maqasid and, together, craft a future that surpasses our grandest dreams. The future is not just upon us; we are actively creating it. Now is the time to act, to embody these principles in our governance, our communities, and our daily lives.

The Role of Technology, Globalization, and Cultural Exchange: The Confluence of Maqasid and Modern Realities

Navigating the Confluence of Tradition and Transformation: The Power of Ethical Adaptation

As we navigate a world where technological advancements, global inter-connectedness, and cultural interactions define our era, the integration of Maqasid's timeless wisdom offers us invaluable guidance. This isn't merely a trend but the defining reality of our times, where tradition and transformation converge to chart a path toward a just and compassionate world.

Embracing the Digital Age with Ethical Principles

Technology's reach reshapes our lives in unprecedented ways. Consider the initiative in South Korea to integrate digital literacy into the education system, aligning with the Maqasid principle of intellect (Aql). This approach promotes not only technological proficiency but also ethical usage, ensuring privacy (Nafs) and community welfare (Ummah). In our information-rich world, empowering individuals and communities with ethical digital literacy is a potent way to harness technology's potential.

Globalization: A Platform for Shared Values

Globalization presents a unique opportunity to apply Maqasid on a global scale. International efforts like the Paris Agreement on climate change exemplify how countries can unite under shared principles such as preserving life (Nafs) and promoting community welfare (Ummah). By advocating for policies that transcend national interests, we can collaboratively address worldwide challenges, embracing globalization as a force for positive change.

Fostering Cultural Exchange for Global Harmony

Cultural exchange, when navigated respectfully, enriches our global community. Programs like student exchange initiatives, which bring together young people from diverse backgrounds, align with Maqasid's emphasis on mutual respect and social harmony (Ummah). These interactions deepen understanding and empathy among cultures, moving us beyond fear and prejudice to a more inclusive world.

Ethical Adaptation for a Future of Convergence

The fusion of Maqasid principles with modern realities is not about conflict but about creating a harmonious future. Ethical adaptation in the digital age, globalization, and cultural exchange allows us to share and amplify the values inherent in Maqasid. Whether it's through ethically guided technological innovations, collaborative global initiatives, or respectful cultural exchanges, these are platforms to showcase our shared human values.

Let us seize this opportunity, approaching these transformations with ethical insight, rooted in Maqasid. The digital age, globalization, and cultural exchange offer not just challenges but also the chance to demonstrate how traditional wisdom can inform and enhance our modern world. It's a call to action to not just coexist with these changes but to actively shape them in ways that foster a just, compassionate, and interconnected world.

Technology: The Engine of Ethical Progress

The Digital Revolution: Balancing Progress with Ethics

In the 21st century, technology has evolved from a mere tool to a cornerstone of progress, deeply influencing economies, societies, and governance systems. However, this transformation brings not only opportunities but also significant ethical challenges. By integrating the principles of Maqasid into our digital landscape, we can navigate these complexities, ensuring that technology not only drives efficiency but also upholds profound ethical standards.

Digital Governance: Merging Efficiency with Ethical Responsibility

Envision governance transformed by digital innovation where efficiency is seamlessly intertwined with ethical stewardship. Aligning Maqasid objectives like preserving intellect (Aql) and wealth (Mal) with digital governance models, we can foster a system that ensures transparency, accountability, and equitable resource distribution. Here, every byte of data is used responsibly, prioritizing public welfare over mere commercial gain. This approach, however, necessitates vigilance against issues such as data privacy violations and the digital divide, ensuring technology's benefits reach all segments of society.

Telemedicine and Remote Learning: Ethical Technology Bridging Societal Gaps

Universal access to healthcare and education is a fundamental right. Telemedicine and remote learning stand as prime examples of technology's potential to fulfill this right, aligning with Maqasid's principles of preserving life (Nafs) and fostering intellect (Aql). Telemedicine's reach to remote areas democratizes healthcare access, while remote learning breaks educational barriers. Yet, we must also be cautious of potential inequalities in access and strive to make these technologies universally accessible.

The Ethical Revolution in Technology: A Call for Responsible Innovation

Technology reflects the values embedded within it. Infusing Maqasid's principles into technological development ensures that progress benefits the wider community. We must consciously create digital ecosystems that respect human dignity and fairness. This ethical revolution in technology is not just about advancement but about progress with a purpose, using technology to enhance the human experience and promote communal well-being (Ummah).

Forging a Future with Ethical Technology

The digital revolution offers immense potential for societal advancement. However, this journey must be navigated with ethical acumen, balancing technological optimism with a realistic appraisal of its risks and challenges. By embracing a framework like Maqasid, we can align our technological strides with enduring values, ensuring that our progress enhances life (Nafs) and intellect (Aql) for future generations. Let's commit to this path of ethical technological advancement, shaping a future where technology is not only a tool of progress but also a beacon of ethical transformation.

Globalization with a Heart: A Vision for Collective Responsibility

In our intricately connected world, globalization is more than an economic trend; it's the defining force shaping our societies and economies. But this leads us to a pivotal question: What kind of globalization do we aspire to? A relentless pursuit of profit, or a more humane approach grounded in ethical progress and collective responsibility? The principles of Maqasid offer us not just a vision but a practical roadmap to achieve the latter.

Global Trade Ethics: Profit with Principles

Globalization need not be synonymous with exploitation and environmental disregard. Integrating Maqasid's principle of wealth (Mal) into global trade can revolutionize our commercial ethos. Imagine trade agreements that mandate fair wages, sustainable practices, and corporate social responsibility. Consider the fair trade movement, which champions these values, showing it's possible to balance profit with ethical considerations. This approach redefines success in global commerce, emphasizing shared prosperity and environmental stewardship.

Humanitarian Leadership: Beyond National Interests

In the realm of international relations, the Maqasid principle of community welfare (Ummah) urges nations to look beyond narrow self-interest. This vision challenges countries to lead humanitarian initiatives, like disaster relief and refugee support, reflecting a shift from power politics to humanitarian leadership. We've seen glimpses of this in international coalitions responding to global crises, suggesting a potential shift in geopolitical priorities towards collective well-being and harmony.

Addressing the Challenges of Ethical Globalization

Realizing this vision of ethical globalization is not without its challenges. Economic disparities, political interests, and cultural differences can impede the path to a more equitable global order. Addressing these issues requires open dialogue, innovative policymaking, and a commitment to finding common ground among diverse stakeholders.

Practical Steps Towards Ethical Globalization

To move towards this ethical paradigm, businesses can adopt more transparent and responsible practices, while consumers can support ethically produced goods. Governments can renegotiate trade agreements to include ethical standards and collaborate on global issues with a spirit of cooperation rather than competition.

A Call to Transform Globalization

The principles of Maqasid don't just offer an idealistic vision for globalization; they provide actionable guidelines for a more ethical, compassionate, and interconnected world. This vision of globalization isn't a zero-sum game but a collaborative effort that benefits all. It's a call for global healing and unity, urging us to rethink how we connect, trade, and interact on the world stage. Let's embrace this imperative, weaving the threads of ethics, equity, and sustainability into the fabric of our global community.

Cultural Exchange: A Tapestry of Shared Values

In today's global landscape, where cultures intertwine more closely than ever, the role of cultural exchange is invaluable. It's within this rich tapestry that the principles of Maqasid can significantly contribute to fostering understanding, respect, and unity across diverse nations and peoples.

Interfaith and Intercultural Dialogues: Overcoming Challenges to Build Bridges

Embracing the Maqasid principle of religion (Din), nations can initiate meaningful interfaith and intercultural dialogues. While such dialogues can be challenging due to differences in beliefs and cultural practices, they offer a platform to address these issues, fostering conversations that promote mutual respect and shared ethical goals. For example, initiatives like the Parliament of the World's Religions showcase how diverse religious communities can come together in dialogue, emphasizing common values and fostering mutual understanding.

Imagine a world where religious and cultural leaders regularly convene to explore shared values that transcend their differences. Additionally, cultural exchange programs, such as student exchanges or international art festivals, can be instrumental in promoting understanding and dismantling prejudices, contributing to a more harmonious global coexistence.

The Universal Language of Art and Media: Beyond Entertainment

Art and media, transcending language barriers, possess a unique capacity to educate and unite. Aligning these cultural forms with the Maqasid principle of intellect (Aql) can create content that entertains, enlightens, and unifies. Consider how international film festivals or collaborative global art projects can showcase diverse cultural narratives, promoting tolerance and a global ethos.

Envision a world where media and art are tools for ethical education, where storytellers and artists are ambassadors of compassion, crafting narratives that resonate with shared human experiences across cultures. This approach not only entertains but also builds bridges of understanding and empathy among diverse audiences.

Realizing the Potential of Cultural Exchange

Cultural exchange, through dialogues, art, and media, has the power to connect and enlighten. Yet, realizing this potential requires intentional effort to overcome challenges like cultural appropriation and ensuring respectful representation. Governments, communities, and individuals can play a role by supporting and participating in culturally sensitive exchange programs and media productions.

A Call to Embrace Diversity and Unity

Cultural exchange is a testament to the adaptability and relevance of Maqasid in our evolving global society. It invites us to embrace diversity, celebrate shared values, and build a more united world. Let's actively engage in and promote cultural exchange, weaving a global tapestry where every thread contributes to a richer, more harmonious picture of humanity.

Imagine a World Where Ethics Drive Progress

Close your eyes for a moment and envision a world where technology enhances, rather than undermines, human dignity. Picture a globalized society prioritizing collective welfare over individual gain, and cultural exchange deepening our shared humanity. This vision for the 21st century is ambitious yet attainable, waiting for our collective effort to bring it into reality.

In this world, technology is a beacon of hope, guided by ethical principles. Innovations, from data privacy to AI, are developed with a deep commitment to human dignity. For instance, initiatives like the EU's General Data Protection Regulation (GDPR) demonstrate how technology can be aligned with ethical standards, protecting personal data and privacy. Artificial intelligence is designed not just for efficiency but to enhance human capabilities and ethics.

Globalization in this vision is reimagined as a force for good. Trade agreements, inspired by Maqasid, balance economic goals with ethical imperatives for fair labor practices and environmental sustainability. Nations lead by humanitarian values, exemplified by efforts like the United Nations Sustainable Development Goals (SDGs), focusing on global welfare and cooperative solutions to shared challenges.

Cultural exchange in this world transcends mere pleasantries. It fosters genuine understanding and appreciation of diversity. Programs like UNESCO's Intercultural Dialogues illustrate how different cultures can collaborate, fostering mutual respect and shared goals. Art and media serve as universal languages, educating and uniting people across cultural divides.

This envisioned world acknowledges the challenges in aligning global progress with ethical values. Economic disparities, political interests, and cultural differences pose significant hurdles. However, by embracing a collaborative approach and learning from existing models, we can navigate these challenges.

To turn this vision into reality, we need concrete actions: businesses must embrace sustainable and ethical practices; governments should create policies that prioritize ethical considerations in technology and globalization; individuals can advocate for and participate in cultural exchanges that promote understanding and respect.

This vision isn't a distant dream but a path within our reach. By aligning the goals of Maqasid with the transformative forces of technology, globalization, and cultural exchange, we can create a model of governance fit not just for the future but to shape it. We can make ethical progress the driving force of our era.

So, let's open our eyes to this potential. Let's commit to this path, fueled by the transformative power of Maqasid. The future is not abstract; it is shaped by our actions today. By embracing these principles, we can create a future that is technologically advanced, ethically enlightened, globally interconnected, and culturally harmonious. This vision is waiting for us to bring it to life. Let's make it happen.

Seize the Opportunity: Forging a Future of Ethical Governance

As we navigate the tides of rapid change, we find ourselves at a crucial crossroads. The evolution of our world presents both unprecedented challenges and profound opportunities. Amidst this transformation, there lies a powerful potential to steer the course of modernity towards a future grounded in ethical governance, social justice, and human well-being.

The Digital Age: Harnessing Technology with Ethical Vigilance

The digital age has ushered in a new era of connectivity, transforming the way information is shared and how we interact. However, this digital revolution also brings challenges such as data privacy concerns and the ethical use of Artificial Intelligence. For example, initiatives like the development of ethical AI guidelines by international bodies demonstrate a commitment to ensuring technology serves humanity's best interests. By applying Maqasid principles, we can ensure that technological advancements respect personal privacy and intellectual property, making every digital innovation a step toward ethical progress.

Globalization: Balancing Economic Growth with Ethical Imperatives

Globalization's reach has been profound, yet its impacts are uneven, often exacerbating inequality. By infusing the principle of wealth (Mal) into global trade agreements, we can foster a more equitable approach. This involves crafting policies that demand fair trade practices, responsible environmental stewardship, and humane working conditions. For instance, the fair trade movement illustrates how global commerce can be both profitable and socially responsible. Nations, driven by collective welfare (Ummah), have the opportunity to lead humanitarian efforts, setting a precedent for a more ethical approach to globalization.

Cultural Exchange: Fostering Unity in Diversity

In the realm of cultural exchange, the opportunities for mutual under-standing and respect are immense. Programs like UNESCO's cultural heritage initiatives show how intercultural dialogue can promote peace and understanding. Art and media, when aligned with the principle of intellect (Aql), become more than entertainment; they are vehicles for education and unity, bridging cultural divides and celebrating our shared humanity.

A Call to Action: Embracing Ethical Governance

Let's embrace this pivotal moment to shape a world where ethical principles guide our advancements in technology, our approach to globalization, and our cultural interactions. It requires a collective will to tackle these challenges, from political and economic hurdles to cultural differences. Governments, businesses, and individuals all have roles to play, from implementing ethical policies to supporting sustainable practices and participating in cultural exchanges that enhance understanding.

The future is not a distant concept; it's the result of our actions today. By weaving the principles of Maqasid into the fabric of our modern world, we can create a future that is not just advanced in technology but enlightened in ethics, not just interconnected but responsible, and not just culturally diverse but harmonious. This vision awaits our collective effort to bring it to life. Let's seize this opportunity and embark on this journey together, forging a world where ethics and progress are inseparable and where our shared humanity is our greatest strength.

Conclusion: The Intersection of Old and New—The Gateway to the Future

As we stand at the historical crossroads, where ancient wisdom meets modern innovation, we are presented with a unique opportunity. Technology, globalization, and cultural exchange are not just phenomena of our age; they are tools that, when wielded with ethical intent, can drive profound transformation. The principles of Maqasid, in this context, become crucial for steering these modern forces towards a future that balances progress with ethics.

Harnessing Modern Tools with Ethical Wisdom

In an era of unparalleled connectivity, the rapid flow of information, goods, and ideas transcends traditional boundaries. Technology empowers us to bridge knowledge gaps and improve lives, yet it also poses challenges like data privacy concerns and digital divides. Similarly, while globalization brings us closer, it also raises issues of economic inequality and cultural homogenization. Cultural exchange, though enriching, requires careful navigation to avoid cultural appropriation and ensure respectful representation.

Applying Maqasid to Modern Challenges

The principles of Maqasid guide us in leveraging technology for the common good, shaping globalization into a force for equitable development, and utilizing cultural exchange as a means of mutual understanding and respect. For instance, initiatives like the global push for sustainable development goals demonstrate how globalization can align with ethical principles to address environmental and social issues. In the realm of technology, the growing emphasis on ethical AI reflects a commitment to align innovation with human values.

A Vision for the Future

Imagine a world where technology champions ethical progress, where global trade is characterized by fairness and sustainability, and where cultural exchanges deepen our collective understanding. This future is not just a dream but a tangible path. It calls for concerted efforts from governments, businesses, and individuals. Governments can enact policies that prioritize ethical considerations in technology and trade; businesses can adopt sustainable and fair practices; individuals can advocate for and participate in cultural exchanges that foster understanding and respect.

Walking the Path Together

This intersection of old wisdom and new realities opens a gateway to a future where ethics and progress are intertwined. Our actions today shape this future. By guiding these actions with the principles of Maqasid, we have the power to forge a world that is not just technologically advanced but also ethically enlightened, not just interconnected but responsible, and not just culturally diverse but harmonious. Let's embrace this opportunity and walk this path together, forging a world where our shared humanity is our greatest strength.

14

The Roadmap Ahead

A Step-By-Step Plan for Governments to Initiate This Transformative Journey: The Tactical Guide for Ethical Governance

The Starting Line: The Urgency of Now

As government leaders, policymakers, and administrators, have you ever pondered the transformative power of ethical governance? The call for a governance model rooted in Maqasid principles isn't just a suggestion; it's an imperative that defines our era. The journey towards this goal is not just possible but necessary, and here's a clear, concise plan to guide you.

1. **Commit to Change:** Ethical governance starts with a firm commitment. Imagine a future where our decisions align with Maqasid's principles, serving society's well-being. This vision must drive our actions.

2. **Establish a Task Force:** Form a group of experts, including scholars and policymakers, to integrate Maqasid into governance. For instance, Singapore's approach in forming specialized committees for policy integration can serve as an inspiration.

3. **Assess and Identify:** Examine existing laws and policies. Identify where Maqasid can be immediately applied and where broader reforms are needed. Think of this as laying the groundwork for transformation.

4. **Engage and Educate the Public:** Use workshops, seminars, and campaigns to explain Maqasid's benefits. Public understanding and support are crucial. Consider Norway's public engagement strategies in environmental policies as a model.

5. **Legislative Reforms:** Collaborate with legislative bodies to introduce necessary reforms. Foster open dialogue to build consensus. Look to Germany's legislative approach to ethical governance as a benchmark.

6. **Pilot Programs:** Implement trial initiatives in sectors like education and healthcare to showcase Maqasid's impact. These pilots can be proof of concept, as seen in Canada's healthcare reforms.

7. **Monitor and Evaluate:** Set up systems to track progress and make adjustments based on feedback. This step ensures continuous improvement and adaptation.

8. **Interdepartmental Collaboration:** Work across different government sectors for a unified approach. Maqasid principles should permeate every aspect of governance, similar to the integrated policies in New Zealand.

9. **International Partnerships:** Forge partnerships with nations and organizations committed to ethical governance. Sharing best practices globally can enhance our strategies.

10. **Educational Integration:** Incorporate Maqasid into educational curricula at all levels, preparing future leaders. Finland's education system offers a blueprint for this integration.

11. **Sustainable Development:** Create a strategy for sustainable development aligned with Maqasid. This plan should cover economic growth, environmental care, and social equity.

12. **Institutionalization:** Make Maqasid an intrinsic part of governance. This is not just an addition but the foundation of our governance

ethos.

This guide provides a strategic, engaging, and visually enriched roadmap for initiating the transformative journey towards Maqasid-driven ethical governance. It's an opportunity to lead in creating a world where governance is synonymous with justice, compassion, and integrity. The time for action is now – are you ready to be a part of this pivotal change?

Phase 1: Preliminary Preparations

The journey towards ethical governance rooted in Maqasid principles commences with a crucial first step: Preliminary Preparations. This phase is foundational, laying the groundwork for the transformative changes ahead. Imagine a governance model where justice, compassion, and social well-being are not just ideals, but realities. Here's how we begin:

1. **Executive Directive:** The journey starts with a bold move – an executive directive. This isn't just a statement; it's a commitment. Think of it as a declaration to the nation and beyond, showcasing our resolve to blend ethics with governance. Consider how New Zealand's government issued directives for environmental preservation, setting a global benchmark for ethical governance.

2. **Consultation with Experts:** Merging ancient wisdom with modern governance complexities is no small feat. We need the brightest minds at our table – scholars, academics, professionals well-versed in Maqasid. Their role is crucial, ensuring that our journey is not just a symbolic nod to tradition but a meaningful integration of values into our everyday governance. Their insights will be the beacon guiding us through uncharted waters.

3. **Public Announcement:** Let's be clear and vocal about our intentions. Announcing this plan publicly is more than a formality; it's an invitation to our citizens to join us on this transformative journey. By openly communicating the benefits – a society rooted in justice,

compassion, and well-being – we build trust. Transparency here is a strategic tool, just as it was when Denmark launched its public initiatives for social welfare, creating a model of citizen engagement and trust.

As we embark on this phase, we are not just setting a tone; we are laying down the very bricks of ethical governance. Embrace this phase with the awareness that it's the groundwork for a future where governance is a reflection of our highest ethical aspirations.

Phase 2: Research & Assessment

As we embark on Phase 2 of our journey towards ethical governance rooted in Maqasid principles, our focus shifts to a critical stage: research and assessment. This phase is pivotal, bridging our foundational understanding with practical application. Let's delve into the key steps:

1. **Policy Audit:** Begin with a comprehensive audit of existing laws, policies, and government programs. This isn't just about identifying areas for the immediate application of Maqasid principles; it's about transforming our entire legal and policy framework. Consider how Sweden conducted a thorough review of its environmental policies, leading to significant sustainable development. Similarly, your goal should be to ensure that every policy aligns with ethical principles, moving beyond symbolism to substantive change.

2. **Stakeholder Analysis:** Remember, effective governance involves various stakeholders. Identify key players – from government departments to community organizations and citizens. For each, understand their roles, interests, and potential contributions. Engage in open dialogue, just like Canada did when reforming its healthcare system, involving stakeholders at all levels to ensure the system met everyone's needs. This inclusive approach is not just about gathering diverse perspectives; it's about building a governance model that truly

reflects Maqasid values and meets community needs.

3. **Resource Allocation:** Now, let's talk resources. To turn our vision into reality, we must secure the necessary financial, human, and technological resources. This means allocating budgets, training personnel in ethical governance, and providing the technology for transparent administration. Think of South Korea's investment in digital governance, significantly enhancing transparency and accountability. Your resource allocation shows your commitment to this transformative journey and prepares you to tackle implementation challenges head-on.

In Phase 2, the convergence of research and assessment informs the practical steps needed to weave Maqasid principles into the fabric of governance. It's about critically examining policies, engaging with all stakeholders, and committing resources to ensure success. With meticulous groundwork, you'll navigate the path towards ethical governance more effectively and confidently. Are you ready to take these crucial steps?

Phase 3: Initial Implementation

As you embark on Phase 3 of your journey towards implementing Maqasid in governance, it's time to bring these principles into real-world practice. This phase is crucial, transitioning from theory to action. Let's explore how to proceed effectively:

1. **Pilot Programs:** Begin by launching small-scale pilot programs in diverse sectors like education, healthcare, and law enforcement. Think of these as your test beds for Maqasid principles. For instance, look at how Finland's education system reform started as small-scale initiatives and later revolutionized national education policies. Your programs should embody Maqasid values, acting as tangible examples of ethical governance. By starting on a smaller scale, you can manage, monitor, and evaluate their impact more effectively, setting the stage

for broader implementation.

2. **Feedback Mechanism:** Establishing a robust feedback system is crucial. Involve both experts in Maqasid principles and community members. You could employ surveys, focus groups, and public forums, much like how Singapore actively gathers public feedback on policy initiatives. This dual approach of expert and public input will provide a holistic view, ensuring that the programs not only adhere to Maqasid principles but also resonate with the community's needs and expectations. Remember, transparency in this process is key to building trust and credibility.

3. **Review and Adapt:** After a period, say 6 to 12 months, thoroughly review these pilot programs. Assess their alignment with Maqasid principles and effectiveness in societal impact. Take inspiration from how South Korea regularly reviews its digital governance initiatives, adapting them based on public feedback and technological advancements. This phase of review and adaptation is vital for fine-tuning your approach. Be flexible and ready to make necessary adjustments, ensuring that your governance model is both dynamic and responsive.

Phase 3 is more than just the beginning of practical application; it's where you start to see the fruits of your efforts in ethical governance. By meticulously designing pilot programs, setting up effective feedback channels, and committing to continuous improvement, you are not just proving the viability of Maqasid-driven governance but also fostering a culture of accountability and responsiveness. This phase is foundational, paving the way for a broader, more impactful implementation in the future.

Phase 4: Expansion & Enhancement

As you progress to Phase 4 in your journey towards Maqasid-based ethical governance, it's time to build on your early successes and broaden your impact. This phase is about turning pilot triumphs into widespread change.

Here's a roadmap for effective expansion and enhancement:

1. **Scale Up Initiatives:** Building on the proven success of your pilot programs, identify those most effective and begin scaling them up. Look at how they can be extended to larger areas or to more diverse sections of the population. Consider Denmark's approach in expanding their renewable energy programs, which started small and now serve as a national model. As you scale, also explore ways to integrate additional Maqasid principles, ensuring your governance model continuously evolves to meet community needs.

2. **Interdepartmental Coordination:** Establish a central coordination body or task force to ensure a cohesive approach across all government departments. This step is vital for avoiding fragmented efforts and for ensuring that Maqasid principles are uniformly applied. Borrow strategies from how Singapore manages its interdepartmental efforts in urban planning, ensuring that different departments work harmoniously towards common goals.

3. **Engage in Public Reporting and Feedback:** Maintain a strong commitment to transparency by regularly updating the public on your initiatives' progress and challenges. Use reports, public meetings, and digital platforms to communicate updates. Additionally, actively seek and incorporate public feedback into further governance improvements, much like how New Zealand engages its citizens in policy development. This open communication builds trust and fosters a collaborative spirit between the government and its citizens.

In this phase, you're not just expanding initiatives but also setting a precedent for ethical governance. By methodically scaling up successful programs, ensuring cohesive interdepartmental collaboration, and committing to transparent and participatory public reporting, you showcase the tangible benefits of Maqasid principles in governance. This phase is critical in solidifying your role as a pioneer in ethical governance and lays the groundwork for its sustained adoption.

Phase 5: Institutionalization & Global Leadership

As you enter Phase 5, you reach the zenith of your journey towards ethical governance based on Maqasid, setting the stage for your government to emerge as a beacon of global leadership. Here's how to solidify these principles within your governance framework and inspire the world:

1. **Policy Codification:** Begin by weaving Maqasid principles into the very fabric of your legal and regulatory systems. This means formally codifying these principles into laws, regulations, and policy documents, akin to how Norway integrated environmental sustainability into its national legislation. This transformation ensures that Maqasid principles become an enduring part of your governance, safeguarding their continuity beyond current leadership and administrative cycles.

2. **International Promotion:** Step onto the global stage as an advocate of the Maqasid model. Share your journey, challenges, and triumphs with international peers. Emulate the approach of countries like Sweden, which has effectively promoted its innovative policies on sustainable development worldwide. Engage in dialogues, form partnerships for collaborative projects, and participate in international forums to showcase the effectiveness of your governance model in addressing global challenges. Your active promotion can inspire other nations and contribute to a global shift towards more ethical governance practices.

3. **Long-term Strategy Development:** Draft a comprehensive, multi-year strategy detailing your vision, objectives, and action plans for embedding Maqasid principles in governance. This strategy should not only be a blueprint but also a living document, adaptable to the evolving landscape of governance. Look at how Japan periodically revises its economic strategies in response to changing global trends. This approach demonstrates a commitment to the sustainability and relevance of Maqasid principles in the long run.

Phase 5 is more than just the final step; it's a legacy-building phase where Maqasid principles become deeply embedded in your governance structure, and your nation rises as a leader in ethical governance on the world stage. Your commitment in this phase extends the impact of your efforts beyond national boundaries, contributing to a more ethical, just, and sustainable world. This is a legacy that will earn admiration and respect for generations to come.

Conclusion: The Ascent Begins

As we draw this discussion to a close, let's take a moment to reflect on the significance of the journey ahead. This is not just an exercise in theoretical governance but a pragmatic, actionable blueprint for societal transformation. As a leader, you are equipped with a comprehensive plan, expert knowledge, and a moral imperative. But have you considered the lasting impact your decisions will make? What legacy do you aspire to create in the realm of ethical governance?

Remember, your role transcends being a mere caretaker of the present. You are an architect of the future. Your actions have the power to not just reshape policies but to redirect the course of civilization itself. The responsibility is immense, the stakes immeasurably high. Every moment of inaction is a missed opportunity to foster a more equitable, compassionate, and ethical society.

Recall the steps we've outlined: from preliminary preparations to the institutionalization and global leadership. Each phase is a building block towards this monumental goal. However, challenges will arise. You may face resistance, resource constraints, or moments of doubt. In these times, remember the importance of steadfastness and the power of collective effort.

Let this era be remembered as a pivotal point when governance regained its moral compass, steering us towards a fairer, more ethical world. The future is not just calling; it is beckoning us to act swiftly and decisively. The journey begins now. Together, let's forge a future where ethical leadership is not an aspiration but a realized, tangible reality. The time for change is here, and you are at the helm, ready to lead the ascent.

V

Conclusion

"Heaven Is Under The Feet Of Governments" outlines an urgent call for transformative governance based on Maqasid principles, emphasizing justice, ethics, and inclusivity. It highlights the necessity of overcoming inertia and resistance to foster a society that values individual dignity, community empowerment, and sustainable progress. This book Calls for strong leadership to adopt tech and social progress for ethical governance, pushing beyond dreams to create a fair, caring society.

15

The Genesis of a New Dawn

A Clarion Call for Change: The Final, Unyielding Invitation to Transform Governance Forever

The Sound of Urgency: A Symphony Awaiting Its Conductor

In the relentless din of our modern world, a distinct sound rises — a resounding call for change that sweeps across every nation. More than a whisper of hope, this is a commanding demand for a new era in governance. An era that reshapes not only the fate of nations but the daily lives of their citizens.

Listen. In the bustling streets of cities, you hear it. It's in the voices of people clamoring for fairness, for equity. It echoes in the serene landscapes of the countryside, where communities seek harmony. This call transcends borders and cultures, finding an echo in the hearts of millions. They dream of a world where governance benefits all, not just a privileged few.

But what does this call truly entail? At its core, it advocates for a governance model inspired by the principles of Maqasid — an approach prioritizing ethics, justice, and inclusivity. For those unfamiliar, Maqasid is a philosophy that emphasizes the well-being of all, ensuring that governance supports the fundamental needs and rights of every individual.

The time for change is now. This urgent symphony beckons us to lead, to become the conductors of this transformative movement. Together, we can forge a future brighter and more just for everyone. It starts with a step, a voice, a decision. The moment to act is here. Let's embrace it.

The Stakes: Nothing Less Than Our Shared Humanity

We stand at a pivotal juncture where our actions transcend administrative tweaks and legislative reforms. We're embarking on a journey to uplift the human spirit itself. Our goal is far-reaching: to reinvigorate the individual's soul, empower whole communities, and invigorate society's very core.

Answering this call for change is not just about adopting a new governance model. It's about aligning with the collective hopes of our people. By joining this cause, you become part of a worldwide movement striving for equity, compassion, and justice. This quest transcends individual ambitions—it's a collective endeavor, a testament to our enduring commitment to human progress.

The ripple effects of our actions will echo beyond our lifetimes, etching a legacy in history's fabric. This journey is more than governance; it's about the heritage we leave—a legacy of ethical leadership, enduring compassion, and respect for every individual's dignity. The stakes are immense, yet so are the potential rewards. We must seize this moment, for the betterment of our shared humanity and for the generations who will inherit our legacy.

The Resistance: The Inertia We Must Overcome

The path to transformation is never without its hurdles. We will encounter challenges, obstacles, and resistance. The comfort of the status quo, fortified by self-interest and tradition, often opposes change. However, encountering resistance should not dishearten us; it should affirm the vital importance of our mission.

Our quest to usher in change will inevitably disrupt established norms.

When we face pushback, it's a testament to the depth of the transformation we seek. The resistance we meet is not a barrier but a benchmark of our journey's significance.

In confronting these challenges, we should remain steadfast. History is replete with examples where monumental change was achieved in the face of fierce opposition. Think of the environmental movement, the push for technological innovation, or the struggle for Indigenous people rights. Each of these, like the civil rights and women's suffrage movements, faced significant resistance yet triumphed.

It's vital to discern which resistance is a sign of meaningful change and which might offer valid criticism worth considering. This discernment is crucial in navigating our path forward.

So, when resistance emerges, view it as a confirmation of your path. It's an opportunity to strengthen our resolve and refine our strategies. Remember, real change is often born out of the crucible of opposition. Embrace resistance not just as a challenge to overcome, but as a crucial part of the journey towards progress.

The Opportunity: An Unprecedented Moment in Time

We are at a unique juncture in history, one brimming with promise for those bold enough to embrace it. Our world is transforming rapidly, with technologies like artificial intelligence and renewable energy revolutionizing how we live and work. Social movements are reshaping our understanding of justice and equality at an extraordinary pace.

This moment is ripe with possibilities, aching for leaders who are ready to harness these changes. The opportunity before us is immense, inviting us to forge a path of transformative impact.

However, such moments are fleeting. History teaches us that opportunities can vanish as quickly as they arise, leaving behind a trail of 'what-ifs.' Time waits for no one, and today's possibilities may soon become tomorrow's lost chances.

The call to action is not a distant dream but an immediate imperative.

The conditions are ideal, the need is urgent, and you, as a leader, are poised to drive this change. With the tools of technology, insights from social progress, and a commitment to ethical leadership, you can spearhead a new era of governance—one that prioritizes the well-being of all.

The world seeks leaders who can transform lofty aspirations into tangible actions, who can actualize the promise of this era. The kind of leaders who recognize the potential of smart cities for sustainable living, who understand the power of digital platforms for inclusive governance, who champion social equity alongside economic growth.

This is your time. The stage is set for you to make a lasting impact. Will you step up to shape a future that is more equitable, just, and sustainable? The moment is now, and the world eagerly anticipates your leadership.

The Action: From Words to World-Changing Deeds

The time for decisive action has arrived. Hearing the clarion call is not enough; we must respond with unwavering commitment. We've explored the principles and potential within these pages; now, we must bring them to life through transformative deeds.

We have a detailed blueprint for ethical and compassionate governance—a guide towards a more equitable future. But remember, a plan is only as good as its execution. It's time to mobilize your teams, galvanize your communities, and embark on this transformative journey. Yes, there will be obstacles, but the path to meaningful change is seldom easy.

Be the initiator of change. Apply the principles of Maqasid in every aspect of governance, from policy-making to everyday decisions. Strive to be a leader who not only dreams of a better world but actively shapes it.

Remember, every significant transformation began with an individual's action—a person who believed in change and stepped forward. You have the potential to be that change-maker in your community, your organization, or your field.

Lead by example and foster collaboration. Urge others to join you in this mission. If you're in education, incorporate ethical values into your curriculum. In business, prioritize sustainable and equitable practices. In governance, ensure policies reflect the principles of justice and compassion.

As we unite in this endeavor, we can make the vision of a just and ethical society a tangible reality. The world needs leaders who challenge the status quo and courageously craft a more equitable and compassionate future. The time to act is now, with the world as our witness.

The Call Resounds: Will You Answer?

A call echoes through our times, a call demanding attention, commitment, and dedication. It's not just any call, but a clarion call to action—a call to shape our future, transform governance, and elevate humanity.

We stand at a crossroads where the future beckons us to honor life, cherish cultural richness, and uphold virtues that define us. Imagine a future where governance transcends bureaucracy and becomes a moral mission, guided by the principles of Maqasid, championing justice, compassion, and ethics.

This call is not a faint whisper but a resonant plea that speaks to the aspirations of many, urging policies that uplift and recognize every individual's dignity. The question now is, will you be the steward of this transformative vision? Will you be the architect of a future revered by generations to come?

The world needs leaders who defy the status quo, who challenge norms, and recognize the immediacy of change. Your response to this call can shape nations' destinies and countless lives.

Let your answer be a resounding "yes." Show your commitment through actions that embody ethical governance. Envision a future where governance equates to compassion, justice, and ethical excellence—a future where policies serve and uplift.

The call is an ensemble, an invitation to join a chorus of change-makers. It's an opportunity to align with like-minded individuals in ushering a new era of governance—one that prioritizes everyone's well-being.

Now is the time to open the door to this future. By answering this call, you join a transformative wave in governance. Let's redefine its narrative, anchoring it in ethics and justice. The stage is set, the call is clear—will you answer?

The Utopian Dream: Not Fantasy but a Feasible Reality

Often, the idea of a utopia—a society where harmony, equity, and prosperity are universal—has been dismissed as a flight of fancy. But what if this vision is not as far-fetched as it seems? What if, instead of a distant mirage, it is a tangible reality that we can actually achieve? It's time to break free from the skepticism that limits our imagination and embrace the potential of a society guided by the enduring principles of Maqasid.

Imagine a world where governance is more than bureaucracy and regulations. Picture a society where policies enhance lives, nurture spirits, and foster purpose. This isn't mere wishful thinking; it's a viable vision, grounded in practicality.

The principles of Maqasid offer a roadmap to such a society—a blueprint that balances the spiritual and material aspects of human existence. This approach values compassion, justice, and ethical excellence, providing a solid foundation for a just and prosperous society.

Consider, for example, communities where participatory governance models have enhanced civic engagement and wellbeing. These instances, though smaller in scale, echo the elements of our envisioned utopia, demonstrating its practicality.

Utopias need not be confined to fantasy. They can be achievable realities. The path to this almost mythical society is intricately woven into the principles of Maqasid. By casting aside doubt, we can embark on a journey toward a utopia that is not just a dream but an actionable and attainable vision.

The Principles: A Guiding Beacon for All of Humanity

Let's pause to appreciate the brilliance of Maqasid, a beacon illuminating our path to a better world. Its principles transcend religious and cultural boundaries, resonating with the core needs and aspirations of all humans.

Take, for example, the principle of preserving life. This universal truth cherishes every life as precious. Imagine governance models that embed this principle deeply within societal structures, prioritizing life in every policy and action.

Consider also the empowerment of intellect. A society where education is accessible to all, not as a privilege but as a fundamental right, aligns with this principle. It's a vision that Maqasid makes attainable, not just idealistic.

The principles of nurturing families and fostering community highlight our interconnectedness. Envision governance that bolsters family structures and builds inclusive communities. This goes beyond mere policy—it's a blueprint for societal harmony.

And the principle of protecting property, advocating for fair economic practices, transcends cultural differences. It's a call for ethical economics, where policies are driven by justice, not greed.

These principles are inclusive and uplifting, belonging to everyone. Adopting them in governance is not optional but a moral imperative. We must now take steps to integrate these truths into the fabric of our societies. This isn't just a lofty vision; it's a practical call to action. Let's work to make these principles a living reality, for the betterment of all.

The Harmony of Spirit and Matter: Where Heaven Meets Earth

In our world, where the pursuit of material wealth often overshadows spiritual fulfillment, Maqasid shines as a model of balance and hope. It advocates for governance that transcends mere economic growth, technological prowess, or military strength, emphasizing instead the soul of a nation — its values, ethics, and spiritual health.

Maqasid prompts a paradigm shift towards a society where technological progress serves both economic and ethical purposes. Picture innovations aimed at social betterment, with their benefits equitably shared. This vision transcends mere prosperity; it champions prosperity with purpose.

Under this model, economic prosperity is redefined. Wealth is not hoarded by a few but shared more equitably, ensuring communal upliftment. Economic drivers are reoriented from pure profit to principles of justice and ethical conduct, fostering shared and sustainable growth.

Cultural richness, too, is reimagined. It becomes a means to enhance spiritual richness, with diversity strengthening understanding and unity. Cultural heritage is celebrated not just for its own sake but for its ability to enrich the human spirit.

In essence, Maqasid beckons us towards a balanced utopia where material and spiritual pursuits are harmoniously integrated. It envisions a world where progress is matched with responsibility and where our defining values are elevated. While this may seem like a lofty goal, practical steps can be taken towards this vision. Implementing policies that prioritize social welfare alongside economic growth, fostering inclusive education that values ethical understanding, and encouraging cultural practices that promote community cohesion are tangible ways to begin this journey.

This isn't merely a dream; it's a practical, achievable reality waiting for us to embrace it, step by step.

The Ripple Effect: From Individuals to the Global Community

The transformative power of Maqasid extends well beyond individual lives, with the potential to reshape communities, nations, and ultimately, the global community. This ripple effect begins with positive change in individuals and cascades upward, profoundly impacting governance and society.

At its heart, Maqasid prioritizes individual well-being, understanding that thriving individuals bolster families, which are the bedrock of strong communities. These communities, in turn, are the pillars of prosperous nations. But this model goes beyond economic growth—it fosters societies where people feel valued and empowered.

The impact of Maqasid doesn't halt at national borders. Its principles echo universal values, resonating across cultures and addressing fundamental human needs. Nations adopting these principles can become exemplars of hope and progress, especially in our interconnected world.

In an era marked by divisive politics and global challenges like climate change, Maqasid offers more than a path—it paves a highway to a more harmonious future. It's a vision that transcends cultural and religious divides, uniting humanity in collective prosperity and ethical progress.

Envision a world where nations collaborate, not compete, focusing on uplifting humanity. Imagine a global community committed to every individual's well-being, where ethical governance is standard. This vision isn't merely a dream—it's a tangible goal.

For instance, consider the potential impact of adopting Maqasid principles in environmental policies, leading to collaborative international efforts in combating climate change. Or envision its application in business, promoting fair trade and ethical labor practices.

To contribute to this ripple effect, individuals can start in their communities, advocating for policies and practices aligned with Maqasid principles. Organizations can adopt ethical frameworks in their operations, and governments can prioritize these values in policy-making.

This vision is an invitation to unite in our diversity, celebrating human richness while striving for a brighter future for all. Let's embrace this opportunity and actively participate in shaping this new trajectory for our world.

The Final Call to Action: The Time for a Utopian Vision Is Now

Now is the time to transcend doubts and embrace the possibility of a better world. The blueprint for a utopian society, guided by the principles of Maqasid, is not a distant dream but an achievable reality. The urgency for such transformation is unprecedented, and the call to action extends to everyone, especially those in governance and influence.

The challenges of social injustice, economic disparity, environmental crises, and political division are formidable but not insurmountable. Maqasid provides a path forward, envisioning a society where every individual's well-being is paramount, and prosperity is equitably shared.

This vision is not fantasy but a practical possibility. It imagines governance as a force for good, leaders who prioritize welfare, and communities that thrive in harmony. This transcends borders and beliefs, uniting us in a mission for humanity's betterment.

The time for this vision is now. It calls for bold action, a challenge to conventional thinking, and a commitment to a future where the human spirit reaches new heights. We must advocate for these principles and implement them in our governance, communities, and lives, becoming catalysts for the change our world needs.

Consider the potential within each of us for compassion, innovation, and cooperation. We can envision a world where dignity is universal, opportunities are accessible, and justice prevails. This future is realizable through our collective efforts.

To bring this vision to life, we must challenge the status quo, confront injustices, and champion policies that prioritize citizen welfare. We must foster a culture of empathy and inclusivity, where diversity is celebrated, and community bonds are strengthened.

The journey ahead is challenging but rewarding, transcending political and cultural divides, uniting us in purpose. Let's not just dream of a utopian society; let's build it with bold steps to transform our world.

This moment is a blank canvas, and we are the artists. History will showcase our masterpiece—a testament to our endeavor and quest for a better world. The future beckons, and the power to shape it is in our hands. Let us unite and paint a portrait of a utopian society that stands as a beacon of hope. Our legacy will be defined not by our words but by the depth of our actions. Together, we can and must create a masterpiece—a symbol of human potential and our enduring pursuit of a better world.

VI

Appendices

These appendices serve as practical guides, providing tools, strategies, and resources to implement the principles discussed in this book. They offer step-by-step approaches for leaders and individuals alike, aiming to translate the theoretical framework of ethical governance into actionable plans. You'll find checklists, case studies, and templates designed to support your journey towards transformative governance, ensuring practical application of these ideals in real-world contexts.

16

Appendix A: Glossary of Terms

Navigating Maqasid: A Comprehensive Guide to Islamic Jurisprudence for Modern Governance

Understanding the language of Maqasid is crucial in grasping its transformative potential in governance. This glossary provides not just definitions but insights into the profound principles of Islamic jurisprudence and their implications for modern governance. As you explore these terms, you're taking a vital step towards comprehending a governance model that serves the higher purposes of humanity.

1. **Maqasid** (*mah-kah-sid*): The overarching objectives of Islamic law (Shari'a), focusing on the preservation of religion, life, intellect, progeny, and property. For example, in environmental governance, Maqasid emphasizes the protection of life and progeny by advocating sustainable practices.

2. **Fiqh** (*feekh*): This is Islamic jurisprudence, the human understanding, and interpretation of Shari'a law. The four major Sunni schools – Hanafi, Maliki, Shafi'i, and Hanbali – each represent different Fiqh methodologies.

3. **Ijtihad** *(ij-tee-had)*: This refers to independent legal reasoning in Islamic law, particularly for cases not explicitly covered by the Quran or Hadith. A notable instance of Ijtihad was the reform of family laws in some modern Muslim countries, reflecting changing societal norms.

4. **Fatwa** *(fat-wah)*: A legal opinion or decree issued by a qualified Islamic scholar. Fatwas play a crucial role in addressing contemporary issues within the Islamic legal framework.

5. **Quran** *(koo-rahn)*: The holy book of Islam, believed to be the literal word of God as revealed to the Prophet Muhammad. It is the primary source of Shari'a law.

6. **Hadith** *(ha-deeth)*: These are recorded sayings and actions of the Prophet Muhammad, serving as a source of guidance in Islamic jurisprudence alongside the Quran.

7. **Shari'a Law**: The moral and legal code of Islam, derived from the Quran and Hadith, covering all aspects of life. Shari'a influences legal systems in various Muslim-majority countries to varying degrees.

8. **Ijma** *(ij-mah)*: The consensus of Islamic scholars on a particular issue, considered a strong source of law in Islamic jurisprudence.

9. **Qiyas** *(kee-yas)*: Analogy or reasoning used to derive rulings for situations not explicitly addressed in the Quran or Hadith. Qiyas is often applied in modern legal issues where direct religious texts are not explicit.

10. **Istislah** *(is-tis-lah)*: Public interest or welfare, a principle used in legal rulings that serve the greater good, even if they don't have a direct basis in the Quran or Hadith.

11. **Istis'hab** *(is-tis-hab)*: This principle involves the presumption of continuity of previous rulings in the absence of specific evidence to the contrary. It ensures stability and consistency in Islamic jurisprudence.

12. **Maslaha** *(mas-la-ha)*: This principle focuses on seeking the common good or public interest in legal and ethical decision-making. It is often used to justify contemporary legal reforms that align with the

overarching objectives of Shari'a.

13. **Haram** *(ha-ram)*: Meaning 'prohibited' or 'forbidden' in Islam. This term is essential in understanding Islamic ethics and law, delineating what is morally and legally unacceptable.

14. **Halal** *(ha-lal)*: The opposite of Haram, this term means 'permissible' or 'lawful' in Islam. It encompasses everything from dietary laws to business practices.

15. **Ijtihad al-Maslahah** *(ij-tee-had al-mas-la-ha)*: This is the use of independent reasoning and judgment to achieve the greater good and fulfill the objectives of Shari'a. It reflects the dynamic nature of Islamic jurisprudence, adapting to changing contexts.

16. **Fiqh al-Maqasid** *(feekh al-mah-kah-sid)*: Jurisprudence that focuses on the objectives and higher purposes of Shari'a, often used in reformative contexts to align traditional laws with contemporary needs.

17. **Fiqh al-Ijtihad** *(feekh al-ij-tee-had)*: This term refers to jurisprudence based on independent legal reasoning, emphasizing the evolving nature of Islamic legal thought.

18. **Ruh al-Quds** *(rooh al-koods)*: The Holy Spirit, believed to be a source of divine guidance in Islam. It is often mentioned in spiritual and mystical contexts.

19. **Tawhid** *(taw-heed)*: The Islamic concept of the oneness of God, forming the foundation of Islamic belief and practice.

20. **Sunni Islam**: The largest branch of Islam, following the Sunnah (traditions) of the Prophet Muhammad. It includes various schools of thought and jurisprudence, like Hanafi and Shafi'i.

21. **Shi'a Islam**: A branch of Islam that emphasizes the leadership of the Imams as spiritual and temporal authorities. It has its own unique practices and interpretations of Islamic law.

22. **Sufism**: Often described as the mystical and spiritual dimension of Islam, Sufism focuses on the inner, personal experience of God and encompasses a variety of practices and beliefs.

23. **Caliphate** *(ka-lif-ate)*: The Islamic system of governance, historically

led by a caliph as the political and spiritual leader of the Muslim community. The concept plays a significant role in Islamic history and political thought.

24. **Ummah** *(um-mah)*: The global Muslim community, transcending national and ethnic boundaries. It represents the concept of a united Islamic identity.

25. **Ismaili** *(is-mai-li)*: A branch of Shi'a Islam, known for its distinct theological and spiritual tradition, and its emphasis on esoteric interpretation of Islam.

26. **Madhhab** *(mad-hab)*: A school of Islamic jurisprudence. The four major Sunni schools – Hanafi, Maliki, Shafi'i, and Hanbali – represent different approaches to Islamic law.

27. **Ibn Rushd** *(ibn rooshd)*: Also known as Averroes in the West, this prominent Islamic philosopher and jurist contributed significantly to Islamic and Western philosophy.

28. **Ibn Sina** *(ibn see-na)*: Known as Avicenna in the West, a renowned Persian polymath whose works in philosophy and medicine were influential in both the Islamic world and Europe.

29. **Sulh al-Hudaybiyyah** *(sul al-hu-day-bee-yah)*: The Treaty of Hudaybiyyah, a pivotal peace agreement between the Prophet Muhammad and the Quraysh tribe. It's often cited as an example of strategic peacemaking in Islamic history.

30. **Ahl al-Bayt** *(ahl al-bayt)*: Referring to the family and descendants of the Prophet Muhammad, this group is especially revered in Shi'a Islam and holds a significant place in Islamic tradition.

Understanding these terms is not just an academic exercise; it's an essential step in embracing a nuanced view of Islamic principles and their application in contemporary governance and ethical decision-making. With this enhanced glossary as your guide, you are better equipped to embark on a transformative journey towards a governance model that aligns with the profound values of humanity.

Through this expanded glossary, you gain a deeper appreciation of the intricacies of Islamic jurisprudence and its application in contemporary governance. Each term opens a window into the rich tapestry of Islamic legal, ethical, and spiritual thought, offering a comprehensive understanding that goes beyond the surface.

17

Appendix B: Case Studies

Maqasid in Motion: Case Studies of Ethical Governance from the Rashidun to the Modern World

In the Pursuit of Transformative Governance Guided by the Principles of Maqasid

These selected case studies, spanning historical and contemporary contexts, offer not just a glimpse into the application of Maqasid principles but also provide a comprehensive understanding of their impact and challenges. They serve as beacons of hope and practical illustrations, demonstrating the versatility and transformative potential inherent in this model.

1. **The Rashidun Caliphs (632-661 CE):** This era represents an exemplary historical model of governance, where leaders like Abu Bakr and Umar ibn al-Khattab emphasized justice, compassion, and the common good. Specific policies, such as Umar's innovative welfare and social security systems, highlight the application of Maqasid in governance, focusing on the preservation of life and property, and the pursuit of justice.

2. **Andalusian Caliphate (711-1492 CE)**: The Golden Age of Islamic Spain, known for its harmonious coexistence of diverse religious communities, is a testament to the Maqasid principle of cultural diversity and intellectual flourishing. This period's advancements in science and philosophy illustrate the compatibility of Maqasid with fostering a vibrant, multicultural society.

3. **Contemporary Malaysia**: Malaysia's integration of Maqasid principles into its governance framework offers insight into modern-day application. Initiatives like the Maqasid-based development index and ethical finance regulations highlight how these ancient principles are adapted to contemporary policy-making, aiming at social justice and equitable development.

4. **Islamic Finance Industry**: This industry is a living example of how Maqasid principles can reshape economic systems. Principles such as risk-sharing and ethical investment demonstrate the alignment of Islamic finance with Maqasid, aiming to achieve financial stability and ethical wealth distribution. However, challenges such as ensuring global regulatory standards and broader acceptance highlight the complexities of implementing these principles in a modern economic context.

5. **Humanitarian Relief Organizations**: In predominantly Muslim countries, various organizations embody Maqasid principles in their missions. They prioritize the preservation of life and social justice, but their effectiveness often depends on navigating complex political and social landscapes, highlighting both the impact and challenges of applying these principles in humanitarian efforts.

6. **Islamic Social Finance Initiatives**: Programs like Zakat and Waqf are rooted in Maqasid. They significantly impact poverty alleviation and community development, exemplifying how these ancient principles can address modern social issues. The success of these programs often lies in their local adaptability and community involvement, showcasing a practical application of Maqasid in social welfare.

These case studies not only demonstrate the practicality of Maqasid principles but also reveal the challenges and complexities involved in their application. From the early Islamic governance models to contemporary policy-making, these examples show a consistent thread of striving for justice, compassion, and well-being, despite varying contexts and challenges. They provide compelling evidence of the feasibility and transformative potential of Maqasid in governance. As we delve into these cases, they inspire us to embrace these principles in our pursuit of ethical governance and reaffirm our belief in humanity's capacity to create a more just and equitable world.

18

Appendix C: Model Policies and Legislation

Blueprints for Justice: Maqasid Principles as Pillars of Progressive Policy-Making

Realizing Transformative Governance Through Maqasid Principles

In our relentless pursuit of ethical and effective governance, Appendix C presents a series of model policies and legislative frameworks that embody the profound principles of Maqasid. These templates are more than theoretical constructs; they represent actionable blueprints designed to empower policymakers in shaping a more just and equitable society.

1. **Preservation of Life Act**: This act enshrines the fundamental principle of safeguarding human life. It integrates comprehensive healthcare, robust safety regulations, and disaster management protocols. For example, similar policies in countries like Denmark have shown remarkable success in public health outcomes, demonstrating

the practicality of such a framework.

2. **Economic Equity and Welfare Act**: Anchored in the Maqasid ideal of economic justice, this policy addresses fair wealth distribution, ethical finance, and social safety nets. It aims to ensure that economic growth benefits all societal layers. However, the challenge lies in balancing economic growth with equitable wealth distribution, a dilemma faced and creatively managed in economies like Sweden.

3. **Family and Community Empowerment Bill**: This legislation focuses on strengthening families and communities, integral components of a cohesive society. It encompasses education, affordable housing, and community initiatives. The success of similar programs in Canada highlights how these policies can be adapted to different cultural contexts.

4. **Justice and Fairness Reform**: This template advocates for a justice system marked by transparency, accountability, and equitable legal aid. While aiming for impartial justice, it acknowledges the challenges, such as the need for judicial independence and combating systemic biases, drawing lessons from reforms in countries like Germany.

5. **Ethical Governance and Transparency Act**: Setting standards for governmental transparency and anti-corruption, this act is fundamental to good governance. The implementation of similar measures in New Zealand, known for its transparency, offers valuable insights into the feasibility of such reforms.

6. **Environmental Stewardship Act**: This policy underscores the necessity of sustainable development and environmental conservation. The integration of green technologies, as seen in the policies of countries like Germany, serves as a practical model for environmental stewardship.

7. **Cultural and Intellectual Flourishing Initiative**: Promoting the arts, culture, and intellectual development, this policy supports educational institutions and innovation. South Korea's investment in cultural industries exemplifies how such policies can enhance a nation's intellectual and cultural wealth.

8. **Humanitarian Aid and International Cooperation Pact**: This legislation guides international humanitarian efforts and cooperation, reflecting global solidarity. The effectiveness of such initiatives, as seen through international bodies like the United Nations, under-scores the importance of global collaboration.

These model policies and legislative drafts, while idealistic, are grounded in real-world applications and challenges. They draw inspiration from global best practices, demonstrating that the principles of Maqasid are not only aspirational but also achievable. As policymakers and leaders consider these templates, they are encouraged to engage in active dialogues, tailor these policies to their unique contexts, and take decisive steps toward redefining governance as a mission for the greater good. Through these concerted efforts, we move closer to realizing a society where justice, compassion, and well-being are not just ideals, but lived realities.

19

Appendix D: Tools for Public Engagement

Cultivating Collaborative Governance: Integrating Maqasid Principles with Public Engagement

Fostering Inclusive Governance through Maqasid Principles

As we embark on this transformative journey towards governance aligned with Maqasid principles, public engagement emerges as a pivotal element. It goes beyond being a mere choice; it's a crucial imperative for building a society grounded in justice, compassion, and collective well-being. Active public involvement is key to making this process of change inclusive and effective.

Here are some refined tools and best practices for effective public engagement, along with examples and strategies to address potential challenges:

1. **Town Hall Meetings**: These meetings offer direct engagement opportunities. Successful examples include the town halls of Norway,

which have utilized technology for wider reach while maintaining face-to-face interactions for those less digitally inclined. Ensuring these meetings are accessible and inclusive is critical for diverse community participation.

2. **Surveys and Feedback Loops**: Regular surveys, like those used effectively in Singapore, gauge public opinion and create responsive feedback loops. Demonstrating how citizen feedback leads to tangible policy changes can enhance engagement and investment in the governance process.

3. **Educational Workshops and Seminars**: These events, much like the civic education programs in South Korea, educate the public about Maqasid principles and their role in governance. They help foster a deeper understanding and empower citizens to actively participate in governance.

4. **Community Outreach Programs**: Tailoring outreach to local needs, as seen in Canada's community-centric initiatives, helps involve people in impactful projects. This approach builds trust and illustrates the practical benefits of inclusive governance.

5. **Social Media and Online Platforms**: Platforms like those used in Estonia's digital governance can engage broader demographics, particularly the youth. Creating diverse content and hosting interactive online discussions can extend reach and foster a more engaged citizenry.

6. **Collaborative Decision-Making**: Involving the public in policy development, similar to the citizen assemblies in Ireland, can foster collective responsibility and ownership. Citizen advisory boards and committees provide valuable input and enhance policy relevance.

7. **Transparency and Accountability**: Following models like New Zealand's open government initiatives, sharing detailed information about policy-making processes and enabling robust accountability mechanisms are essential for maintaining public trust and engagement.

8. **Cultural Sensitivity and Inclusivity**: Recognizing diversity within

the community is crucial. Strategies should be culturally sensitive and inclusive, ensuring all voices are heard, especially those from marginalized or underrepresented groups.

9. **Empowering Local Leaders**: Identifying and supporting local influencers, akin to community leadership programs in the United States, can significantly boost public engagement efforts. Their endorsement can enhance the credibility and reach of governance initiatives.

10. **Continuous Communication**: Consistent and open communication, as demonstrated in the United Kingdom's public information services, keeps the public informed about progress and upcoming changes. Regular updates enhance trust and maintain long-term engagement.

Public engagement is a continuous and evolving process. It's about nurturing a collaborative relationship between the government and its citizens. By incorporating these enhanced strategies, we ensure that policies and reforms resonate with the community, fostering a sense of shared responsibility. As we integrate these tools with empathy, compassion, and a genuine desire to honor both the spirit and matter of human existence, we move closer to realizing a governance model that benefits every member of society.

20

Appendix E: Recommended Reading and Resources

Navigating Governance with Maqasid: A Resource Guide for Ethical Policymaking

Enhancing Your Journey with Maqasid Principles in Governance

Your dedication to understanding and applying Maqasid principles in governance is admirable. To aid in this endeavor, we have compiled a curated list of diverse and insightful resources. These selections offer a range of perspectives and focus on both the theoretical understanding and practical application of Maqasid principles.

Books

1. **"Maqasid Al-Shariah Made Simple"** by Mohammad Hashim Kamali - This book provides a concise and accessible introduction to Maqasid principles, ideal for beginners.

2. **"Maqasid Al-Shariah as Philosophy of Islamic Law"** by Jasser Auda - Auda delves into the ethical foundations and philosophical underpinnings of Islamic law, offering deep insights into Maqasid.

3. **"Reforming Modernity: Ethics and the New Human in the Philosophy of Abdurrahman Taha"** by Wael Hallaq - This critical analysis examines the works of Abdurrahman Taha, a key figure in contemporary Maqasid scholarship.

4. **"Islamic Law and International Human Rights Law"** by Anver M. Emon - A compelling exploration of the intersections and tensions between Islamic law, including Maqasid, and international human rights norms.

5. **"The Closing of the Muslim Mind: How Intellectual Suicide Created the Modern Islamist Crisis"** by Robert R. Reilly - This book provides historical and philosophical perspectives on the evolution of Islamic thought and governance.

Academic Journals

1. **Journal of Islamic Ethics** - Focuses on contemporary applications of Islamic ethics, including articles and papers on Maqasid. **Link to Journal**

2. **Journal of Maqasid Studies** - Dedicated to exploring both theory and practical aspects of Maqasid. **Link to Journal**

Online Resources

1. **Maqasid Institute** - A comprehensive platform offering articles, courses, and seminars on Maqasid. **Visit Website**

2. **Stanford Encyclopedia of Philosophy - Islamic Ethics** - Offers in-depth articles on various aspects of Islamic ethics, including Maqasid. **Read Articles**

3. **Academia.edu** - A hub for academic papers and articles on Maqasid and Islamic governance. **Explore Research**

4. **YouTube Lectures and Talks** - Search for lectures by reputable scholars like Jasser Auda and Tariq Ramadan for diverse perspectives on Maqasid.

Interactive and Community Resources

- Participate in online forums and discussion groups focused on Maqasid.
- Enroll in online courses and webinars that offer practical insights into implementing Maqasid in governance.

Your journey in implementing Maqasid principles is a continuous learning process. These resources will provide a strong foundation and ongoing support as you strive to create a just and ethical society. Stay dedicated, engage with diverse perspectives, and let your actions reflect the transformative power of Maqasid. Together, we can build a future guided by these profound values.

21

Appendix F: Assessment Metrics and KPIs

Maqasid Metrics: Assessing the Impact of Islamic Jurisprudential Principles on Governance

Evaluating Progress in Implementing Maqasid Principles

To effectively implement Maqasid principles in governance, it is crucial to have a robust framework for assessment. The following metrics and Key Performance Indicators (KPIs) are designed to gauge progress, success, and areas for improvement. They are adaptable to various cultural and societal contexts and provide a comprehensive view of governance impact.

Human Dignity and Well-being

- *Quality of Life Index*: Assess improvements in overall quality of life, with benchmarks set according to regional and global standards.
- *Life Expectancy*: Monitor increases in life expectancy, reflecting advancements in healthcare and living conditions.

Social Equity

- *Income Inequality Index*: Evaluate the reduction in income disparity, setting targets in line with national goals and international averages.
- *Access to Education*: Track the increase in equitable access to quality education, ensuring inclusivity across all socio-economic groups.

Ethical Governance

- *Transparency Index*: Assess the openness and accountability of government institutions, with goals based on global best practices.
- *Corruption Perceptions Index*: Measure reductions in corruption, aiming for continuous improvement towards international benchmarks.

Environmental Stewardship

- *Carbon Footprint Reduction*: Monitor reductions in greenhouse gas emissions, setting targets in alignment with international climate agreements.
- *Natural Resource Conservation*: Evaluate efforts in sustainable management and conservation of natural resources.

Community Cohesion

- *Social Cohesion Index*: Assess improvements in social harmony and integration, taking into account local cultural dynamics.
- *Community Engagement*: Monitor participation rates in civic activities and community development projects.

Economic Prosperity

- *GDP Growth*: Analyze economic growth, ensuring it is inclusive and equitably distributed.
- *Unemployment Rate*: Evaluate reductions in unemployment and under-employment, aiming for benchmarks reflective of economic health.

Family and Individual Well-being

- *Family Stability Index*: Measure the strength and stability of family units, considering local cultural definitions of family.
- *Mental Health and Well-being*: Assess improvements in mental health support and outcomes.

Legal and Judicial Reforms

- *Access to Justice Index*: Evaluate the accessibility, fairness, and efficiency of the legal system.
- *Rule of Law*: Monitor adherence to legal principles, ensuring justice is upheld uniformly.

Cultural and Heritage Preservation

- *Cultural Heritage Index*: Assess efforts in protecting and promoting cultural heritage.
- *Promotion of Arts and Culture*: Measure investment and engagement in arts and cultural activities.

Public Trust and Satisfaction

- *Public Opinion Surveys*: Conduct regular surveys to gauge public trust and satisfaction, adapting questions to be culturally sensitive.
- *Citizen Feedback Mechanisms*: Monitor the effectiveness of feedback

channels in influencing policy and governance.

Implementing and Interpreting Metrics

- Data should be collected and analyzed regularly, with frequency depending on the specific metric.
- Challenges such as data availability, cultural nuances in interpretation, and ensuring consistent measurement standards need consideration.
- Case studies, such as the implementation of similar metrics in countries like Singapore and Denmark, can provide practical insights and inspiration.

These metrics and KPIs are not just indicators but tools for continuous improvement in governance. By regularly assessing these areas, Maqasid principles are transformed from ideals into actionable strategies, leading to tangible benefits for society. Remember, the journey towards ethical and just governance is ongoing, and these metrics are crucial in steering and refining this path.

22

Appendix G: Frequently Asked Questions (FAQs)

Maqasid in Modernity: Unpacking the Role of Islamic Jurisprudential Principles in Contemporary Governance

This section aims to clarify common queries about Maqasid, offering insights into its relevance and application in modern governance. We hope these answers provide a deeper understanding and encourage further exploration of Maqasid principles.

Q1: What is Maqasid, and why is it relevant to modern governance?

A1: Maqasid refers to the higher objectives of Islamic law (Shari'a), focusing on principles like justice, equality, human dignity, and social welfare. In modern governance, it offers a holistic ethical framework that resonates with universal aspirations of a just and compassionate society.

Q2: Is Maqasid only applicable to Muslim-majority countries?

A2: No, Maqasid's universal principles are relevant beyond Muslim-majority contexts. They emphasize values like ethical governance and social justice, making them applicable and beneficial to diverse societies globally.

Q3: Does implementing Maqasid mean imposing Islamic law (Shari'a) on a society?

A3: Implementing Maqasid doesn't mean imposing Shari'a law. It's about embracing ethical and universal principles from Maqasid to foster a just and equitable society, respecting the rule of law, human rights, and diversity.

Q4: How does Maqasid address the separation of religion and state?

A4: Maqasid supports ethical governance and justice, irrespective of government forms. It respects the separation of religion and state, focusing on ethical principles compatible with various governance models.

Q5: What are some practical steps to implement Maqasid principles in governance?

A5: To implement Maqasid:

- Educate policymakers and the public about its principles.
- Draft policies aligned with Maqasid values like justice and social welfare.
- Ensure transparency and accountability in governance.
- Prioritize initiatives in social welfare and environmental sustainability.
- Promote public participation in governance.

Q6: Are there real-world examples of countries successfully implementing Maqasid principles?

A6: Yes, countries like Malaysia and Jordan have incorporated Maqasid elements into their governance systems. These examples show how Maqasid can inform policies and legal frameworks, leading to more equitable societies.

Q7: Does Maqasid conflict with democracy and individual freedoms?

A7: Maqasid aligns with democratic values and individual freedoms. It emphasizes justice and human dignity, integral to democratic systems. Balancing these within ethical governance frameworks is key.

Q8: How can I contribute to the implementation of Maqasid principles in my community?

A8: To contribute:

- Educate yourself and others about Maqasid.
- Engage in dialogues advocating for ethical governance.
- Participate in community initiatives upholding justice and social welfare.
- Hold policymakers accountable for ethical decisions.

Q9: What challenges might arise in implementing Maqasid, and how can they be addressed?

A9: Challenges include cultural misconceptions and resistance to change. Addressing these requires open dialogue, education, and demonstrating the universal benefits of Maqasid principles.

Q10: Where can I find more resources on Maqasid?

A10: Explore academic journals, books on Islamic jurisprudence, and online platforms focusing on Maqasid. Engaging in forums and discussions with scholars and practitioners can also be enlightening.

Q11: Are there different interpretations of Maqasid within Islamic thought?

A11: Yes, various schools of thought offer different perspectives on Maqasid. These interpretations enrich the understanding and application of Maqasid principles in diverse contexts.

Understanding Maqasid and its applicability to modern governance is a journey of continuous learning. By exploring these principles and their diverse interpretations, you can advocate for and contribute to ethical governance in your community and beyond.

23

Appendix H: Contact Information and Networks

Maqasid Synergy: Building Networks for Ethical Governance and Social Justice

Embracing ethical governance through Maqasid principles requires a strong network of informed individuals, organizations, and scholars. This guide provides you with essential contacts and resources to enhance your journey.

1. International Organizations

- *Organization of Islamic Cooperation (OIC)*: Engage with OIC's initiatives in ethical governance. Contact: **www.oic-oci.org**
- *United Nations (UN)*: Connect with UN programs on ethics, human rights, and sustainability. Explore: https://unsdg.un.org/2030-agenda/universal-values/human-rights-based-approach

2. Think Tanks and Research Institutions

- *Center for the Study of Islam and Democracy (CSID)*: Research on Islam and democracy. Visit: https://www.csid-online.org/
- *Brookings Institution*: Expert analysis on governance. Explore: https://www.brookings.edu/programs/governance-studies/

3. Academic Scholars

- *Dr. Jasser Auda*: Influential Maqasid scholar. Follow: @JasserAuda on Twitter
- *Dr. Tariq Ramadan*: Renowned Islamic thinker. Explore: https://tariqramadan.com/

4. Local and National Organizations

- Seek out NGOs focused on ethical governance and social justice. Check local directories and community boards for contacts.

5. Online Communities

- *LinkedIn*: Join groups dedicated to ethical governance and Maqasid. Search: 'Maqasid Governance' groups
- *Twitter*: Stay updated with hashtags like #Maqasid and #EthicalGovernance.

6. Academic Journals and Publications

- *The American Journal of Islamic Social Sciences*: Access: **www.ajiss.org**
- *International Journal of Islamic Thought*: Visit: https://www.ukm.my/ijit/

7. Seminars and Conferences

- Attend events on ethical governance. Websites like **www.eventbrite .com** often list relevant seminars and webinars.

8. Local Initiatives

- Engage with community projects promoting ethical governance. Volunteering can open doors to collaborative opportunities.

9. Networking Tips

- Approach contacts respectfully, with clear intentions.
- Ask specific questions and seek collaboration opportunities.
- Attend networking events and engage in discussions.

10. Inclusivity and Accessibility

- Check if resources are available in multiple languages or accessible formats.

11. Post-Contact Actions

- Propose collaborative projects or research initiatives.
- Stay in touch through regular updates or joint activities.

These contacts and networks are your gateway to a deeper understanding and impactful application of Maqasid principles in governance. Actively engage with these resources, build meaningful relationships, and leverage this network to drive transformative change. Together, we can foster a just, ethical, and prosperous society.

24

Additional Resources for Further Study

Maqasid and Governance: A Continuous Learning Guide for Ethical Policymaking

As this book concludes, remember that your journey into the depths of Maqasid and ethical governance is just beginning. This is not merely the final chapter but an open door to an expansive realm of knowledge, rich with opportunities for deeper understanding and broadened perspectives.

To quench your ever-growing thirst for wisdom, consider these additional resources as invaluable companions on your voyage:

1. **Diverse Reading Materials**: Delve into books like "Islam and Good Governance" by M. A. Muqtedar Khan and "The Spirit of Islamic Law" by Bernard G. Weiss for deeper insights. Explore articles in academic journals such as the "Journal of Islamic Studies" for contemporary analysis.

2. **Engaging with Experts**: Connect with thought leaders and scholars in the field. Attend lectures by figures like Dr. Tariq Ramadan, or participate in discussions and workshops led by experts in Islamic governance.

3. **Interactive Learning Platforms**: Join online courses offered by universities or platforms like Coursera and EdX, which often feature modules on Islamic ethics and governance. Engage in forums and discussion groups to exchange ideas and viewpoints.

4. **Critical Engagement**: As you explore these resources, practice critical thinking. Question assumptions, engage in debates, and contribute your perspectives to online discussions.

5. **Practical Application**: Seek opportunities to apply your learning in real-world scenarios. This could involve participating in community governance projects, volunteering with NGOs, or starting a study group to discuss and implement ethical governance practices in your community.

6. **Podcasts and Multimedia**: For diverse learning experiences, listen to podcasts on ethical governance and watch relevant documentaries that offer practical insights into the implementation of Maqasid principles.

Remember, these resources are like a well of knowledge - deep, refreshing, and endlessly enriching. They are not just for reading or passive consumption; they are tools for active engagement and practical application. By diving into these texts, engaging with thought leaders, and applying what you learn, you become a vital participant in the ongoing discourse shaping the future of governance.

This quest for a governance model that uplifts humanity is a collective endeavor. You are now equipped with a rich arsenal of tools and resources to navigate these waters confidently. Embrace this journey with an open mind and a commitment to action. Let these resources guide you, inspire you, and empower you to contribute meaningfully to a more just and ethical world.

Your journey towards a new era of governance is illuminated by this wealth of knowledge. These resources are your guiding light, leading you towards a future where the principles of Maqasid are not just concepts but living realities in the governance of societies. The path is set, and the journey awaits.

Books

Embarking on the transformative journey of governance through the lens of Maqasid principles, these books are not just collections of pages; they are gateways to wisdom. Let's explore each one, with added insights into their accessibility and context:

1. **"General Philosophy of Islamic Law (Maqāsid) and Laws of Priorities (Fiqh al-Awlawiyāt)" by Dr. Sulaiman Lebbe Rifai**: This foundational work is key to understanding Maqasid's ethical underpinnings. Dr. Rifai, a renowned scholar in Islamic jurisprudence, offers a comprehensive guide that is accessible for readers at various levels of expertise. *Available in digital and print formats, this book is suited for those beginning their exploration of Islamic law and governance.*

2. **"God and the EU: Faith in the European Project (Routledge Studies in Religion and Politics)" by Jonathan Chaplin and Gary Wilton**: While focusing on European governance and virtue ethics, this book offers valuable insights that resonate with Maqasid principles. It discusses how moral values influence governance, an aspect crucial to understanding Maqasid. *Critically acclaimed for its interdisciplinary approach, it's suitable for readers interested in comparative governance studies.*

3. **"The Boundaries of Meaning and the Formation of Law" by Sharron Gu**: Central to Maqasid is the pursuit of justice, which Gu's book explores deeply. This book navigates the practical implementation of justice in Islamic law, aligning with Maqasid principles. *Geared towards readers with some background in law or Islamic studies, it's available in various libraries and online stores.*

Complementary Materials

- Explore articles in the *Journal of Islamic Studies* for academic discussions related to these topics.
- Watch the documentary series *"The Caliph"* for historical context on Islamic governance.
- Attend webinars or lectures by these authors, often available through academic institutions or online platforms like *Coursera*.

Critical Perspectives

- Engage with book reviews and academic critiques of these works to gain a well-rounded understanding.
- Participate in discussion forums or study groups to debate and analyze the themes presented in these books.

These books and resources are your compass in the vast ocean of governance and Maqasid principles. Each offers unique perspectives, equipping you with the knowledge to advocate for a governance model rooted in ethics, justice, and social welfare. Dive into these texts with an open mind, engage critically with their content, and let the wisdom they offer fuel your journey towards transformative governance.

Academic Journals

In your quest to deepen your understanding of Maqasid and ethical governance, these academic journals are not just collections of scholarly articles; they are reservoirs of insightful and transformative knowledge. Let's delve into each one, highlighting their accessibility and key articles:

1. **Journal of Islamic Ethics (Published by Brill)**: A vital resource for exploring ethics in the Islamic world, this journal covers a range of topics from governance to policy. Notably, its open-access articles,

like "Ethical Dimensions of Islamic Governance" provide crucial insights into Maqasid principles. Access at Brill's website

2. **Islamic Law and Society**: This journal offers scholarly articles intersecting with Maqasid principles. It's a hub of rigorous research, including articles like "Contemporary Applications of Maqasid in Governance." Note that access may require a subscription or academic library membership.

3. **Harvard Journal of Law and Public Policy**: Broadening your perspective, this journal examines the intersection of law, ethics, and governance. While not exclusively focused on Islamic principles, articles such as "Ethical Policy Making in a Global Context" offer valuable insights. Available through most academic libraries

Additional Resources

- **Interdisciplinary Journals**: Expand your reading to include journals in political science and international relations, which often discuss ethical governance in a broader context.
- **Digital Platforms**: Utilize platforms like JSTOR or Google Scholar for accessing a wide array of related articles and journals.

Engaging with the Material

- **Critical Reading**: Approach these journals critically, comparing methodologies and perspectives to gain a well-rounded understanding.
- **Notable Articles**: Start with landmark articles or special issues that have been widely cited or discussed within the academic community.

These academic journals are more than repositories of information; they are dynamic spaces that challenge and refine your understanding of governance and ethics. By engaging with these resources, you will not only gain academic insights but also practical knowledge that can inform your advocacy for Maqasid principles. Each article read and critically analyzed is a step forward in your journey to transform governance for the better.

Online Courses

In today's world, where learning is more accessible than ever, online courses stand out as pivotal tools for personal and professional development. Particularly for those exploring Maqasid and its impact on governance, these courses offer invaluable insights and expertise.

"Islamic Legal Philosophy"

- Offered on platforms like Coursera and EdX, this course shines a light on the ethical foundations of Islamic law, with a special focus on Maqasid.
- It's designed to provide a comprehensive understanding of the moral underpinnings guiding governance decisions.
- Accessibility features include subtitles in multiple languages, making it suitable for a diverse global audience.
- Interactive elements like discussion forums and live Q&A sessions enrich the learning experience.

"Ethics and Governance"

- Available on platforms such as Udemy and FutureLearn, this course provides a broad context for understanding ethical governance, complementing Maqasid-focused studies.
- It covers essential principles of ethics in public administration and policy-making.
- The course is structured to cater to learners at various levels, from beginners to advanced professionals.
- Features testimonials from past students who have successfully applied these principles in their careers.

Expanding Your Learning Horizon

- Consider courses on related topics like public policy analysis, international relations, and leadership ethics available on these platforms.
- Check for flexible learning options, including self-paced modules and part-time schedules, to accommodate different lifestyles and commitments.

Why Enroll

- These courses are not just for academic enrichment; they're stepping stones to practical application in governance.
- Each module equips you with knowledge and tools to be an effective advocate for ethical governance.
- The courses often include real-life case studies, providing a tangible connection between theoretical principles and their application in the real world.

Take the Step: Embrace these online courses as opportunities to expand your understanding and amplify your impact in the realm of governance. They are more than educational endeavors; they are pathways to becoming a catalyst for change. Enroll in these courses, engage with their teachings, and harness the knowledge to be an advocate for a governance model that uplifts and serves humanity.

Your journey towards a just, compassionate, and ethical world begins with this decision to learn. Are you ready to take that step?

Websites and Blogs

The digital world is ripe with resources that can enrich your understanding of Maqasid and ethical governance. Here are some standout websites and blogs that offer valuable insights:

Cordoba Academy's Maqasid Studies Center

- Visit **Cordoba Academy** for a comprehensive exploration of Maqasid.
- This platform provides articles, seminars, and lectures, creating a rich learning environment.
- It's a vibrant community where you can interact with scholars and peers through discussion forums and live webinars.
- Regularly updated, the content here offers fresh perspectives and practical applications of Maqasid principles.

Islamicity Indices

- Explore **Islamicity Indices** to understand how different countries implement Islamic principles, including governance and ethics.
- The site offers an innovative approach to comparing governance models, complete with detailed analyses and rankings.
- This resource is updated annually, ensuring current and relevant insights into global governance trends.

Maqasid Journal Online

- **Maqasid Journal** offers a range of scholarly articles and blog posts on various aspects of Maqasid and governance.
- It features diverse viewpoints, fostering a comprehensive understanding of the subject.

Ethics and Governance Blog

- For broader ethical governance discussions, visit the **Ethics and Governance Blog**.
- This blog is updated frequently with posts from various contributors, offering a multifaceted look at ethical governance issues.

Engagement and Interaction

- These platforms are more than just informational; they encourage active participation. Engage in the comment sections, contribute to discussions, and even consider writing guest posts or articles.

Starting Points

- On Cordoba Academy, begin with their introductory seminars on Maqasid.
- On Islamicity Indices, start with their latest country rankings and accompanying analysis.

These websites and blogs open doors to a dynamic and interactive world of learning about Maqasid and ethical governance. They are not just repositories of information but active communities where ideas are exchanged, and knowledge is constantly evolving. Dive into these resources, engage with their content, and join the global conversation on transforming governance. Your journey of discovery and impact in the realm of Maqasid is just a click away.

Documentaries and Webinars

As you delve into the realm of ethical governance through Maqasid, a variety of documentaries and webinars can offer you deeper, more immersive insights. These resources combine visual storytelling and expert discussions to enhance your understanding:

"Ethical Governance: An Islamic Perspective" (Webinar Series)

- Available on the **Islamic Governance YouTube Channel**, this series of webinars features contemporary discussions by leading scholars in the field.

- Topics range from the application of Maqasid in modern governance to ethical policy-making.
- These sessions often include interactive Q&A segments, allowing for engagement with experts.
- Accessibility features like subtitles in multiple languages make it approachable for a global audience.

"The Golden Age of Islam" (Documentary)

- Produced by History Channel, this documentary offers a historical exploration of Islamic governance during its golden era, highlighting the application of Maqasid.
- It can be accessed through platforms like **History Vault** or educational libraries.
- The documentary helps draw parallels between historical and contemporary governance, providing valuable lessons for today's context.

Expanding Your Learning

- Explore other documentaries like "Islamic Art: Mirror of the Invisible World" for cultural context related to Maqasid principles.
- Engage with webinar series such as "Ethics in Public Life" offered on platforms like **Coursera**.

Additional Formats

- Listen to podcasts like "Islamic Thought and Governance" for insights on the go.
- Attend online talks and panel discussions hosted by universities and think tanks on related subjects.

Engaging Critically

- As you watch these documentaries and attend webinars, practice critical thinking by questioning assumptions and considering multiple perspectives.
- Participate in online discussions or forums to debate and analyze the concepts presented.

Documentaries and webinars are not just passive sources of information; they are gateways to a dynamic and interactive world of learning. They provide a rich, multi-dimensional approach to understanding Maqasid and its application in governance. As you embark on your advocacy journey, these visual and auditory resources will not only inform but also inspire you to contribute to a more ethical and just society.

Conferences and Seminars

Elevate your understanding of ethical governance and Maqasid by participating in a variety of conferences and seminars. These platforms offer not just learning opportunities but also the chance to connect with a community of experts and enthusiasts. Let's explore how you can make the most of these events:

International Conference on Islamic Governance

- This annual event, held in cities like Doha or Kuala Lumpur, brings together leading academics and practitioners.
- Look out for its next iteration on platforms such as **Eventbrite** or **ConferencesAlerts.com**, where you can find details and registration options.
- To maximize your experience, plan which sessions to attend in advance and don't hesitate to engage in discussions and networking opportunities.

Maqasid Workshops

- Hosted by various Islamic institutions and think tanks, these workshops delve into Maqasid's principles and applications.
- Local universities or Islamic study centers often announce such workshops, so keep an eye on their websites or newsletters.
- These workshops are ideal for hands-on learning and practical insights, often featuring case studies and group discussions.

Expanding Your Horizons

- Seek out regional seminars or online webinars if traveling to international conferences is not feasible.
- Diverse events like the "Ethical Governance Forum" or "Maqasid Online Webinar Series" can also be valuable.

Tips for Active Participation

- Network effectively by preparing a brief introduction about your interest in Maqasid and ethical governance.
- Engage speakers and attendees with thoughtful questions and share your perspectives.
- Collect contact information for future collaborations or discussions.

Post-Event Engagement

- Follow up with new contacts through LinkedIn or email.
- Apply learned concepts in your community or workplace and share your experiences with peers or through a blog.

Conferences and seminars are dynamic avenues for broadening your knowledge and joining a larger conversation on Maqasid and ethical governance. They provide platforms for deep engagement, critical learning, and fostering collaborations. As you attend these events, remember they are just the beginning. The real impact lies in how you apply and share this knowledge, contributing to the advancement of ethical governance. Embrace these opportunities, and let them guide you on your journey to becoming an informed and active participant in this transformative field.

25

Templates and Checklists for Policy Makers

Empowering Policy Makers: Streamline Your Transformative Initiatives with Practical Templates and Checklists

As you navigate the complex world of policy-making with an aim to integrate Maqasid principles, having practical tools at your disposal is crucial. This toolkit, comprising detailed templates and comprehensive checklists, is designed to bridge the gap between visionary ideals and tangible policies. Let's explore how these resources can empower your policymaking process:

Templates for Policy Development

- These templates provide structured frameworks for formulating policies across various sectors such as social justice, economic equity, and ethical governance.
- For example, a template for social justice policy might include sections on objective setting, stakeholder analysis, and impact assessment.

- Available for download from platforms like Resources for Public Policymakers, these templates can be customized to suit local contexts and specific policy objectives.

Checklists for Evaluation

- Use these checklists as a guide to evaluate the effectiveness and ethical alignment of your policies.
- They include items for tracking progress, identifying improvement areas, and ensuring adherence to Maqasid principles.
- These checklists can also serve as a tool for engaging with stakeholders, gathering feedback, and iterating on policy design.

Alignment with Maqasid Principles

- Each tool is grounded in the core values of justice, compassion, and ethical governance, ensuring that your policies reflect these tenets.
- They encourage consideration of the broader societal impact and promote policies that are inclusive and equitable.

Accessibility and Inclusivity

- These tools emphasize policies that cater to all segments of society, especially focusing on the needs of vulnerable groups.
- They guide you to craft policies that are not only effective but also accessible and inclusive.

Ethical Oversight and Implementation Challenges

- The toolkit includes guidance on maintaining integrity and ethical oversight throughout the policymaking process.
- It also addresses common implementation challenges, offering strategies to overcome obstacles and ensure successful policy rollouts.

This toolkit is more than just a collection of templates and checklists; it's a comprehensive guide for enacting meaningful change through policy. These tools not only assist in crafting policies aligned with Maqasid principles but also ensure that your strategies are practical, effective, and inclusive. They empower you to navigate the intricacies of policymaking with confidence and conviction, helping you leave a lasting legacy of ethical governance. Embrace these resources, and let them guide you towards creating policies that resonate with the spirit of Maqasid, uplift societies, and foster a world governed by principles of justice and compassion.

Policy Template: Maqasid Aligned Policy Draft

Title of the Policy: [Insert Title]
   Date: [Insert Date]

Policy Overview

- **Objective:** Craft policies aligned with Maqasid to uphold the highest ethical standards, prioritizing citizen well-being.
- **Scope:** Impacts various governance areas including social justice, economic equity, and ethical governance.
- **Duration:** Ongoing implementation with periodic assessments for relevance and effectiveness.

Maqasid Principles Addressed

- **Din:** Promote moral values and religious tolerance.
- **Nafs:** Enhance citizen safety and healthcare.
- **Aql:** Boost education and innovation.
- **Nasl:** Strengthen family structures and support gender equality.
- **Mal:** Ensure equitable economic growth.
- **Watan:** Maintain homeland security through diplomacy.
- **Ummah:** Foster community cohesion.

Implementation Steps

1. Review existing policies for Maqasid alignment.
2. Collaborate with departments, experts, and stakeholders for policy recommendations.
3. Present the draft for legislative approval.

Monitoring and Assessment Metrics

- **KPIs:** Establish Key Performance Indicators for social, economic, and ethical impact.
- **Feedback Channels:** Enable citizen feedback for ongoing policy development.
- **Review Process:** Regularly assess policy effectiveness and make necessary adjustments.

Stakeholders Involved

- Involve government departments, NGOs, religious leaders, scholars, and citizens. Identify specific stakeholders in the policy development phase.

Examples and Case Studies

- Include examples like [Country/Region]'s approach to [specific policy area] that aligns with Maqasid principles.

Flexibility and Adaptability

- This template can be adapted to various policy areas by altering the scope and specific Maqasid principles addressed.

Conflict Resolution Guidance

- Offer strategies to navigate conflicts between modern governance challenges and Maqasid principles.

References and Supporting Documents

- Attach relevant data sets, previous policy papers, or academic research.

User-Friendly Formatting and Accessibility

- Format as a downloadable PDF or an interactive web tool for easy access and use.
- Ensure language is accessible and consider providing translations where necessary.

Policy Makers' Checklist: Ensuring Maqasid Compliance

For policymakers committed to aligning their initiatives with Maqasid principles, this comprehensive checklist ensures that every policy is rooted in ethical governance and serves the collective well-being.

1. **Identify the Maqasid Principle(s)**: Determine which Maqasid principles your policy aligns with. For instance, a public health initiative might primarily address 'Nafs' (Preservation of Life).
2. **Stakeholder Analysis**: Identify and consult with all relevant stakeholders. Utilize surveys or focus groups to incorporate diverse views, ensuring policies are inclusive and comprehensive.
3. **Resource Allocation**: Evaluate the resources required for policy implementation. For example, assess the budget and workforce needed for a new educational reform.
4. **Public Engagement**: Develop a plan for public involvement, using town hall meetings or online platforms for wider participation and

transparency.

5. **Ethical Auditing**: Review the policy for ethical considerations. Conduct impact assessments to ensure alignment with ethical standards and Maqasid principles.

6. **Implementation Strategy**: Outline a clear implementation plan, detailing action steps, timelines, and responsibilities. Refer to successful models from other regions or sectors for structure.

7. **Monitoring Mechanisms**: Set up KPIs to measure impact. For instance, use community health indicators to assess the effectiveness of a healthcare policy.

8. **Legal Review**: Ensure the policy complies with national and international laws. Consult legal experts to address any potential legal conflicts.

9. **Feedback Loops**: Implement systems for ongoing feedback, using digital platforms for ease of access and broader reach.

10. **Review and Renewal**: Establish regular review periods to evaluate and update the policy. Adaptive policies remain relevant and effective over time.

11. **Adaptability to Contexts**: Consider cultural, economic, and geographical factors in policy development. Adapt your strategies to local contexts for better efficacy.

12. **Navigating Challenges**: Prepare for potential obstacles, such as resource limitations or stakeholder resistance, by developing contingency plans and maintaining open channels of communication.

13. **Digital Integration**: Utilize digital tools for efficient policy management, monitoring, and community engagement.

This checklist is a dynamic tool for crafting policies that are not only ethically sound but also practical and impactful. By diligently applying these steps, policymakers can create initiatives that resonate with Maqasid principles and foster a governance model that uplifts and nurtures society. Remember, effective policy-making is an evolving process that thrives on adaptability, ethical integrity, and community involvement.

Transforming Governance with Practical Tools: A Guide for Policymakers

As you embark on the challenging yet rewarding journey of ethical governance, consider these templates and checklists your practical allies. They are more than administrative aids; they are instruments designed to translate the lofty vision of Maqasid into effective, real-world policies. As a policymaker, your decisions shape societies. It's imperative that these decisions are steered by a moral compass pointing towards justice, welfare, and human dignity.

Practical Application of Tools

- Use these templates not just to draft policies, but to envision and create a future that aligns with the highest ideals of human civilization.
- For instance, a template focused on environmental policy can guide you through incorporating sustainability principles in line with Maqasid.
- In areas like public health, checklists can ensure that ethical considerations are central to your approach.

Navigating Complexities with Realism

- While these tools streamline policy formulation, be mindful of the complexities and challenges in governance.
- Utilize the checklists to identify potential obstacles and use the templates to strategize solutions, ensuring a realistic and effective policy-making process.

Adapting to Diverse Policy Areas

- These resources are versatile and can be adapted to various domains—from education reform to economic development—ensuring that Maqasid principles are embedded in all facets of governance.

Fostering Collaborative Efforts

- Effective governance is a collaborative endeavor. Engage with experts, community leaders, and stakeholders to enrich your policies with diverse perspectives.
- Use these tools to facilitate dialogue and build consensus among different parties.

Emphasizing Continuous Improvement

- Remember, policy-making is an evolving process. Regularly revisit and refine your policies using these tools to respond to new challenges and changing societal needs.

As you wield the pen of policy-making, let these templates and checklists empower you to lead with integrity and vision. They are your guides in building a world that's not just efficient but profoundly ethical. The transformation towards a just, equitable, and compassionate society begins with your actions. Embrace these tools with determination and a commitment to bettering the world.

Emboldened with these resources, your role in governance transcends administrative duties. You become a steward of societal upliftment, crafting policies that protect the vulnerable and promote the common good. The toolkit in your hands is a gateway to creating a brighter future for all. Let's journey together on this path of ethical governance, for the benefit of humanity and the well-being of all citizens.

Why This Book is Your Call to Action: An Invitation to Transform Governance and Humanity

This book is more than a source of knowledge; it's a practical guide to inspire a profound shift in governance and societal well-being. We're not just rearranging the furniture; we're reimagining the entire structure of governance and ethical leadership.

A Visionary yet Accessible Approach

- This book provides a clear, actionable roadmap for integrating Maqasid principles into modern governance, tailored to both novices and experts in the field.
- It breaks down complex concepts into accessible language, ensuring that the transformative vision it presents is understandable and applicable to a diverse range of readers.

Practical Application in Real-World Scenarios

- Each chapter includes real-life examples, case studies, and practical exercises that guide you in applying the principles to your unique governance challenges.
- From crafting policies to engaging with communities, the book offers step-by-step strategies for bringing ethical change to governance structures.

Navigating Skepticism and Challenges

- The book acknowledges potential barriers and skepticism, offering strategies to address common challenges and misconceptions.
- It provides a section on how to effectively communicate and implement these ideas in environments resistant to change.

Embracing Diverse Perspectives

- Readers are encouraged to bring their own experiences into their application of the book's teachings, enriching the process with diverse perspectives.
- Interactive elements like reflection questions and discussion prompts foster a deeper, personalized engagement with the content.

Fostering Community and Collaborative Change

- The book emphasizes the importance of community involvement and collaborative efforts in transforming governance.
- It guides readers on how to build coalitions, engage stakeholders, and create inclusive platforms for dialogue and action.

This book is not just a call to action; it's a comprehensive guide for anyone ready to play a role in shaping a more ethical and just society. It empowers you to take concrete steps towards governance transformation, offering tools and insights that bridge the gap between theory and practice.

As you delve into these pages, you're embarking on a journey that goes beyond personal enlightenment. You're joining a community of change-makers committed to elevating humanity through ethical governance. Embrace this journey with open-mindedness, practicality, and a commitment to collaborative action. Together, we can redesign the foundations of governance and build a future where ethical principles guide our societies. The transformation starts with you.

Challenge Your Views, Expand Your Horizons

The aim of this book is not merely to enlighten but to fundamentally challenge and expand your views on governance. This journey is not about incremental reform; it's about embracing a complete paradigm shift in how you perceive the role and potential of governance.

Embracing the Challenge with Guidance

- While challenging your long-held beliefs can be daunting, this book provides a supportive framework to guide you through this transformative process. It encourages you to question assumptions while offering insights to navigate the complexities of these new perspectives.

Introducing New Ideas with Practical Examples

- The book presents innovative ideas such as integrating ethical considerations into policy-making, illustrated through real-world examples and case studies. These practical insights demonstrate how a shift in perspective can lead to meaningful change in governance.

Fostering Collaborative Learning

- Engage with a community of readers and thinkers. Join online forums or local discussion groups to explore these concepts collaboratively, enriching your journey with diverse insights and shared experiences.

Respecting Diverse Perspectives

- This book values a multitude of viewpoints, incorporating diverse perspectives on governance. It invites you to consider and respect different approaches and ideologies, broadening your understanding of what ethical governance can entail.

Applying New Understandings in the Real World

- Beyond theoretical knowledge, the book encourages you to apply these new perspectives in real governance scenarios or in your civic engagement, making the concepts tangible and actionable in your community and professional life.

As you delve into this book, open your heart and mind to the possibility of a radically different approach to governance – one that is deeply ethical, morally driven, and profoundly impactful. Let this book be your guide as you explore uncharted intellectual territories, challenge your preconceptions, and imagine a world where governance transcends administrative duties to become a noble, ethical endeavor.

This is more than a reading experience; it's an invitation to be part of a larger movement towards ethical governance. By embracing these new ideas and participating in this journey, you contribute to a broader vision of governance – one that prioritizes the well-being and dignity of all. The path ahead is bold and requires courage, but the reward is a transformative understanding of governance that aspires to the extraordinary.

The Seven Pillars: Your Blueprint for Heavenly Governance

The seven pillars of Maqasid—Din (religion), Nafs (life), Aql (intellect), Nasl (lineage), Mal (wealth), Watan (homeland), and Ummah (community)—are more than philosophical concepts; they are actionable pillars that provide a robust framework for building a just and virtuous society. These pillars serve as guiding principles, transforming governance from administrative duties into a mission that enriches and uplifts humanity.

Balancing Vision with Real-world Challenges

- While these pillars outline an ideal form of governance, it's important to recognize the challenges in applying them across diverse political and cultural landscapes. Practical strategies must be developed to navigate these complexities.

Incorporating Diverse Perspectives

- Understanding that different cultures may interpret and apply these principles in varied ways is crucial. This diversity enriches the implementation of Maqasid, allowing it to be adaptable and inclusive.

Practical Applications and Case Studies

1. **Din (Religion)**: Example - A policy ensuring religious freedom and interfaith dialogues, contributing to societal harmony.
2. **Nafs (Life)**: Case Study - Healthcare reforms focused on both physical well-being and mental health.
3. **Aql (Intellect)**: Example - Investment in education and critical thinking programs.
4. **Nasl (Lineage)**: Case Study - Family support initiatives that emphasize the welfare of children and gender equality.
5. **Mal (Wealth)**: Example - Economic policies that address wealth distribution and poverty alleviation.
6. **Watan (Homeland)**: Case Study - Balancing national security with human rights and cultural preservation.
7. **Ummah (Community)**: Example - Community development programs that foster unity and social justice.

Navigating Conflicts and Interconnectedness

- Acknowledge potential conflicts between pillars, such as economic growth versus environmental protection, and provide strategies for balancing these interests.
- Emphasize how these pillars are interconnected, working collectively to create a holistic governance model.

Imagine a world where governance prioritizes these seven pillars—a world where policy-making is a profound moral and ethical undertaking.

This is the promise of Maqasid: to create governance systems that not only provide services but also cultivate environments where individuals, families, and communities can thrive. These pillars, when implemented thoughtfully, can transform our earthly governance into a model that closely resembles an ideal, harmonious society. Embrace these pillars as part of your governance strategy, and join in building a future that aspires to the extraordinary.

Be the Change-Maker: Usher in a New Era of Compassionate and Effective Governance

The call to action is clear and urgent. Whether you're a policymaker, academic, student, or an engaged citizen, you possess the unique power to be a catalyst for transformative change. This book isn't just a compilation of ideas; it's a toolkit for action, designed to help you build a world that is not just more just but profoundly ethical; not only more equitable but deeply compassionate; not merely more efficient but profoundly humane.

Why Answer This Call to Action?

1. **Transformative Power**: Your individual actions have the potential to uplift communities, protect the vulnerable, and foster opportunities for all.
2. **Legacy of Compassion**: Embracing Maqasid-based governance means creating a legacy of justice and ethical values for future generations.
3. **Resilience in Society**: Ethical policies enhance societal cohesion and resilience, preparing communities to face diverse challenges.
4. **Global Influence**: Your commitment can inspire change beyond borders, contributing to global justice and compassion.
5. **Personal Fulfillment**: Engaging in ethical governance can bring a deep sense of satisfaction and purpose.
6. **Redefining Governance**: Maqasid offers a unique lens to rethink

governance, prioritizing holistic well-being over conventional metrics.

Practical Steps for Diverse Roles

- **Policymakers**: Integrate Maqasid principles into policy drafts and decision-making processes. Utilize the templates and checklists to align policies with ethical standards.
- **Academics and Researchers**: Conduct studies and publish findings on the impact of Maqasid principles in governance. Offer workshops and seminars to spread knowledge.
- **Students**: Engage in courses and research projects related to ethical governance. Participate in internships or volunteer with organizations that align with Maqasid principles.
- **Concerned Citizens**: Advocate for ethical governance in your community. Participate in public consultations and policy discussions.

Navigating Challenges

- Recognize and prepare for challenges such as bureaucratic resistance or limited resources. Develop strategies like building coalitions or leveraging community support to overcome these barriers.

Fostering Collaboration and Inclusivity

- Collaborate across sectors and communities to implement ethical governance. Encourage diverse voices and perspectives in policymaking.

Commitment to Continuous Learning

- Embrace ongoing education and adaptation. Stay informed about the latest developments in ethical governance and be open to revising approaches as needed.

This book is your invitation to be part of a transformative journey. It's a call to build governance models that are not just administratively competent but morally and ethically profound. The path ahead is one of bold action and collaboration. Seize this opportunity to be a leader in this new era of governance – one that honors compassion, justice, and human dignity.

The journey towards a more compassionate, just, and humane world begins with each of us. Take up this mantle of change-maker, and let your actions resonate both now and in the future as a testament to your commitment to a better world. The time to act is now, and the future of ethical governance is in your hands. Let's embark on this transformative path together, for the benefit of all humanity.

Let's Usher in a New Era of Governance: Where Love, Liberation, and Inspiration Prevail

In the realm of governance, audacity is essential. It's time to embrace a bold vision, where governance transcends traditional power structures and becomes a profound manifestation of love for humanity, justice, and individual well-being.

Integrating Love with Practical Governance

- Imagine policies crafted not just as regulations but as expressions of care and empathy. However, translating this love into practical governance requires concrete steps: policies that directly address social issues, programs that genuinely support community needs, and a leadership style that prioritizes empathy and understanding

457

in decision-making.

Unyielding Commitment to Ethical Governance

- Our dedication to principles like justice and integrity must be un-wavering. We need to incorporate transparency, accountability, and fairness in all aspects of governance. This might involve establishing robust anti-corruption frameworks or ensuring equitable resource distribution.

Liberation as a Guiding Principle

- Governance should be a pathway to liberation, empowering communities to thrive. This involves creating policies that enhance individual freedoms and support community growth, such as inclusive education systems and economic policies that foster independence and creativity.

Inspiration Through Governance

- Governance should inspire hope and positive action. Showcasing successful stories of ethical governance, engaging citizens in policy-making, and celebrating community achievements can ignite a spirit of active participation and hope.

Acknowledging and Overcoming Challenges

- Realizing this vision will have challenges, from systemic inertia to cultural barriers. We must identify these hurdles, openly discuss them, and collaboratively develop strategies to overcome them.

Embracing Diverse Perspectives

- Recognizing that diverse cultural and societal contexts will influence the application of these principles is crucial. Policies should be adaptable to different communities, respecting their unique values and needs.

Fostering Collaboration for Collective Action

- Achieving this vision requires collaborative efforts across various sectors – government, civil society, private sector, and citizens. By working together, pooling resources and ideas, we can create more impactful governance.

Commitment to Continuous Learning

- This journey requires ongoing learning, adaptation, and reflection. Staying informed about global governance trends and being open to revising strategies as situations evolve is essential.

The journey to a new era of governance – driven by love, liberation, and inspiration – is challenging but profoundly rewarding. Let's stand together, driven by our audacious aspirations and a strong commitment to ethical governance. With love, liberation, and inspiration as our guiding principles, we can forge a world that is more just, equitable, and humane. The future of governance is in our collective hands, and it's time to act with courage and conviction.

Embark on a Transformational Journey: From Ordinary to Extraordinary, from Policies to Lives

This book is more than just a read; it's an expedition into transformative governance. It invites you on a journey from the ordinary to the extraordinary, a path that promises not just to change policies but to transform lives.

Vision of Transformative Governance with Practical Steps

- Imagine governance as a force for positive transformation, where policies are living instruments of profound impact. This book provides practical steps to realize this vision, guiding you through the implementation of compassionate and ethical governance practices.
- For example, it offers frameworks for policy development that prioritize social equity and environmental sustainability, urging you to apply these in your context.

Collective Journey Embracing Challenges

- You are not alone on this journey. It's a collective endeavor, inviting policymakers, academics, students, and engaged citizens to unite their wisdom and passion.
- The book acknowledges the challenges in this transformative process, such as institutional resistance or resource limitations, and provides strategies to navigate these obstacles effectively.

Incorporating Diverse Perspectives for Inclusive Governance

- Emphasizing the need for diverse perspectives, the book encourages inclusive policy-making that reflects a range of cultural and societal needs.
- It guides you in engaging with different communities to ensure that

policies are equitable and representative.

Continuous Learning and Real-World Application

- This journey is about continuous learning and adaptation. Stay informed about evolving governance practices and be prepared to adjust your approaches as needed.
- Real-world case studies in the book illustrate how ethical governance principles have been successfully applied, serving as both inspiration and a practical guide.

Immerse yourself in this book and let it be a catalyst for your active role in governance. Let its ideas fuel your determination to make a tangible difference. As you turn each page, envision yourself as part of a movement shaping a world where governance uplifts and empowers.

Together, we can turn the ordinary into the extraordinary, transforming policies into tools of positive change. We have the opportunity to shape a world where governance is not only efficient but also enriches lives. The journey starts now, and it begins with your commitment and action. Will you answer the call to be a part of this transformative era in governance?

The Responsibility of a Lifetime: Be the Change-Maker for a Transformed World

This moment is more than an opportunity; it's a profound responsibility calling us to action with urgency. We stand at a pivotal point in history, where our choices will echo through generations. This is not merely a proposal, but a solemn commitment to create a world that marries spiritual richness with material well-being, where governance is a sacred duty, and policies are instruments of upliftment and common good.

Inclusivity in Our Transformative Journey

- We welcome diverse voices and perspectives in this quest. Recognizing that the richness of our collective experience strengthens our approach to ethical governance is crucial. Every individual, irrespective of background or position, contributes uniquely to this transformative vision.

Practical Steps Toward Change

- Start by engaging in community dialogues to understand local needs.
- Advocate for policy changes that reflect Maqasid principles in your area of influence, whether it's your workplace, local community, or through social media.
- Educate yourself and others about the principles of ethical governance and their real-world applications.

Overcoming Challenges with Resilience

- We must acknowledge and prepare for challenges such as institutional resistance or resource constraints. Develop strategies like forming alliances with like-minded individuals and organizations to navigate these challenges effectively.

Collaboration and Community Engagement

- This journey is not solitary. It thrives on collaboration and community involvement. Participate in or organize forums, workshops, and collaborative projects that aim to implement ethical governance practices.

Commitment to Continuous Learning

- Embrace a mindset of continuous learning and adaptation. Stay informed about developments in governance and be prepared to evolve your approaches as new challenges and opportunities arise.

As we embark on this path, let us not be mere spectators to the challenges of our time. Let's seize this moment to be architects of a more just, compassionate, and humane world. The blueprint is laid out, and the tools are in our hands. The time for action is now. Will you take that transformative step? Together, we have the power to make a lasting impact, creating a legacy of ethical and effective governance for future generations. Let's take this step together, for a world where our collective aspirations become a reality.

Epilogue

Navigating Towards Ethical Governance

As we turn the final page of "Heaven Is Under The Feet Of Governments," it becomes evident that the journey to weave the Maqasid model into the fabric of governance transcends ambition—it is a critical endeavor for the prosperity of communities across the globe. Our exploration has highlighted the undeniable power of governance infused with ethical principles and spiritual values to confront the complex challenges of our era.

Reflecting upon the insights and narratives presented, this epilogue acts as a catalyst for change. It is a call to governments, policymakers, and individuals alike to reconceptualize governance as a profound responsibility to uplift humanity. By adopting the Maqasid framework, we are guided towards a governance model that seeks not only administrative efficiency but the comprehensive welfare of all citizens.

This envisioned approach to governance escapes the confines of theory, proposing practical and implementable strategies. Through the Maqasid principles, we envision a future marked by compassion, justice, and sustainability—a mirror of our collective humanity and mutual reliance.

Standing at a pivotal moment in history, we are faced with a decision. Do we persist on the familiar path of conventional governance, or do we embrace the transformative potential offered by the Maqasid wisdom? The fate of our societies, our planet, and the essence of our being is at stake.

May this book serve not merely as a record of potential but as a rallying cry for those who champion a governance model that places humanity's noblest values at its heart. Together, we can herald the arrival of a new era, where governance transcends resource management to celebrate and cultivate the spirit and capabilities of every person.

In heeding this higher calling, we pay homage to the pioneers who have set the groundwork and lay a robust foundation for future generations to flourish. Despite the hurdles that lie ahead, the journey is ripe with potential. Let us step forward with bravery, honesty, and a steadfast dedication to ethical governance. Herein lies the seed of a world that embodies the pinnacle of our collective potential.

Afterword

A New Horizon in Ethical Leadership

As we conclude our journey through "Heaven Is Under The Feet Of Governments," we reach the culmination of an engaging narrative that advocates for weaving the principles of the Maqasid model into the very essence of contemporary governance. This exploration has transcended mere academic inquiry, serving as a deep-seated call to recognize and embrace the inherent duties of governance.

This work delves deep into the essence of ethical governance, drawing from the rich spiritual and moral teachings of Islam to present a blueprint for societies striving towards holistic well-being. It has vividly illustrated that the true measure of a society's success is not in its accumulation of wealth or power but in its unwavering commitment to justice, compassion, and the collective good.

As this journey of enlightenment concludes, our aspiration is that "Heaven Is Under The Feet Of Governments" ignites a transformative spark. It is a fervent hope that this book will inspire both leaders and citizens to reimagine governance as an embodiment of our noblest pursuits—where decisions are made not just in the interest of the present but as a legacy for future generations.

The principles championed in these pages extend beyond theoretical ideals; they represent a clarion call to reshape our world. This is an invitation to challenge the status quo, to dare to envision governance as a conduit for moral and ethical progress.

Let the insights from this book fuel ongoing discussions, stimulate further research, and inspire actionable steps towards the realization of ethical governance worldwide. The end of this book marks the beginning of a collective journey towards a new dawn in leadership—a journey that beckons each of us to contribute towards creating a world that mirrors our highest aspirations for justice, peace, and human dignity.

With every step taken towards ethical governance, we pave a path to a future radiant with the promise of equity, empathy, and shared prosperity. Let us embark on this path with determination, guided by the principles of Maqasid, to forge a legacy of ethical leadership that will illuminate the way for generations to come.

Legal Disclaimers

GENERAL DISCLAIMER

This book is a work of synthesis and analysis based on extensive research and the author's insights into integrating Maqasid (objectives of Islamic law) into governance practices. The views expressed herein are those of the author and are not necessarily intended to reflect or represent the policies or viewpoints of any specific government, organization, or religious group. Readers should critically assess the applicability of any insights or recommendations to their own contexts.

CONSULT PROFESSIONALS

This publication is intended for informational purposes only. While it discusses principles of governance and policy-making, readers are encouraged to consult with professional advisors or experts in public administration, law, or relevant fields to understand the implications of these principles in their specific legal, institutional, or cultural contexts.

LIABILITY DISCLAIMER

The author and publisher disclaim any liability for any direct, indirect, incidental, or consequential damages or losses that may result from applying the ideas and strategies discussed in this book. The information provided is on an "as is" basis, and the author does not guarantee the accuracy, completeness, or usefulness of any information on these pages or that the use of such information will meet any reader's requirements.

EARNINGS DISCLAIMER

This book does not promise or guarantee any specific outcomes in terms of policy success, economic development, social improvement, or otherwise, resulting from the application of the concepts and models discussed. Real-world governance and policy-making outcomes depend on a wide array of factors beyond the principles covered in this publication.

PANDEMIC DISCLAIMER

Given the evolving nature of global challenges such as pandemics, the strategies and recommendations presented in this book should be considered in light of the most current public health guidelines and within the framework of legal and policy responses to such crises.

NOT A BUSINESS OPPORTUNITY

The book discusses governance and policy-making principles and does not offer business opportunities. Any references to economic or financial models are for illustrative purposes only and should not be construed as investment advice or business proposals.

NOT A FRANCHISE

This publication does not offer a franchise or a business model that can be replicated for commercial gain. The principles of Maqasid discussed are intended for the enhancement of governance and public policy.

AFFILIATE DISCLAIMER

This book may reference other works, studies, or publications. These references do not imply any affiliation with or endorsement by the authors or publishers of such works, unless explicitly stated. The author and publisher are not responsible for the content of external sites or publications referenced within this book.

About the Author

Abdellatif Raji stands as a beacon in the landscape of Islamic thought and governance, distinguished by his pioneering efforts to meld the wisdom of ancient traditions with the demands of modern society. His unique perspective, grounded in a comprehensive understanding of law, sociology, and spirituality, equips him to devise innovative solutions to today's multifaceted societal issues. Raji's writings strike a balance between scholarly depth and accessibility, inviting a wide audience into a thoughtful conversation about reforming governance with a foundation of ethical integrity and compassion.

In his seminal work, "**Heaven Is Under The Feet Of Governments**," Raji articulates a vision that transcends traditional governance models. This book is more than just a compilation of ideas; it serves as Raji's clarion call for a society striving for justice, operational excellence, and moral leadership. His prose does not merely illuminate; it galvanizes, encouraging us to pursue tangible reforms. Through Raji's narrative, a vision unfolds of governance that elevates society, emphasizing the importance of spiritual values alongside material advancement.

Delving deeper into Raji's interdisciplinary approach reveals how his integration of varied fields of study lays the groundwork for a governance system that is as ethically sound as it is effective. He challenges the prevailing notion that compassion and ethical governance are incompatible with efficiency and practicality, proposing a model where these elements coexist harmoniously. His advocacy for such a balanced approach encourages a departure from conventional views, urging a reevaluation of governance's potential to foster a society that cherishes both the soul and its civilizational achievements.

Raji's influence extends beyond academic circles, offering hope to those seeking a more harmonious world. His work is not just an academic endeavor but a passionate call to action, inviting us all to partake in a global movement toward ethical governance. By engaging with Raji's visionary ideas at www.abdellatifraji.com, readers can discover specific strategies for contributing to this shift, including forums for discussion, resources for deeper learning, and platforms for collaborative action.

You can connect with me on:

- https://heavenisunderthefeetofgovernments.com
- https://twitter.com/i/communities/1760086099014160422
- https://www.facebook.com/HeavenUnderGovernmentsFeet
- https://www.linkedin.com/groups/12993934

Subscribe to my newsletter:

- https://www.abdellatifraji.com

Index

www.ingramcontent.com/pod-product-compliance
Lightning Source LLC
Chambersburg PA
CBHW052117270326
41930CB00012B/2665